THE BRIGHTON POLICE SCANDAL

DICK KIRBY
has also written:

Rough Justice: Memoirs of a Flying Squad Officer

The Real Sweeney

You're Nicked!

Villains

The Guv'nors: Ten of Scotland Yard's Finest Detectives

The Sweeney: The First Sixty Years of Scotland Yard's Crimebusting
Flying Squad 1919–1978

Scotland Yard's Ghost Squad:
The Secret Weapon against Post-War Crime

The Brave Blue Line:
100 Years of Metropolitan Police Gallantry

Death on the Beat:
Police Officers killed in the Line of Duty

The Scourge of Soho:
The Controversial Career of SAS Hero Harry Challenor MM

Whitechapel's Sherlock Holmes:
The Casebook of Fred Wensley OBE, KPM, Victorian Crimebuster

The Wrong Man:
The Shooting of Steven Waldorf and the Hunt for David Martin

Laid Bare:
The Nude Murders and the Hunt for 'Jack the Stripper'

London's Gangs at War

Operation Countryman:
The Flawed Enquiry into London Police Corruption

Scotland Yard's Gangbuster:
Bert Wickstead's Most Celebrated Cases

The Mayfair Mafia:
The Lives and Crimes of the Messina Brothers

Scotland Yard's Flying Squad:
100 Years of Crime Fighting

Scotland Yard's Murder Squad

The Racetrack Gangs:
Four Decades of Doping, Intimidation and Violent Crime

IRA Terror on Britain's Streets 1939–1940: The Wartime Bombing Campaign
and Hitler Connection

Scotland Yard's Casebook of Serious Crimes: 75 Years of No-Nonsense Policing

The Brighton Police Scandal

A Story of Corruption, Intimidation and Violence

DICK KIRBY

PEN & SWORD
TRUE CRIME

First published in Great Britain in 2021 by
Pen & Sword True Crime
An imprint of
Pen & Sword Books Ltd
Yorkshire – Philadelphia

ISBN 978 1 39901 728 2

Printed and bound in the UK by CPI Group (UK) Ltd,
Croydon, CR0 4YY.

Pen & Sword Books Limited incorporates the imprints of Atlas,
Archaeology, Aviation, Discovery, Family History, Fiction, History,
Maritime, Military, Military Classics, Politics, Select, Transport, True
Crime, Air World, Frontline Publishing, Leo Cooper, Remember
When, Seaforth Publishing, The Praetorian Press, Wharncliffe Local
History, Wharncliffe Transport, Wharncliffe True Crime and White
Owl.

For a complete list of Pen & Sword titles please contact

PEN & SWORD BOOKS LIMITED
47 Church Street, Barnsley, South Yorkshire, S70 2AS, England
E-mail: enquiries@pen-and-sword.co.uk
Website: www.pen-and-sword.co.uk

Or
PEN AND SWORD BOOKS
1950 Lawrence Rd, Havertown, PA 19083, USA
E-mail: Uspen-and-sword@casematepublishers.com
Website: www.penandswordbooks.com

To Ann

You must never go down to the end of the town
If you don't go down with me.

Disobedience
A.A. Milne, 1882–1956

Praise for Dick Kirby's Books

'He treats criminals the only way they understand. His language is often shocking, his methods unorthodox.' **NATIONAL ASSOCIATION OF RETIRED POLICE OFFICERS' MAGAZINE**

'The continuing increase in violent crime will make many readers yearn for yesteryear and officers of Dick Kirby's calibre.' **POLICE MAGAZINE**

'His reflections on the political aspect of law enforcement will ring true for cops, everywhere.' **AMERICAN POLICE BEAT**

'Its no-nonsense portrayal of life in the police will give readers a memorable literary experience.' **SUFFOLK JOURNAL**

'A great read with fascinating stories and amusing anecdotes from a man who experienced it all.' **SUFFOLK NORFOLK LIFE MAGAZINE**

'A gritty series of episodes from his time in the Met – laced with black humour and humanity'. **EAST ANGLIAN DAILY TIMES**

'This is magic. The artfulness of these anti-heroes has you pining for the bad old days.' **DAILY SPORT**

'Crammed with vivid descriptions of long-forgotten police operations, races along like an Invicta tourer, at full throttle.' **DAILY EXPRESS.**

'Rarely, if ever, have I been so captivated and moved by a book... the way in which Mr Kirby has gone about it is exceptional'. **POLICE MEMORABILIA COLLECTORS CLUB**

'Dick Kirby has chosen his fascinating subject well.' **LAW SOCIETY GAZETTE**

'Thrilling stories of gang-busting, murder and insurrection'.
BERTRAMS BOOKS

'Ascrupulously honest and detailed account of the unfortunate events leading to police shooting an innocent man . . . nobody is better qualified to write an account of this story than Dick Kirby.'
LONDON POLICE PENSIONER MAGAZINE

'Dick Kirby knows his stuff!' **surrey-constabulary.com**

'Kirby looks to untangle facts from speculation and questions everything.' **GET WEST LONDON**

'Murder, torture and extortion all feature prominently as Mr Kirby investigates some of the most famous incidents of the post-war era.' **THE MAIL ONLINE**

'Only an insider with the engaging style of Dick Kirby could have produced this nakedly forthright page-turner.'
JOSEPH WAMBAUGH, AUTHOR OF THE CHOIRBOYS

'Kirby's wit and extremely dry humour comes on straight away as early as the prologue which, of course, makes heavy reading subjects easier and creates a relationship between the author (narrator) and the reader.' **THE LOVE OF BOOKS**

'Dick Kirby's book gives precious insight into its exploits for over a century.' **PAUL MILLEN, AUTHOR OF CRIME SCENE INVESTIGATOR**

'Dick Kirby has written a book that all crime aficionados will want to read.' **WASHINGTON TIMES**

'Kirby does not hold back in detailing the grisly parts, bringing home to the reader the harsh reality that these ruthless killers had no boundaries.' **LONDON POLICE PENSIONER MAGAZINE**

Contents

Acknowledgements   xi

Preface   xiii

Introduction   xvii

PART I ARRIVING

Chapter 1   The Slimy Conman   3

Chapter 2   The Bucket of Blood   9

Chapter 3   Protection – at a Price   19

Chapter 4   Abortionists and Burglars   25

Chapter 5   An Informant and a Receiver   31

Chapter 6   The Lorry-load of Snout   37

Chapter 7   A Wild Goose Chase   41

Chapter 8   Undercover Work and Search Warrants   45

Chapter 9   Call in Scotland Yard!   49

Chapter 10   Helping Police with their Enquiries   55

Chapter 11   Questions – Pointed Ones – are Asked   61

Chapter 12   Arrests   65

Chapter 13   A New Appointment   71

Chapter 14   Court Appearance – and Threats   75

Chapter 15   Alan Bennett Speaks out . . .   81

Chapter 16   . . . and so does Wenche Bennett   85

Chapter 17   More Fuel for the Fire   89

Chapter 18   The Receiver's Version   93

Chapter 19   Stolen Consignments   97

Chapter 20   Dynamite Evidence   101

Chapter 21   Committal   107

Chapter 22   The Trial Commences   111

Chapter 23   'Brighton Police Were Crooked'   115

Chapter 24   '£5 Notes in a Newspaper'   121

Chapter 25   An Unwelcome Visitor   125

Chapter 26   'A Gentlemen's Agreement'   127

Chapter 27   The Close of the Prosecution   131

Chapter 28   Heath's Defence   137

Chapter 29   Three More Defences   141

Chapter 30   Ridge's Defence   145

Chapter 31   Final Speeches   151

Chapter 32   The Judge's Summing-up   161

Chapter 33   The Verdicts and Sentences   165

PART II LEAVING

Chapter 34   The Aftermath   171

Chapter 35   Page's Downfall   177

Chapter 36   Some Went on to Greater Heights . . .   185

Chapter 37   . . . and Others Didn't   189

Chapter 38   A Fall from Grace   195

Chapter 39   Conclusions and Suppositions   205

Epilogue   211

Bibliography   213

Index   215

Acknowledgements

First and foremost, I should like to thank fellow author David Rowland for his enormous, generous and well-researched input into the book; it has proved invaluable. My thanks, as ever, go to Brigadier Henry Wilson of Pen & Sword Books for his help and encouragement, as well as to Matt Jones, Tara Moran, Jon Wilkinson for his splendid, imaginative illustrations and George Chamier for his lynx-eyed editing.

Next, the following people provided great assistance: Russ Allen; Julie Bedford, Data Protection Unit, Sussex Police; Ian Borthwick; Philip Bye, Senior Archivist, Elizabeth Hughes and Andrew Lusted of East Sussex Record Office; Andrew Cook; Bob Fenton QGM, The Ex-CID Officers' Association; John Kalber; Martin McKay, British Transport Police History Group; Phillip Meeson, Vice-Chairman of the Old Police Cells Museum, Brighton Town Hall; Alan Moss of History by the Yard; the late John Rigby; Susi Rogol, editor of the *London Police Pensioner* magazine; Tim Sargeant; Peter Scott; Jenny Stacey; Michelle Sutton, British Transport Police; the late Frank Wensley; Giles York QPM, Chief Constable, Sussex Police.

My thanks to David Rowland and Martin McKay for the use of some of the photographs; others are from the author's collection, and whilst every effort has been made to trace the copyright holders of all images, the author and the publishers apologise for any inadvertent omissions.

As always, my thanks go to my daughter, Suzanne Cowper, and her husband Steve, for guiding me though the minefields of computer-land, and for the love and support of their children, Emma, B Mus, Jessica, B Mus and Harry, MTheatre; also to my other daughter, Barbara Jerreat, her husband Rich and their children Sam and Annie Grace; and to my sons Mark and Robert. They have all faced up to the Covid 19 pandemic with courage and fortitude.

Most of all, I thank my dear wife Ann, who for well over half a century has stuck with me, during the good times and the bad.

Dick Kirby
Suffolk, 2021

Preface

Corruption in a police force is a pernicious disease. Not only does it bring public disquiet and distrust upon the police in general (and hysterical pleasure to Marxists and other anti-police organizations), it also pervades the ranks of the police itself. Honest officers do not know whom to trust; other officers become ensnared by their crooked counterparts. A classic case came in the 1970s, when a trustworthy officer was posted into the ranks of Scotland Yard's Obscene Publication Squad (OPS) and was horrified when he saw the amount of orchestrated bribery and corruption – literally on the industrial level of a Mafia operation – that was going on. He went to the officer in charge, Detective Chief Superintendent 'Wicked Bill' Moody, and requested an immediate transfer; in keeping with a Mafia *capo dei capi*, Moody told the officer that his relocation would cost him £500.

Crooked officers working alone and taking money from criminals in return for watered-down charges, or leaving out evidence and obtaining money in return for bail: these were bad enough. Far worse were the officers who interfered with their honest colleagues' cases, tipping off the criminals concerned about impending searches or arrests, stealing vital evidence or statements for cash. Worse still were those officers who took bribes while saying that they were acting on behalf of an officer – an honest and unwitting one – to whom they would pass on the money. This was reflected in an old Flying Squad verse:

> . . . and to his eternal shame
> copped his dough
> in another man's name.

So when it becomes clear that corruption is at work, it must be addressed immediately and expeditiously eradicated.

In 1928 it was discovered that Station Sergeant George Goddard was taking mountainous bribes from nightclub owners for turning a blind eye to gaming, the staging of erotic cabarets and flouting of the licensing laws. He was able to buy a house for £1,850 and a £400 car, both for cash, he financed two pawnbroker's shops and he had bank accounts containing £2,700 and a cash deposit box with £12,000 – all on his weekly wage of £6 15s 0d.

Fred Wensley OBE, KPM, the Chief Constable of the CID, immediately put Charles Cooper, the head of the Flying Squad, in charge of the investigation, and within a very short space of time the venal club owners were convicted, and Goddard appeared at the Old Bailey, was sentenced to eighteen months' hard labour, fined £2,000 and ordered to pay the costs of the prosecution.

It was a textbook operation and one that should have acted as a template for any further investigations of that kind. Unfortunately, that was not always the case.

The matter of 'Wicked Bill', referred to above, was an appalling case involving the heads of the OPS, who had not only accepted bribes but were also instrumental in recycling pornographic material to bookshops and arranging 'licences' for pornographers to run them. In the 1960s, the going rate for a licence had been £100 per month; by the 1970s, one particular transaction cost a pornographer £1,000, and this was in addition to handing over a percentage of the profits. The Flying Squad was accused of accepting bribes as well. It was a matter that demanded the most prompt and searching investigation by the most experienced detectives. It did not get it.

The new Commissioner, Sir Robert Mark GBE, QPM, hated and despised CID officers. Instead of swallowing his prejudices and asking for sound advice to choose detectives whose honesty was beyond reproach to head the investigation, he instead selected senior uniform officers. They, together with the head of the enquiry, Assistant Commissioner Gilbert Kelland CBE, QPM, who after thirty-one years' service in the uniform branch suddenly became head of the CID, knew little or nothing of criminal investigative work.

Kelland simply did not have a clue. For his main prosecution witness he used pornographer Jimmy Humphreys, who immediately identified Kelland as a dope and proceeded to run rings round him, sulking, pouting and picking and choosing who he would give evidence about. It took five years from the time that these allegations were first made for some of the officers to be convicted.[1]

Even worse was 'Operation Countryman'. Accusations of corruption were levelled first at CID officers from the City of

1 For further information on these matters, see *Scotland Yard's Gangbuster: Bert Wickstead's Most Celebrated Cases*, Pen & Sword Books, 2018

London police force, and later at Metropolitan Police officers. Dorset police were called in by the Home Office to head the enquiry, and the detectives on that investigation were few and far between. The majority were uniform or traffic officers, who were allowed to insert 'detective' in front of their upgraded rank and launched into an enquiry which was way beyond their experience or capabilities. A traffic sergeant, able to spot a worn tyre at 50 yards, became overnight a detective inspector who, as one senior Scotland Yard detective stated, 'knew as much about criminal investigation as my arsehole knows about steam navigation'. Wily criminals correctly identified the team as a bunch of mugs and provided them with a mixture of lies, rumours and bullshit rather than evidence, which these gormless officers, without any verification, accepted as the truth. Few of them had any knowledge of the criminal law or the rules of evidence, and they blundered from one investigation to another. Eventually, having destroyed the careers of any number of honest CID officers as well as letting scores of guilty criminals go free, the eight Metropolitan Police officers whom they managed to put on trial were all acquitted. Just two City of London police officers were convicted of corruption, and that was due to the superlative investigative techniques of the newly appointed head of that force's Criminal Investigation Department. He was, by the way, a former Metropolitan police officer. The shambles that was 'Operation Countryman' had cost the taxpayer £4 million and, with a workforce of over ninety officers, had lasted for four years.[2]

Therefore, it's refreshing to recount the story of an investigation into corruption in 1957 that was a success. From beginning to end it took six months, it was accomplished by ten Metropolitan police officers who interviewed over 200 people, took 150 witness statements and called 64 of them to give evidence; and it started in a provincial town 47 miles south of London.

---

2 For further information about this pernicious enquiry, see *Operation Countryman: The Flawed Enquiry into London Police Corruption*, Pen & Sword Books, 2018

Introduction

On England's south coast, in the county of East Sussex, is the city of Brighton and Hove. It is situated beneath a gentle slope and protected from the north wind by the high ground of the South Downs immediately behind it. A popular holiday destination, its shingle beach is almost 5½ miles long.

It is estimated that 11–16 per cent of the city's population over the age of sixteen are gay, bisexual or lesbian, and it has the highest percentage of same-sex households in the United Kingdom. Understandably, it has been termed 'The unofficial gay capital of the UK'. Additionally, it has been described as 'The happiest place to live in the UK'. Despite the bustling activity of the shops in its quirky streets and the effervescent nightlife, this is a view that might not be shared by everyone.

Brighton has been described as the country's 'most godless' city, and in 2001, thanks to the *Star Wars* franchise, 2.6 per cent of the population declared that their religious affiliation was that of 'Jedi Knight'. Others elsewhere also adopted this idiotic concept, but Brighton's devotion to this faith was the highest in the United Kingdom. The city has the worst rate of homelessness (4,095 persons) outside of London, suggesting that one in every sixty-nine people in Brighton is homeless. Three areas within the city's boundaries were rated in the top ten nationally for deprivation.

If this paints a grim picture of this seaside metropolis, it was not always the case. During the nineteenth century, Brighton – it acquired city status in 2000 – was regarded as a spa town, a health resort, where people came to bathe in the sea, believing that immersion in the waters might cure their ailments.

And as the great and the good arrived, so did the architecture. In the early part of that century, the Royal Pavilion was built for the Prince Regent by the architect John Nash. To accommodate those of slightly less than royal status, the Grand Hotel was erected in 1864; with its 201 rooms, contained behind six levels of balconies, it was the first hotel outside of London to possess lifts, which were referred to as 'ascending omnibuses'.

From 1883, Magnus Volk's Electric Railway, powered by a 1½ hp engine, transported thrilled passengers as it thundered along at 6mph from the Palace Pier (built, with Brighton's Marine Palace, in 1899) to the Marina. The previous year, the Brighton Clock Tower was erected to celebrate Queen Victoria's jubilee.

And as the years went by, the tourists, day-trippers and those wanting a longer stay (especially for naughty weekends) flooded into the town, to enjoy the sunshine, the candyfloss and the bathing.

After the end of the Second World War (and the austerity which followed it), Brighton appeared to be a pretty law-abiding town. The salutary sentences imposed on the London thugs following 'The Battle of Lewes Racetrack' in 1936 had brought systemic violence under control, and although the feared gangland boss 'Darby' Sabini had taken up residence in the town's Old Shoreham Road, he mercifully passed away in 1950. Obviously, criminality still existed, but the records show that whereas the number of crimes recorded in 1948 had been 2,183, offences by 1956 had decreased to 1,674. The detection rate increased from 43.8 per cent to 61.3 per cent, and arrests during that period were up, too, from 453 to 638. The force had been split into two divisions in 1949: 'A' Division, whose headquarters was at the Town Hall, and 'B' Division at Wellington Road, which housed the traffic offices, the information room, criminal records office and the social club.

By the time a new Chief Constable was appointed on 1 July 1956, the retiring incumbent had left a record for the previous year which brought gasps of adulation from members of Brighton Town Council. The establishment of the police force had increased to 277 men and six women (of whom twenty-seven men were appointed to the CID), and they were easily able to deal with any tiresome Teddy Boys who started trouble in the dancehalls. A total of 7,475 '999' calls had received prompt attention. There had been 4,586 enquiries regarding lost property, and of 6,440 articles found in the street, 2,107 were restored to their owners. Proactive policing resulted in the serving of 3,233 summonses, as well as 829 warrants being executed. Soon, police working hours would be reduced to an 88-hour fortnight, and the fleet would comprise fifteen cars and vans, plus five motorcycles, all of which were equipped with two-way radios.

And the new Chief Constable (who acquired a grey horse from the Metropolitan Police stables at Imber Court, to parade along the promenade) was taking decisive action regarding traffic, which on one day in August 1956 had become so congested that it had come to a complete standstill.

'Authority cannot afford to face another holiday season without formulating definite schemes for a constructive solution', he thundered to the Watch Committee, adding, 'While the police will continue to play their part in endeavouring to maintain unobstructed movement of traffic, their task will continue to be more and more difficult.'

He suggested the banning of all parking on the south side of the sea front, that pedestrian subways should replace zebra crossings at the aquarium roundabout and that concrete rafts should be placed on the beach to accommodate parking for 200 cars. With these innovative suggestions, it appeared that vehicular traffic would park neatly and flow freely, and the streets would not be clogged up with cars.

On 29 March 1957, uniform officers lead by Superintendent Thomas Hill raided a bookmaker's office in Duke Street, arresting the staff and thirty-eight punters. Eight months later, thirty members of the Chez-Moi club were caught drinking after hours, and the club was struck off. Therefore, amidst the population of approximately 160,000, it appeared that under the leadership of the newly appointed and farsighted Chief Constable law and order was being well maintained.

Don't you believe it.

As Marcellus said to Horatio in *Hamlet*, 'Something is rotten in the state of Denmark'; and 828 miles west of Helsingør, where those words were allegedly uttered, it appeared that certain sections of Brighton's CID were not smelling too sweetly, either.

In fact, if all the rumours that were circulating could be believed, they hadn't been for some time.

PART I

ARRIVING

'Ride on! Rough-shod if need be, smooth shod if that will do,
but ride on! Ride on over all obstacles, and win the race!'

Charles Dickens (1812–1870)

David Copperfield

CHAPTER 1

The Slimy Conman

The story begins with a seedy crook, a conman whose name was Isaac Rosenbaum. By the time he was thirty-two he had acquired six convictions, two for begging, three for fraud and one for perjury, so on 14 June 1938 he decided to renounce his baptismal name and adopt a new identity as Richard Isaac Rose. He was also known as Isaac (or 'Ike') Rose and, for the purposes of the frauds he was about to carry out, Frank Rose.

In 1942, Rose set up two companies, the first styled Loyal Service Handicrafts (Brighton) Ltd and the second, British Disabled Ex-Servicemen's Industries, which he ran from 3 and 4 Cannon Place, in the north of Brighton. He employed about a dozen disabled ex-servicemen, but this was a token gesture. They were there to manufacture items such as garden chairs and other furniture, but these were shoddy goods indeed, and customers were led to believe that these so-called charitable concerns were in existence to assist disabled ex-servicemen. This was at a time when, of course, practically everyone in the country knew of at least one person who had suffered disabilities due to war service; in 1955 alone, 16,682 ex-servicemen were registered as disabled. In fact, the British Legion was fiercely campaigning on their behalf to have their inadequate pensions raised to 90 shillings per week, so everyone was aware of their plight. In the midst of this very helpful publicity, Rose employed canvassers – not ex-servicemen at all but just as smooth-tongued as himself – who took with them gruesome photographs of disabled ex-servicemen to acquire potential customers. Much favoured were photographs of disfigured RAF personnel at the Queen Victoria Hospital at East Grinstead, prior to the brilliant Sir Archibald McIndoe working the magic of his plastic surgery on them.

Customers were required to pay cash in advance for the goods, and that was the last they saw of their money. They would repeatedly write to Rose, but these letters were ignored, and eventually most customers simply gave up. Seldom did the goods arrive, but if and when they did they were found to be of very inferior quality; customers complained, but it did them no good at all.

Sometimes there was a variation on the theme of the swindle: Rose asked customers for loans which, he stated, were needed to keep disabled servicemen in employment – and again, that was the last they saw of their money.

But sometimes dissatisfied customers contacted the Brighton police; however, since the detectives in the Criminal Investigation Department who dealt with these letters were astonishingly corrupt, action – other than marking Rose's cards – was seldom taken. It was only if the person complaining was influential – and this could be deduced from their social standing and their letter-heading – that Rose would be advised that it might well be sensible to return the money.

Those repayments, however – few as they were – were a drop in the ocean; in the fifteen years of the companies' existence, Rose took £40,000 per year, of which £25,000 was siphoned off into his private bank account.

This was brought to the attention of the Official Receiver on 10 January 1956, and when it was discovered that no proper books of the transactions had been kept and after Rose's bank accounts had been scrutinized, the companies were wound up. Findings by the Official Receiver were often referred to the Department of Trade and Industry, although sometimes the matter was passed to the Director of Public Prosecutions, as it was on this occasion. That department, in turn, referred it to Scotland Yard's latest crime-fighting arm, which had been formed in February 1946. This was COC6 Department, or The Metropolitan and City Police Company Fraud Department, more colloquially known as 'The Fraud Squad'. It investigated such matters as mock auctions, share-pushing, fraudulent take-over bids, long firm frauds, fraudulent conversions, falsification of accounts, embezzling, forgery and the issuing of false balance sheets. It also dealt with fraudulent mail-order concerns, which fitted the bill perfectly so far as Rose's case was concerned.

Detectives from both the Metropolitan and the City of London Police staffed the Fraud Squad; one of them was Detective Inspector Ernest George William Millen.

* * *

Ernie Millen had just celebrated his forty-sixth birthday when he was called into the office of the squad's head, Detective Chief Superintendent Colin MacDougall, and handed the Rose docket. Millen was an accredited fraud investigator who had

taken crash courses in accountancy and banking even before
the Fraud Squad was formed; that had assisted materially when
he investigated the activities of the Revd Harry Clapham, 'The
Embezzling Vicar', who owned nine houses and whose ninety-
seven bank accounts were dotted around the United Kingdom.
Millen proved twenty-one cases of fraudulent conversion and
falsification of accounts, which resulted in Clapham being sent
to penal servitude for three years at Parkhurst prison, ordered
to pay prosecution costs of £1,000 and, despite the best efforts
of 'Sister Connie' Owens who tried to clear his name, being
defrocked by his Southwark diocese.[1]

But Millen, coming to the end of his three-year tenure with the
Fraud Squad, was no pen-pushing, sober peruser of columns of
disputed figures; he had served on the Flying Squad as a detective
sergeant (first class) for two and a half years, and at half an inch
over six feet, he was a pretty tough customer.

Just as tough was the officer he selected to accompany him
on the Rose investigation. Detective Constable Ernest Radcliffe
Bond had joined the police in 1946, having served as David
Stirling's sergeant in the Western Desert's wartime Special Air
Service Brigade. Bond was now coming to the end of a two-year
posting at the Fraud Squad and, aged thirty-eight, was awaiting
promotion to detective sergeant; he had already been commended
by the commissioner on eight occasions, six of them for fraud
investigations, the last of which included commendations from
the bench at Halifax Magistrates' Court, the trial Judge at Leeds
Assizes and the Director of Public Prosecutions.

But the stink of corruption from Brighton Borough Police
Force was wafting north, into the offices of the Director of Public
Prosecutions (DPP) and New Scotland Yard, and not for the first
time, either. Allegations of corruption had already been made
to the DPP by a respected Brighton solicitor named Howard
Sidney Johnson, who had been fed information by a disgruntled
officer from 'A' Division. Johnson, who died on the Isle of Man in
September 2000, never divulged the name of his source. His name
is still kept secret.

The outgoing Chief Constable's replacement was the Deputy
Chief Constable, Detective Superintendent Charles Feild Williams
Ridge, who had been selected by the Home Office following the

---

1 For further information on this pilfering priest, see *The Guv'nors: Ten of
Scotland Yard's Greatest Detectives*, Pen & Sword Books, 2010

recommendation of Brighton Watch Committee on 22 February from a shortlist of five strong contenders.

Certainly, given his experience in the borough, Ridge seemed the suitable candidate. There was a dissenter; it came in the form of an anonymous letter, oddly signed by someone who described himself as 'A brother West Indian (Trinidad)'. In it, he wrote:

> Ridge is not a popular man, except with the local businessmen who put him there for their own purpose. It is not considered policy to appoint a local man, for very obvious reasons.

The letter was dismissed by the Watch Committee, who appended it to the file which made its way to the Home Office, where due to its lack of evidence, plus the anonymity of the writer, it was again ignored, and the committee's recommendation was rubber-stamped. So if, amongst others, the finger of accusation was pointing at Ridge – although the enquiry got nowhere – perhaps it wasn't far wrong. But one thing the resentful former officer was sure of: that Rose's criminal activities had gone on unabated because someone in the CID office at Brighton was tipping him off.

With all that in mind, Millen and Bond set off for Brighton.

*   *   *

It would have been usual for the host police force to provide an office at the police station for the visitors from London to work from; but with the accusations of corruption, this was, of course, the last thing that Millen wanted. Instead, he set up office at the Official Liquidators Office at 44–46 Old Steyne in the town which also contained a safe in which to deposit the statements and documents he was accruing. It was not too long before the crooked cops came calling: Detective Inspector John Richard Hammersley, deputy head of the CID, and his trusted assistant, Detective Sergeant Trevor Ernest Heath. They expressed delight at the arrival of 'The men from the Yard' and unctuously offered them every assistance. This especially applied to Ernie Bond, to whom they offered an oily friendship and from whom they tried to extract both information and copies of the statements obtained. With Millen's agreement, Bond fed them snippets of information which were of no relevance whatsoever, and they lost interest – just for the time being.

With access to Rose's bank accounts, Millen obtained a considerable wealth of damning evidence as well as statements from the defrauded persons, and he paid a call on Rose at his sumptuously furnished apartment at Flat 1, 17 Cannon Place, a salubrious thoroughfare which led down to Brighton's sea front. Rose, who described himself as a company director and was carrying on a business as a jeweller and antiques dealer from that address, was not particularly perturbed when Millen showed him a large number of cheques which had been made out to his company but had found their way into his account. As accuser and accused sipped their tea, Rose made a statement of admission. He must have known the game was up but perhaps he felt that the local police contacts he had made would prevent him going to prison; and he was nearly right.

Millen now submitted his file back to the DPP, who authorized prosecution in the case and drew up the informations to present to the Magistrates' Court. Millen then applied to Brighton Magistrates' Court for fifteen summonses against Rose; one was for carrying on the company for fraudulent purposes and another was for failing to keep proper books of account. The next eight summonses were for fraudulently converting sums of money to the tune of £884 17s 6d, and the last five were for obtaining a total of £1,372 10s 0d by means of false pretences.

Whenever officers from Scotland Yard travelled to the provinces to carry out criminal investigations which reached a successful conclusion, it was accepted that a local officer should be responsible for charging the offender. It was good for public relations; it showed that the local police had been working closely with the Metropolitan officers, and that the latter were not being 'Clever Dicks' or suggesting that they had achieved something that their constabulary colleagues had been unable to.

But when Inspector Hammersley asked Millen if he might serve the summonses on Rose, it raised an immediate question mark. Why should he make such a request in respect of an investigation which he had not in any way been party to? Millen wanted to know what Rose would say when he was officially served with the summonses and wanted the details of any previous convictions. But then again, Hammersley was a local officer and, after all, was second-in-command of the CID; so Millen handed the items to him.

When Hammersley returned he stated that Rose had no record of convictions. Unlike the charging of a suspect, when fingerprints were taken, this did not happen when a summons was served. But Millen was convinced that Rose *must* have previous convictions; common sense dictated that one simply did not commence a complex charity fraud lasting fifteen years having lived a blameless, temperate life beforehand. So Millen got to work . . .

Meanwhile, Rose appeared at Brighton Magistrates' Court, and after a two-day hearing finishing on 3 July 1957, Mr Anthony Harmsworth QC (representing the DPP) called a number of witnesses to say that they had paid cash in advance to canvassers for goods which had not been delivered. Then there were others who had lent money to Rose after he had told them that he urgently needed capital to keep disabled ex-servicemen in employment. Rose was committed on bail to Sussex Assizes for trial, and Mr L. J. Stroud, who appeared for Rose, informed the bench that his client would be pleading guilty to all the offences.

So far, so good – for Rose. Matters changed dramatically after Millen, who had checked with all of the Criminal Records Offices in the country, received a telephone call from the office in Liverpool. It revealed not only Rose's convictions but his photograph as well.

On 24 July, as Rose confidently walked up the steps of the Assize Court he was stopped by Millen and Bond, and the contented smile on his face was abruptly wiped off when Millen produced his previous convictions and the photograph. He admitted that the youthful photograph and the convictions belonged to him, and then he said something else: 'Did you get that from Brighton?'

This was a decisive moment. It meant that while Millen had been searching the country for any details of Rose's convictions, they had been known to officers at Brighton all the time; and Hammersley had stated that he could find no trace of any convictions.

Rose pleaded guilty to everything and was sentenced to three years' imprisonment. Both Hammersley and Heath were present in court; neither of them had anything to say to Millen.

But within a month of commencing his sentence, Rose, from the confines of his Maidstone prison cell, was feeling badly let down by the crooked cops who were supposed to be looking after him. Unlike his two dodgy associates, he had plenty to say; and he started talking ...

CHAPTER 2

The Bucket of Blood

The playwright Keith Waterhouse once said, 'Brighton is a town that always looks as if it is helping police with their enquiries', and now it's time to find out why.

The Astor Club had originally opened in 1924 as the Astra Club, where the Happy Four Orchestra was said 'to set one all a-twiddle' and the audience was mesmerized by the likes of Miss Bobbie Macauley, who was described as being 'light of foot and supple of limb'. It all added up to an evening's entertainment which was probably regarded at the time as being slightly saucy but nothing more. The club changed hands, names and addresses several times over the years until November 1954, when as the Astor Hotel it opened its doors at 61 King's Road, courtesy of a highly disreputable character named Alan Roy Bennett, who between 1931 and 1948 had acquired fourteen previous convictions. He was known by a number of other names, as the hotel had been. Later, it became colloquially known as 'The Bucket of Blood' and, more than anything else, it cast a shadow over the town, as it would continue to do for years to come.

★   ★   ★

Following a twelve-month sentence, Bennett had been released from prison in February 1949. His wife and two children had been jettisoned along the way, and in Oslo in 1951, legally or perhaps not, he married a Norwegian girl named Wenche, who was commonly known as 'Winkie', and they honeymooned in Nassau.

After purchasing the hotel, 36-year-old Bennett – and although he was now using the name 'Brown', one of his ten aliases, to prevent confusion he will continue to be referred to as 'Bennett' during this narrative – converted the hotel's basement into a drinking establishment known as the Astor Club. It opened at Easter 1955 and was subject to the usual club hours, closing at 10.30pm on weekdays. Bennett was visited by an old friend, Anthony John Lyons, the 59-year-old owner of nearby Sherry's Bar in West Street, who had held an on-license for the previous eight and a half years. He had also been co-owner of Tony Lessells' Salon de Paris hairdresser's at 9 Ship Street for three years and was now living at Marine Gate, Brighton, a block of luxury flats built in 1939 which nowadays fetch up to half a million pounds. Lyons asked Bennett how he wanted to run the club, telling him, 'If you're not greedy, you can serve drinks all night and nobody will bother you.'

Bearing in mind Bennett's character and background, it is somewhat surprising that this had not occurred to him without Lyons' help, but within a few days Lyons brought Ridge – then a detective superintendent – to the club, where he was introduced to Bennett and his wife.

Charles Ridge, impressively tall at 6 feet 2 inches and a Freeman of the City of London, was then aged fifty-seven. Born in Ffestiniog, Porthmadog in May 1899, he had seen active service in the First World War, when he had been gassed, and he joined the police in 1925 as a constable, transferring after a year to Brighton. Within three years he was appointed to the CID and in 1935 he was promoted detective sergeant. Further promotion to detective inspector followed in 1948, to detective chief inspector in 1949 and then to detective superintendent in 1950; he had also been commended on four occasions.

It was agreed that Ridge would be paid 'a score' – £20 per week – for Bennett to drive a coach and horses through the licensing laws pretty much as he pleased, and that was exactly what happened. Lyons would bring his customers to the club as soon as his own club had closed, and drinks were sold until 2.00–3.00am. It was a drunken, noisy establishment which often witnessed fights; due to the rowdy, blood-spattered combatants staggering out into King's Road in the early hours of the morning, the club became known as 'The Bucket of Blood'. But never once was it prosecuted.

Ridge would arrive at the club on a weekly basis to collect his bursary, sometimes with Lyons but often alone, usually at about 5.00pm because nobody else would be in the club at that time; there was little point in it opening before 10.30pm, because it only made money after that hour. On one occasion, Ridge admired Bennett's gleaming Mark VII Jaguar parked outside the club.

'That's a nice motor car', commented Ridge. 'I can't afford one like that; I don't know how you do it.' He later added, 'My wife likes nice things.'

'So does mine', replied Bennett, 'but don't worry; it'll be taken care of.'

Bennett paid his weekly subscription to Ridge – always £20 in £5 notes – on six or seven occasions. The last occasion he personally paid Ridge the money was in Lyons' Sherry's Bar, when he passed it over, wrapped in a newspaper, just prior to Ridge going on holiday to Spain. This was observed by Harry Waterman, who helped out at the Astor Hotel and lived there rent-free; he had also seen Bennett put money in an envelope and hand it to Ridge at the Astor. He was in good company with Bennett; a fellow crook, Waterman had twice been convicted of receiving stolen property, once in 1948 and then again the following year, when he was sentenced to twelve months' imprisonment.

After Ridge's holiday, the collection procedure changed. Detective Sergeant Heath arrived, telling Bennett that from now on, he was to be calling for the 'present'.

'Did Ridge send you?' asked Bennett, to be told, 'Yes.'

Born in 1921 in Epsom, Trevor Heath had been with the Force for fourteen years, having served as a sub lieutenant in the Royal Navy during the war and commanded a landing craft on D-Day. Six feet tall, he had been appointed to the CID in February 1948 and prior to his promotion to detective sergeant had made more arrests than any other detective constable on the Force, as well as having been commended on eleven occasions.

The usual £20 was handed over, and the collections continued on a weekly basis, with Heath either receiving the money personally or it being left for him in an envelope behind the bar. From time to time, Bennett would also slip Heath one or two £5 notes for himself and he purchased several expensive ties for him from Mayfair's Burlington Arcade. He also gave him items of clothing, including a shirt and a jacket, some of which were his own cast-offs.

Matters started to change when Heath visited Bennett at the club and asked for a quiet word. They went into Bennett's private room, where Heath produced a ten-year-old police photograph of Bennett.

'We're rather surprised', said Heath, to which Bennett asked, 'Who's we?'

'The guv'nor and I. We're surprised; we didn't expect this.'

Bennett stated that he was a businessman, the chairman of a few companies and asked what Heath wanted. Was it blackmail?

But Heath simply and enigmatically replied, 'The guv'nor's sent me.'

If it was blackmail, Bennett was a prime candidate for it; his convictions included larceny, false pretences, stealing by a trick, stealing a handbag from a woman, receiving, taking and driving away a motor car, posing as a pilot in the RAF, being found in a house for an unlawful purpose, housebreaking, shop-breaking and unlawful wounding.

These were not just one-off offences; in 1939, Bennett was part of an organized four-man gang – one of them had just been discharged at the Inner London Sessions for receiving seventy-four suits and another had been convicted in three cases of attempting to bribe a police constable – who had stolen travellers' cars under cover of darkness and relieved them of their contents, which they then sold. These included women's coats and dresses, children's clothing, jewellery and typewriters, valued in excess of £1,000. Bennett – he was then calling himself variously Alan, Allen and Austin Roy Ferguson, was living at 11–13 Talbot Road, Stretford, Manchester and was said to be working as a chef – already had a number of convictions recorded against him. At Manchester City Sessions on 28 September 1939, Bennett asked for six other offences to be taken into consideration, and the Recorder, Mr Noel B. Goldie KC, MP, saying that these offences were 'a despicable form of crime', sent the four men to prison, with Bennett receiving the heaviest punishment of twelve months' hard labour.

Called up for wartime service with the RAF, Bennett impersonated an officer and moved around the country obtaining property by false pretences. When he appeared at Uxbridge Police Court, now using the name Allen Roy Brown, in August 1941 he asked for thirteen more offences – committed at venues which included Leicester, Paignton, Sheffield, Kingstown and Pinner – to be taken into consideration and was sentenced to twelve months' imprisonment. The following February, he was back at the same court, demanding that the sum of £40 7s 2½d found in his possession should be returned to him, since police were unable to prove it was stolen. A solicitor appearing for the Commissioner of the Metropolitan Police argued that the money should be distributed amongst the defrauded persons. Someone thought to be rather more deserving was Bennett's (or Brown's or Ferguson's) wife, who with two young children had written to her local police in Manchester requesting the money which she knew he had in his possession, because she was on the point of appealing to the Public Assistance Committee. Since the sum represented £2,140 at today's value, it would certainly have kept the wolf from the door of the abandoned Mrs Ferguson. His application having been refused, Brown was dragged from the dock, noisily informing the arresting officer, 'I'll get you yet!'

These were just two of ten periods of imprisonment, including a sentence of penal servitude, that Bennett had served. If he were to be further convicted of crime, with his form he could expect to go away for a very long time.

Bennett certainly believed Heath's words to be blackmail, because that's precisely what he furiously told him: 'This is nothing but blackmail; go and tell your guv'nor to jump off Brighton Pier! Not another penny, and I've a good mind to write a letter to the commissioner!' – although he would later change this to say that it was the Home Secretary to whom he would complain.

Heath and his crooked cohorts were getting greedy. Quite apart from money they were obtaining elsewhere from other criminals, the regular income of £20 per week from Bennett – worth almost £530 at today's value – was quite a respectable sum to someone like Heath, whose weekly wage as a detective sergeant was only £14 8s 7d.

So it was that on this occasion Bennett did not part with any money for Heath; but that would soon change.

Just before Ascot week 1955, a man named Alan Walker arrived at Bennett's hotel. He was flush with money, as well he might have been, because he had stolen a large sum of it from a premises in East Anglia. On 13 July Bennett's wife accompanied Walker when he went out to dine, but she later returned, alone.

Heath, together with two other detectives, arrived at the hotel and told Bennett, 'We've arrested Alan. Your wife was with him.'

'What's my wife got to do with Alan being arrested?' asked Bennett, to be told that Walker had been arrested for larceny and that 'matters could be made very difficult for her.' The officers had let Bennett's wife go free, but Heath then said, 'Just give us our whack of the grand.'

For the benefit of those unused to the language of the criminal classes, 'a whack' in this instance meant 'an illicit share of' and 'the grand' was £1,000. This was the stolen money which Walker had kept in his bedroom and which was now allegedly missing. The imputation was that Bennett had stolen it, which he denied, saying that he had been at Ascot all day. However, Heath persisted in referring again and again to receiving his whack, in which case the matter would be forgotten, but Bennett protested that 'there was no grand out of which to get a whack.'

An inspector from Lowestoft later arrived to look round the hotel, and after he left, Heath turned up, told Bennett, 'He doesn't believe you've not had it; and neither do I', and once more demanded his whack.

Had there been £1,000 in Alan Walker's bedroom, and if so, had Bennett helped himself to it? Whatever the case, the matter was resolved by Bennett parting with £30–£40, so that Walker's name would not appear in the press as staying at the hotel and so that Wenche Bennett's name would similarly not feature in connection with Walker's arrest. It could be that this transaction was not fully to Heath's satisfaction, since Bennett would later say that Heath continually kept repeating the demand for 'his whack of the grand, from that day to this'.

If Bennett – by a long stretch of the imagination – could be thought to be an innocent party in that matter, he was not when Detective Sergeant Arthur Broadbent-Speight of the Leeds City Police investigated a matter of obtaining property by means of a dishonoured cheque. This had been issued by a man named Austin Ferguson, which coincidentally was one of Bennett's many aliases, and on 23 August 1955 the officer wrote to Brighton police asking them to interview the culprit.

In Bennett's private room at the hotel he was seen by Heath, who told him, 'There's an enquiry for you, out at Leeds, about a forged cheque.'

Bennett protested that he had not been to Leeds for twenty years (although to issue a fraudulent cheque he didn't necessarily need to have been), but nevertheless, Heath persisted: 'You'll have to go, you know.'

'I've done nothing', protested Bennett. 'It's ridiculous. I can't go at the height of the season', but Heath repeated his mantra: 'You'll have to go.'

Instead, he parted with £15–£20 and he did not have to go. Bennett heard no more about it, and neither did Detective Sergeant Broadbent-Speight of the Leeds City Police.

When Heath wanted a deposit for a car which cost £300, he offered a diamond ring to Bennett – he was unable to take it to a jeweller's, the reason he gave being because 'they know me there' – who gave him £70 for it.

Bennett shut up the club and never reopened it. However, the lawlessness regarding 'The Bucket of Blood' did not end there.

Mrs Blanche Josephine Cherryman had lived in the Astor Hotel and had sometimes acted as an unpaid receptionist. She had lent Bennett £2,000, which he had never repaid. She had never known the Astor Club to close prior to 1.30am and she knew it had a very bad name, with fights breaking out and trouble with women; she had also seen Heath and Lyons there, had seen Heath receive money and was 'shocked and worried about it'. One night, she had received a telephone call for Bennett; the caller said, 'Close the club, tonight', adding, 'Say it was Charlie.'

On 4 October 1955, feeling that she could not trust anyone in the CID, she went to police headquarters, where she asked to

see the Chief Constable, Ridge. She told him of the misbehaviour
at the club, plus the warning telephone call, and Ridge, giving a
knowing look to another officer present, replied that he would
'look into it'.

The club was reopened in January 1956 by Mary Mason.
She knew Tony Lyons, who told her that Bennett paid £20 per
week to do as he liked – but not, mind you, to the police. Lyons
told her that the money was paid to him to encourage his own
customers to go to the Astor and that Bennett knew someone
who was able to tell him when a raid was going to take place,
whereupon he would shut the club for a day or two. However,
Mrs Mason did not pay any money to either Lyons or the police;
she was raided in August 1956, and the club was struck off. She
was an excitable lady, especially when drink had been taken;
she blamed Lyons for the demise of her club and, visiting The
White Horse public house, she loudly informed the clientele of
her suspicions. At Sherry's Bar, where she denounced Lyons as
'a bastard', he denied any knowledge of her downfall.

Back now to Bennett who, following the closing of the Astor
Bar, went abroad to conduct business in Norway and other
European countries; whatever that business was, it was obviously
quite lucrative, because by the time he returned he was driving a
Rolls-Royce. On 19 June 1956, he had arrived in Brighton, had
just completed a business transaction and was about to leave,
when he heard a voice call out, 'Alan!' He turned and saw it was
Heath, who said, 'Just a moment. There's an enquiry out for you.'

'Where from?' asked Bennett and was told, 'Bournemouth'.

Heath went on to say that there had been a burglary at
Stewart's, a jeweller's shop in Bournemouth, by means of
duplicate keys on 30 April 1956, and property valued at £8,000
had been stolen. Bennett said he had gone to Belgium on the
day prior to the burglary, but on 1 May, message No. 1,043 had
been received at Brighton police station in respect of the theft, in
which Heath said the enquiry related to Bennett and asked for
him to be interviewed.

Let's just pause for a moment. The message was sent within
two days of the shop-breaking, naming Bennett (under his current
alias of Brown) as a suspect, so the police at Bournemouth must
have had very reasonable grounds for doing so. Furthermore,
jewellery valued at £8,000 had been stolen, a pretty tidy sum
for 1956 (and at today's values, some £211,280), and bearing
in mind the distance between the two towns was less than
100 miles, one would have thought that Bournemouth officers
(who knew the ins and outs of the case) would have got into a

car or jumped on a train and interviewed Bennett themselves. But the fact was, constabularies were quite parsimonious regarding their expenditure in those days, and if they wished an offender in a different police area to be brought to court, often for quite serious offences, a summons would be sent through the post requesting the malefactor to show up at a specified date and time. Therefore, the concept of the outlay incurred by sending one or two officers simply to interview a suspect, when this could be carried out by an unknown, but quite obviously upright, honest CID officer of a different constabulary stationed 100 miles away, would undoubtedly have brought the treasurer of Bournemouth's Watch Committee into a state of frenzied conniptions.

'You must be completely mad', said Bennett in response to Heath's statement, but rather than listen to Bennett's reply, Heath's attention was drawn to Bennett's car. 'You look to be doing all right with your big Rolls-Royce', he said, enviously.

'I get by', replied Bennett, to which Heath retorted, 'More than I do; things are very bad.'

Bennett took the hint, gave Heath £10 and asked him to make enquiries, which he did; this was the first time Heath had seen Bennett since the shop-breaking so he telephoned the police at Bournemouth. The message which Constable Charles Ronald Bodger recorded was Heath asking, 'Brown is calling to see me . . . are you still interested? He is driving a £7,000 Rolls.'

Bodger's response was that Bennett should be interviewed regarding his movements at the time of the shop-breaking and his present address and means of livelihood should be discovered.

Bennett later went to the CID office at Brighton where, in the presence of Heath, he saw Hammersley, who said, 'Hello, Alan.'

'You know John', commented Heath, and Bennett replied, 'Yes. The last time I saw him, he was in uniform.'

Hammersley was one of two detective inspectors at Brighton; he had been promoted to that rank in 1956. Tall, with a toothbrush moustache, he had been born at Barnet in 1919, joined the force in 1937 and had served as a captain with the Corps of Military Police in the Second World War, during which he had been Mentioned in Dispatches.

'Now he's an inspector', said Heath; since August 1948 he and Hammersley had worked together continuously, hence the familiarity.

Bennett asked Hammersley the nature of the trouble in Bournemouth, but before he could answer, sharp-eyed Heath (referring to Bennett) said, 'He's got a cake of notes in his back pocket', which was true – he had about £500.

'About the Bournemouth job – we'll find out about it', said Hammersley, adding, 'It has nothing to do with us.'

Heath left the office, ostensibly to make a telephone call, although Bennett was of the opinion that he had gone to inspect his car. He was half right. The message that was received by Detective Inspector Frederick John Tilling of Bournemouth Borough Police was that Bennett had been interrogated by Brighton Police but that they had got nowhere. Bennett, said Heath, was out of the country at the time of the offence, his car's registration number was OLK 800 and his address was Radnor Mews, London, W2.

When he returned, Heath told Bennett, 'Everything is all right.'

'What, just like that?' exclaimed Bennett, to be told, 'Yes, just like that.'

After some further conversation, Bennett was about to leave when Heath said, 'Don't forget John', and Bennett screwed up a couple of £5 notes and dropped them on the floor.

'Thank you, Alan', remarked Hammersley.

We might speculate that if Bennett had been responsible for the shop-breaking and had disposed of the jewellery on the continent, it could well have funded the purchase of his Rolls-Royce. That had certainly been a busy time for Bennett, because (if he were to be believed) ten days prior to the jeweller's being broken into, he had been in Monaco for the wedding of Grace Kelly to Prince Rainier. He had also, apparently, hired a yacht for a tour of the Mediterranean; perhaps these expensive expeditions had left him short of money, hence his sudden return to England, prior to 29 April.

But what is astonishing about that encounter at Brighton police station is not the bare-faced illegality of it; but that in respect of an £8,000 theft Bennett was given his impunity for a total bursary of twenty miserable quid.

Just six days later, on 25 June, Bennett in London made a telephone call to Heath, at Heath's request on Brighton 21730, the direct line to the CID office – this meant it did not go through the station's switchboard, Brighton 24141 – and Heath told him, 'There's a 'W' [warrant] out for you', adding that it was in respect of 'a screwing job at Folkestone'. The offence had occurred on 30 May 1956, Bennett had been picked out by his photograph and 'he was in plenty of trouble.'

Heath wanted Bennett to come to Brighton immediately, saying that he would be in the Bodega public house in Ship Street, but Bennett failed to turn up. Instead, the following day, he spoke to a former lawyer named Jasper Addis in the Wig & Pen public house, told him what had happened and asked Addis what he should do.

'If it was me, I would go and see the Yard', was Addis' advice, and at 5.00pm Bennett went to New Scotland Yard, where he spoke to Detective Sergeant Frederick Powell of the Fraud Squad. It appeared there was no warrant in existence in Bennett's name, and he told Heath so.

'Have you been told that by a rozzer?'[1] asked Heath and, told that was the case, he continued, 'Can you trust him, because it's different from what I hear? Half a ton[2] will put it right down here.'

But half a ton would not put it right in Brighton. On 12 July, Detective Constable Richard Crane of Kent County Police, who had obtained a warrant on description of a man responsible for an attempted shop-breaking at Folkestone, arrested Bennett, who appeared at the local Magistrates' Court the following day. It was finally dealt with on 10 August, when the magistrates declined to commit Bennett for trial and he was discharged.

And now, on the same day and with the greatest secrecy imaginable, Scotland Yard was about to get involved. But before that happened, it's time to look at whatever else had been going on in that sunny seaside town.

---

1 'Rozzer' being the slang term for a police officer; to be scrupulously correct, the nickname for a CID officer was 'Cozzer'.

2 'Half a ton' represented £50.

Chapter 3

Protection – at a Price

A father and son named Harry and John Leach both had premises at 74 West Street, Brighton. Harry Leach, aged sixty-four, ran a fishmonger's; in 1951, next door at No. 74a, his son John, aged forty, opened a drinking establishment which was known as the Burlesque Club. Both father and son (plus some other people) had a financial interest in the club, and John looked after the administrative side. In 1954, John loaned money to one of his customers named Michael Roberts on security of three watches and a travelling clock. Roberts was a thief; later, he and another thief named Roy John Mitchell broke into a shop, and John bought items which resulted from the breaking: rings, wristwatches and gold coins.

On a Saturday in December 1954, Hammersley and Heath paid a visit to John Leach's club. This was just after John had been fined £15 on each of two summonses and ordered to pay £1 2s 6d costs for selling liquor without a licence at the Burlesque Club, after Police Constable Hopper and Policewoman Morgan, telling the steward, 'We're down for the weekend', had been served drinks. Whilst the Bench at Brighton Magistrates' Court had ordered the confiscation of liquor worth £75 they had rejected an application for the club to be struck off the register. The previous year, John had been questioned regarding the possession of uncustomed cigarettes, and during the war he had been prosecuted for nine cases of using petrol unlawfully when acting as chauffeur to his father. It could not be considered a criminal record of alarming proportions, but those past brushes with the law, plus being in possession of stolen property, nevertheless put John Leach in a rather vulnerable position.

He admitted the purchase of the jewellery, described Roberts and, the next day, the two officers returned; after John had made a statement, they took away two rings, a wristwatch and some coins.

The following day – Monday – a caller arrived at Harry Leach's address. The father was deeply concerned about his son's plight and was told, 'This case can be straightened out, you know. Shall I try and do it for you?'

The caller was Samuel 'Sammy' Pisoner Bellson, an unlicensed bookmaker with an unsavoury reputation. Born in August 1915 in Mile End, London, Bellson had convictions for being a suspected person, being found on enclosed premises for an unlawful purpose and attempting to steal women's coats, and he had served two terms of hard labour, the last being in 1942. Leaving the family home at 271 Queens Road, West Ham, he moved to Brighton, where he ran a chain of gambling establishments, including the Lonsdale Club – it shared an address with the Burlesque Club, of which he was part-owner – and he was what was known as 'a fixer', someone who acted as a go-between 'twixt police and criminals. Leach senior certainly wanted matters straightened out, and he gave Bellson £50. But within half an hour Bellson was back, saying, 'That's not enough.' Leach gave him another £50, but when Bellson returned he told Leach that when he had placed the £100 on the errant officer's desk, the sum had caused much amusement. This infuriated Leach, who told Bellson, 'They can do their worst, we'll fight them.'

Ridge – then a detective superintendent – called on Leach Senior and commiserated with him, saying he was sorry to see his son in trouble. Leach told him, 'Well, Charlie, we all make mistakes. All I ask is for you to do the best you can.'

To this, Ridge replied, 'Whatever you do, Harry, keep within the law' – or it could have been, 'keep in with the law', which, if that was said, cast a completely different meaning on Ridge's parting words.

Two days later, Hammersley and Heath returned a fob watch to John Leach, and Hammersley told him that Micky Roberts was calling him 'The biggest receiver in Brighton', adding, 'If you have to go to court you will have to have a solicitor and maybe a barrister, and that may cost you £300 to £400.'

'What can I do?' asked John and received the reply, 'Well, for £250 the evidence can be taken down and slung in the sea.'

But John Leach refused to pay up; he was brought before the magistrates in January 1955 and for receiving a gold watch and a diamond ring, valued together at £150, was sentenced to concurrent terms of three months' imprisonment. He later appealed to the court of quarter sessions and was successful, with costs being awarded against police, and the Recorder, Sir Charles Doughty QC, MP, commenting that 'He would not be likely to commit a criminal offence for a "tuppenny-ha'penny" profit, and that if he had known the property was stolen he would have tried to dispose of it, but that he did not attempt to do.'

Afterwards, Ridge invited John Leach to his office, saying, 'I don't want you to have any feelings about this, because one day you may be on the Watch Committee', before burning Leach's fingerprint form as a sign of his good faith. Leach may not have been aware that due to his successful appeal, the regulations stipulated that it should be destroyed anyway.

Bellson was a handy conduit for the crooked officers. Two years previously, he had appeared at court on 3 August 1953, when a former police officer (and now an enquiry agent), Mr Harold Frederick Charles Barnard, had served a writ on him after Bellson had been pointed out to him by Heath. A few days later, when Barnard was driving his car, he saw that a police car was following him. He stopped and went into a public house. Within a few moments Hammersley and another officer entered the pub and told him, 'Watch your step. We have to look after Sammy Bellson. You'd better keep your mouth shut.' They then went on to threaten Barnard, saying he would be framed if he did not.

Bellson was, indeed, being looked after.

* * *

William Albert Page was the father of Jill Day, a popular singer, film, television and radio performer, which was to his credit, although little else was. A large, bombastic bookmaker with a mouthful of rotting teeth, Page had come to the notice of the authorities when, on 14 July 1944, he had been sentenced to fifteen months' imprisonment and fined £1,000 for conspiracy to dope greyhounds; thereafter he had been warned off greyhound and horse-racing tracks. With a string of convictions for running illegal betting shops, and a habit of cowing people into submission by roaring, 'Do you know who I am?', he was more closely associated with Chief Constable Charles Ridge (he had his home telephone number) than the Watch Committee might have thought desirable. In April 1957, he went into Ridge's office, ordered out Superintendent Hill – 'I don't want to speak to him. I've come here to speak to you personally' – and told Ridge, 'I've come to help you clean up the town.'

Unsurprisingly (albeit inaccurately), Ridge replied, 'I never said the town wanted cleaning up.'

'But I think it do', replied Page ungrammatically. He went on to cite an instance of one of Ridge's officers taking £50 off a person and then having him convicted, and also mentioned another officer who had had the impudence to interview a youth whom Page had 'helped'. Asked the names of those officers, Page pompously replied, 'At the proper time and place.'

No doubt there would have been many officers (senior or otherwise) of that era who, being addressed in such an insolent, hectoring manner, would have taken the opportunity to smash what remained of Page's disintegrating teeth straight down his throat – but not Ridge. It appeared that Page certainly had the upper hand, because in a conciliatory tone Ridge said, 'Pagey, put your cards on the table; tell me what you want.'

'You've summonsed a man for aiding and abetting me. This is a liberty. This man has a wife and three children. He's going into hospital with suspected cancer of the throat. It's not right for you to summon him.'

'What can I do?' asked Ridge.

'I don't know, *you* know what you can do.'

'I can have a word with the Magistrates' Clerk and get him the minimum fine.'

'I don't want that. Why should this man have a conviction when Bellson's club has been raided five times and the landlord has never had a conviction? I'll bet you don't prosecute Leach, who's the owner of the Burlesque.'

So this was a power struggle between Page and Bellson; but it appeared that it would be Bellson who was going to be looked after.

On 4 June 1957, Police Constable Frank Knight of Brighton police was one of two officers deployed in plain clothes to carry out observations on betting houses and licensed premises. One of the clubs was the Burlesque in West Street – also known as the Lonsdale Club – and since the owner was Sammy Bellson, its clientele more familiarly referred to it as 'Sammy's Place'.

Knight was just about to go on duty at 6.00pm, to work until 2.00am, when he was called to the CID office to see Heath. Knight's partner, Police Constable Vernon Tullett, waited outside the office.

'Are you interested in earning a tenner a week?' asked Heath, and when Knight asked what he meant, Heath told him, 'Mr Hammersley has asked me to see you. Sammy will pay you a tenner a week just to keep him informed when his club is going to be done.'

'I'm not interested', replied Knight, to which Heath told him, 'It'll be all right, your job won't fall flat and you won't be in the cart because the frequenters will be there.'

Once more Knight told Heath he wasn't interested, and Heath replied, 'All right, it's up to you. I was to get a fiver a week out of it for fixing it up, but that won't break me', and added, somewhat surprisingly to a straight cop who had rejected his advances, 'I have my other fiddles, you know that.'

In fact, Knight was unaware of any other fiddles with which Heath was involved, but Heath told him not to speak to anyone regarding that conversation and, as Knight was about to leave the office, he said, 'If Vernon wants to know about it, say it's about Weaver being in and out of West Street.'

But as soon as he left the office, Knight told Vernon Tullett precisely what had transpired.

In fact, Heath's offer had the ring of authenticity about it. When Bellson had a club on the seafront, it had been raided twice; the Burlesque Club in West Street had been raided three times, the latest of which had been on 21 June 1956, when Bellson had been fined £75 on each of two charges of using the premises for betting. It would have been worth a tenner a week to have been forewarned of police action by bunging a venal cop – but not PC Knight.

CHAPTER 4

Abortionists and Burglars

Mrs Alice Florence Brabiner was, not to put too fine a point on it, an abortionist. She had a conviction for stealing women's clothing from Brighton goods yard in 1941 for which she had been fined £5, but in 1949 she had been convicted of procuring an abortion, an offence for which, perhaps surprisingly, she had been conditionally discharged. She lived with her daughter, Mrs Iris Karrouze, at a basement flat in Regency Square, Brighton. On 26 November 1956, she met a woman, Mrs Gwladys Mabel Elizabeth 'Betty' Lawrence, who asked her to go to her flat at Vernon Terrace, Brighton to perform an abortion on a young girl. A plump, motherly-looking figure, Betty Lawrence did not fit the traditional picture of an abortionist's assistant, but that is what she was, and she supplied the syringe necessary for the illegal operation.

On Christmas Eve, Mrs Lawrence was summonsed to the police station's CID office by Heath, who told her that he knew of the abortion that had been carried out; the young woman concerned had provided all the details, and Mrs Lawrence admitted her part in it and made a statement.

The same evening, Mrs Brabiner received a visit from Heath, whom she knew. He told her that he was aware that she had been to Vernon Terrace for the illegal operation, something she denied and made a statement to Heath.

On 30 December, Mrs Lawrence saw Heath again, this time in a public house, and he demanded the syringe that had been used; rather than let Heath come to her flat (in which case her husband would have been made aware of her part in the illegal act), she agreed to bring it to Heath the following day, which she did.

A little later, in Sherry's Bar, she saw Heath talking to Lyons at the bar. She approached Heath and asked if her name would be published in the newspapers; Heath told her to go and speak to Lyons, and that evening, in the same bar, she did.

'You're in a spot of bother, Betty', said Lyons, to which Mrs Lawrence replied, 'Yes. I understand you can help me.'

'Yes', replied Lyons. 'It'll cost you a ton.'

Mrs Lawrence had no idea what 'a ton' was, so Lyons explained it was £100. She replied that she hadn't got that amount of money but that she might be able to borrow £50; however Lyons stated, 'That won't be any good.'

When she phoned Heath at the CID office, he met her, told her not to telephone him at the office in future and gave her his home telephone number. The next time she met Heath was in his car outside the GPO office, when she told him she could not get the amount of money that Lyons had demanded.

'If you can get £50, that will suit me', said Heath and asked Mrs Lawrence how she would acquire it.

'I have a friend in London who'll be down the following week and he'll probably lend me the money', she replied, and she was right; Arthur Thorn was the friend who gave her £25, which she duly passed to Heath.

'That's not enough, I don't want that', said Heath, telling her, 'The guv'nor will want more than that.'

Early in the New Year, Heath returned to Mrs Brabiner's flat with another detective; Heath asked Mrs Karrouze to go into the kitchen and make him some tea, and in her absence he told Mrs Brabiner that if she paid him he might be able to help her.

'In what way could you help?' she asked, to be told, 'If you pay me, it'll go a long way. Even if you won the football pools, it couldn't keep you out of the trouble you're in, but I'll help if you pay me.'

On both occasions, a certain Reginald Betts – he was also known by his stage name of Max Ray and was often referred to as 'Maxey' – was at Mrs Brabiner's flat. He was not present when the conversations took place with Heath, but after Heath left, Betts noticed that Mrs Brabiner was very white and shaken. Her daughter confirmed the effect Heath had had upon her mother; after each visit her nerves were bad, and on one occasion she fainted.

A week later, she and her daughter went to the Celebrity Club, where she saw Betty Lawrence; after a conversation, Mrs Brabiner sent her daughter home, and when she returned she handed her mother £25 in an envelope, which she gave to Betty Lawrence, who left. Following a conversation with her, Mrs Brabiner's daughter acquired another £25, and after Heath was telephoned at the police station he went to the club, where she handed the money over to him in his car. Heath told her that Betty Lawrence had asked if he could tear up the statement Mrs Brabiner had made, but he had told her he could not.

He also asked if 'Maxey' was present, because he did not want him to witness the passing over of the money. Mrs Brabiner said that he had left the club, but in fact he had been there, she had shown him the envelope containing the £5 notes and Betts saw her get into Heath's car.

After that, she saw Heath at her flat several times a week, and on one occasion he told her she was eligible for corrective training, for which she could go to prison for fourteen years; in order to stop him serving the necessary papers on her, she paid him approximately £15.

Heath's demand was, in fact, nothing more than extortion. Corrective training had been placed on the statute books in 1948 and it catered for persons between the ages of twenty-one and thirty who, being convicted of an offence carrying two years' imprisonment or more and having been convicted on two previous occasions, could be sentenced to not less than two years' corrective training and not more than four. Aged forty-eight, Mrs Brabiner was far too old to qualify for that type of punishment, as well as it being impossible for her (or anybody else) to receive fourteen years' imprisonment for corrective training; and Heath knew it.

Meanwhile, Heath's extortion of Mrs Lawrence was moving on apace. He altered one paragraph of her statement in her favour – it was to do with the acquisition of the syringe – and he wanted to know when she would be able to raise the rest of the money, telling her, 'The guv'nor's getting very annoyed and impatient.' On 8 February, she gave evidence at Brighton Magistrates' Court against Mrs Brabiner, who was committed for trial. She had by then been given the extra £25 by Mr Thorn, but although Heath pestered her for the money, she gave him £10, deciding not to give him the balance until the case at the assize court had been completed.

The day before her trial, Mrs Brabiner gave Heath another £8; she asked if he could wait until after the trial for any more money, but as Heath pragmatically told her, 'You don't back a horse after the race.'

The following day, 2 April 1957, she was sentenced to fifteen months' imprisonment.

At the time of Heath's approach to her she knew nothing about corrective training or the possible resultant sentences; she was enlightened about both by her fellow inmates when she was serving her time.

Following the trial, Heath saw Mrs Lawrence in a public house, where she passed over the remaining £15; Arthur Thorn was with her and he heard Heath say to her, 'The money has been worth it.' Mrs Lawrence may have thought the £50 had been worth it; as far as Heath was concerned, the case certainly had been – he had accumulated £118, which at today's values represents £2,425.

*   *   *

Mr and Mrs Swaby of Gloucester Terrace, London W2 could not be described, by any stretch of the imagination, as a reputable couple. Plump, 26-year-old Sheila Swaby possessed over fifty convictions for soliciting prostitution over a period of three years, and her husband, James Thomas Swaby, had fourteen convictions to his name, including assaulting the police in 1944, larceny in 1947 and 1952, shop-breaking in 1950, being a suspected person in 1952 and, more recently, living on immoral earnings. So when he appeared at Brighton Quarter Sessions on 20 June 1957, pleaded guilty to housebreaking and asked for one other matter to be taken into consideration, he was sentenced to five years' imprisonment; most people would have said that, given his record, that was not a day too long. In fact, Swaby was the exception, because he appealed against his sentence. That made matters rather worse for him, because the sentence of imprisonment was replaced with one of five years' preventative detention.

However, before that sentence was imposed there had been a great deal of horse-trading, attempted horse-trading and downright chicanery between the Swabys and a certain Detective Sergeant Heath.

James Swaby was circulated as being wanted for the house-breaking offence at Brighton and on 22 May 1957 he was detained by the Metropolitan Police and was taken to Paddington Green police station. It was there that he was seen by Detective Constable Raymond Hovey from Brighton police, transferred to Brighton and, on the following day, appeared at the local Magistrates' Court, where he was remanded in custody until 28 May. He was seen in the cells at the court by Heath, who was the officer in the case, and Swaby asked if 'anything could be done' in respect of the charges by way of leaving out the convictions.

'Can you help me?' he asked Heath, who replied, 'That's up to you.'

Asked what he meant, Heath replied, 'Come on, lad, don't let's beat about the bush; you've been around.'

Swaby then extracted two £5 notes which he had wrapped around a pen and slipped into the hem of his raincoat. Heath took these and inserted them into the folder of his case papers but told Swaby that he would require £50 more. Swaby, in turn, suggested that Heath should speak to his wife.

'What do you think my husband's chances are?' asked Mrs Swaby and was asked in turn by Heath, 'How are you fixed for £50?' The matter was then temporarily left in abeyance after Mrs Swaby said, 'I'll have to speak to my husband.'

Heath and Hovey later went to Lewes prison, where Swaby was being held on remand; this was to serve the necessary forms on him, since he was certainly eligible for preventative detention. This form of punishment had replaced penal servitude: if a person over the age of thirty had been sentenced on three occasions to borstal training, imprisonment or penal servitude, he could be sentenced to not less than five years and not more than fourteen years' preventative detention for the protection of the public. The possibility of a sentence of preventative detention (or 'PD' as it was known) was greatly feared by members of the underworld.[1]

Hovey heard Heath say something to Swaby along the lines of 'for a pony[2] something could be done about his last conviction'. This was a reference to the offence of living on immoral earnings.

On 20 June, Swaby appeared at Brighton Quarter Sessions. Hovey took Mrs Swaby down to the cells to have a few words with her husband, after which he brought her back into court and sat down next to Heath.

'Go outside and take Mrs Swaby with you and see if she's brought me anything', Heath told Hovey who, being Heath's subordinate, did as he was told.

However, she had nothing for Heath, and when Hovey relayed the news to Heath, he was aware that Mrs Swaby had arrived at court with a number of friends.

'Go and tell her to ask them if they can help', said Heath, and adopting the same racing terminology he had used with

---

1 Many people, especially criminals, thought that 'PD' was unfair; on one occasion, an old lag was released from prison and almost immediately nicked a pint of milk from a doorstep and was caught; he was sentenced to eight years' preventative detention.

2 A racing term, meaning £25.

Mrs Brabiner, added, 'Tell her it's no good backing the horse after the off.'

But Mrs Swaby told Hovey it was 'hopeless' or 'useless' and Heath was made aware of this. Then Swaby's case was called, he pleaded guilty, Heath gave his antecedents, which included all of his convictions, and Swaby received the five-year sentence.

Mrs Swaby was understandably upset, and Hovey helped her from the court, after which Heath told her, 'You see now what's happened? You didn't look after me so I didn't look after you.'

Eight days after his sentence, Swaby wrote to the Chief Constable of Brighton, complaining about Heath and using the word 'conspiracy'. It would lead to Heath's arrest, but not until four months later, and when that happened, the recipient of Swaby's letter, the Chief Constable, would be arrested as well.

CHAPTER 5

An Informant and a Receiver

S ince time immemorial, detectives of police forces all over the world have used informants to provide them with intelligence on the whereabouts of stolen and prohibited items and wanted persons. Used properly and skilfully, informants – otherwise known as 'snouts' or 'grasses' – can be utterly invaluable to detectives. At New Scotland Yard, there was an Informants' Fund so that snouts could be paid a modest amount to encourage them to continue their activities, with the tacit promise of more largesse to come. Constabulary forces had more modest purses to reward their officers' informants. In addition, insurance companies or loss adjusters would pay a reward of 10 per cent of the value of recovered stolen property.

Certainly, up until the mid-1970s in the Metropolitan Police, the identity of his snout was a secret closely guarded by the officer running an informant. To honest officers, that was an admirable arrangement. Information came in, searches were carried out and arrests were made. A report, using the snout's pseudonym, was submitted, and the informant was paid after signing an invoice using the same alias. As long as the detective remembered that he and the informant – who almost inevitably was a criminal – should remain on separate sides of the fence, all would be well.

However, not all officers were trustworthy, either in the Met or elsewhere. Stolen property which had been recovered might be split between the informant (who might also be the thief) and the officer; so might the reward money. What was more, the theft might have been carried out in the first place with the connivance of a crooked detective. A fraction of the remaining stolen property could be entrusted to a disposable 'mug', who would then be arrested and take the blame for the theft or burglary. That done, the crime would be cleared up and the 'guilty' person punished. All sorts of skulduggery might take place, and it could be difficult (sometimes impossible) to differentiate between cop and crook; which brings us rather neatly to the matter of Ernie Waite.

* * *

Described as 'a greengrocer, poulterer, an undischarged bankrupt and a receiver of stolen goods' and later, by the Solicitor General, as 'obviously a scoundrel', Ernest Edward Waite, born in 1912, could also be referred to as a payer of bribes to corrupt police officers and someone with his finger in any number of dodgy pies.

Waite's criminal record was not initially an impressive one: fined £3 in 1933 for stealing, he received two months' hard labour the following year for stealing a handbag.

Then in May 1945, for causing unnecessary suffering to three calves by 'unreasonably killing them in an improper manner', he was fined £15; and five months later at Steyning Petty Sessions, for unlawfully acquiring 14 gallons of petrol, he was sent to prison for six months. In 1947, for black market offences, he was sent to prison for nine months, and he received another six-month sentence at Brighton Quarter Sessions in August 1948, as well as being fined £250 with £50 costs, for dealing in black market calves and chickens. The Recorder informed him that in default of payment he would serve an additional twenty-one months' imprisonment, and in consequence of that stern warning, Waite coughed up. It bankrupted him.

Those prison sentences had a salutary effect on Waite; he resolved not to spend one more day in gaol, and he didn't. His cunning went into overdrive, and whenever criminal proceedings beckoned thereafter, he greased his way out of them by perjury, skulduggery or bunging the police.

Divorced, Waite – as well as being an industrious black marketeer – had been a receiver of stolen goods since 1934 and had lived at 155 Preston Road, Brighton since 1950. In September 1956, a Mrs Joan Watson had taken over a shop at 39 New England Road as a greengrocer and poulterer, and Waite managed it.

Waite had an acquaintance named Matheson, who kept a shop in Marine Gardens and sold meat suitable only for consumption by cats and dogs. As a sideline, he also sold illegal meat for human consumption, supplied by Waite. It was there that, in about 1949, Waite first met Ridge, who would collect food for animal consumption, plus some meat for himself, usually on a Friday evening; there was never any question of payment.

When officials from the Ministry of Food made inspections in Brighton, Waite got to know of it via Matheson, who had been tipped off. On those occasions, Waite kept his meat out of Matheson's shop; but if the tip-off came too late and he was unable to retrieve the crooked meat in time, it was simply sprayed with green dye to show that it was the same as the rest on sale, for animal consumption only.

At about the same time, Waite got to know Hammersley and later, Heath. They both came to his shop, where they would order meat, vegetables and other foodstuffs to the value of £2–£3, pay with a ten shilling note – and wait for change. The same happened at Mrs Watson's shop in New England Road. This was done on a weekly basis – and 'at odd times' both officers received cash gifts from Waite.

The reason for Waite's apparent beneficence was because the officers knew that he was a receiver of stolen goods. They didn't just turn a blind eye to his activities, they openly encouraged him and, what was more, laid down guidelines. The system was quite simple: Waite was allowed to receive stolen property which was stolen in areas other than Brighton. Anything stolen within the area that came to his attention he was to have no dealings with, because the officers wished to keep themselves clear of local complications; but Waite was encouraged to pass on information about such thefts.

It was a handy arrangement; little wonder there was a healthy arrest rate.

In October 1949, Waite received 137 cartons each containing forty-eight tins of Nescafé, valued in total at £521 12s 0d – almost £18,000 by today's standards – which had been stolen from a lorry in London. He discussed this with Hammersley and Heath, and they suggested someone who could get rid of it. This person was Norman Kensett, the proprietor of general stores at Southwick, a small town some 5 miles west of Brighton. Waite told Kensett it was export stock which had not gone through due to a strike; Kensett refused to buy it but permitted Waite to store the cartons in a garage.

Later, on 1 November, Waite was arrested; he told Detective Sergeant Grant that three men had offered him the cartons, saying they were bankrupt stock, but while he had refused to buy it, he nevertheless had offered to find storage for it. While he was on bail he met up with Hammersley and Heath, who told him that a man involved with the case would turn Queen's evidence. Therefore, they suggested, Waite's defence should be that that man was the receiver. He adopted the suggestion, telling the jury that he had never told Kensett that it was export stock or, indeed, that he had any interest in it. On 12 January 1950, the jury at the West Sussex Quarter Sessions disagreed; at the second trial, on 20 April, Waite was acquitted.

Waite was lucky; judging by the sort of sentences that were being dished out at that particular court of quarter sessions at that time, had he been convicted he would have been looking at a five-year prison sentence – and a couple of bent coppers would have been denied a lucrative source of income.

Some cigarettes which had been stolen during a breaking at the Cooperative Stores in Lewes Road, Brighton came into Waite's possession; he informed Hammersley, who took money but no action, and the tobacco was sold. Waite also provided the names of the persons responsible. One of them was Roy John Mitchell who, besides having a number of criminal convictions, had also escaped from Eastchurch Prison in 1952.

Mitchell told Waite that he next intended to break into Davis, a jeweller's shop in Brighton. It would appear that this was an imprudent move, but he wanted Waite to agree beforehand to fence the property that he intended to steal. Nevertheless, it was still a very risky business, because although Mitchell was aware that Waite was a police informant, he didn't believe that Waite would grass him up.

Well, he was wrong. The following day, Mrs Watson answered a telephone call from one of the men and she later went to the house where the two thieves were living. They were not there, and she left; but later that evening, Hammersley and Heath arrived at Preston Road. Hammersley told her that the telephone call had been intercepted and recorded; she had been extremely lucky, Hammersley told her, that she had not been arrested when she called at the thieves' house. The £25 reward that Waite received did not last long. Money changed hands between Waite and Hammersley; no charges were brought against Mrs Watson. They were, however, against Mitchell, who was caught with the stolen watches and jewellery before they could be handed over to Waite.

While Mitchell was on remand in Lewes Prison he received a visit from Hammersley and Heath.

'Of course, you know you can help yourself', said Heath, to which Mitchell replied, 'I know what you're on about. I don't want to know anything about it; I'm skint.'

Later, on 3 October 1957, Mitchell pleaded guilty to a number of offences, asked for three others to be taken into consideration and was sentenced to two years' imprisonment.

During Whitsun 1956, Waite and Mrs Watson went to Quaker Street, behind Petticoat Lane in London's East End, where they met a man named Ackerman in a café. He took them to a garage and a yard in which were two sheds full of stolen groceries, the property of Kearney & Tongue, including bacon and butter. The goods were loaded on to a lorry, in which Mrs Watson returned to Brighton; Waite went ahead by car.

Hammersley received £50 for his trouble; he had also arranged for a friend to provide the lorry. He also came to Waite's house – 'I see you've got the goods all right' was his comment – and helped himself to butter, bacon and several tins of peaches from the consignment, the rest of which was later sold on.

At 11.00pm on 9 December 1956, a lorry-load of stolen groceries arrived at Waite's house at Preston Road. He was expecting a consignment of Libby's corned beef, but in the event, the lorry contained tinned tomatoes and peaches. The load was big enough to require six men to unload it, and they made a great deal of noise in doing so. A constable walked up the drive, and Waite made himself scarce, staying away for an hour. When he returned, the lorry, his helpers and the policeman had all gone; the lorry's contents were left on his lawn and he had to carry them into an outhouse. Mrs Watson helped, but this took from midnight until 4 o'clock in the morning.

There was then further help from Mrs Olive Tarff, who was also living at Waite's address with William Watson, employed by Waite as a van driver. The day after the lorry's arrival, Watson and Waite brought a large quantity of butter to her room. Unwrapping and re-wrapping it took her three days.

A week later, Hammersley arrived; Waite told him he was concerned in case the constable had made a report about the stolen property. Helping himself to some stolen tins of peaches, Hammersley said that he would make the report. Waite need not have concerned himself; when Police Constable Harold Kerry had arrived at the scene, he had seen the lorry, Waite, the six men (all of whom were wearing gloves) and the merchandise on the lawn. But he was only concerned about the noise; he spoke to 'somebody', and when the noise abated, he continued on his beat.

Two of Waite's helpers were brought in for questioning. One of them was Frederick Ketley, who at the time was working as an assistant in Mrs Watson's shop and was aware of the existence of the peaches at Waite's address. He decided upon a little public-spirited grassing and went to see Heath, whom he knew as 'Trev'. This took some considerable time, and when he did, Heath wanted to know if the information was in respect of cigarettes, only to be told it was regarding peaches. Given the significant amount of dodgy property circulating from Waite's premises, it was an understandable mistake.

Heath took a statement from Ketley, and within hours, unsurprisingly, Waite was aware of it and confronted Ketley, who wisely denied going to the police at all.

The whole matter was obviously too hot for Heath to handle personally, so it was turned over to Detective Sergeant Robert Johnson for investigation. He was shown Ketley's statement and he interviewed William Watson. As a result, he was unable to deduce that a consignment of tinned peaches and tomatoes had been stolen. He knew nothing of the lorry which had been stolen, or that it had been abandoned at Redhill. There was a section at Criminal Records Office, New Scotland Yard, known as 'Property Index'. When large, identifiable quantities of goods were stolen, it was there that they were registered; it was open to enquiries made by police officers from all over the United Kingdom. Property Index was not a closely guarded secret.

So the position was this: a police constable had seen a load of suspicious-looking gear on a front lawn, in the middle of the night, with half a dozen men unloading it, and did nothing about it; then two of the men present that night made statements to police, but the investigating officer decided not to interview the prime suspect, because he was unable to discover that the goods were stolen.

OK then.

The word was that Waite's time was up – but not to those in the know, it wasn't. Hammersley was not going to nick him; instead he received £50 from Waite.

CHAPTER 6

The Lorry-load of Snout

Between 1 and 2 August 1957, a trailer containing 305 cartons of cigarettes and tobacco, valued at £15,000, was stolen from a goods depot at Bishopsgate. This was investigated by the British Transport Commission Police, and the officer in charge was Superintendent Edwin Moody, who had served with the Royal Artillery in Palestine and France during the First World War and joined the Great Northern Railway Police in 1922. During thirty-seven years he had served with great distinction as both a uniform and CID officer throughout many branches of the British Transport Commission Police.

Moody was one very straight cop. He did not like cops who weren't.

★ ★ ★

During the August Bank Holiday of 1957, Waite had dealings with two men, Ackerman once more, and separately another named Edward George Wyatt. Two days later, Waite saw Hammersley and told him he had been offered a quantity of stolen cigarettes. Hammersley said nothing at the time but about five days later he told Waite that the cigarettes had been stolen from a goods yard at Bishopsgate and that one of the railway detectives had been involved with the men who had stolen them. (In fact, two officers were said to be involved in the theft.) Hammersley told him, 'I think we'll be on a good thing there if we can get the cigarettes. We should get about £1,500 from the insurance company.'

But in the meantime, Wyatt, a newsagent and tobacconist of Upper Gloucester Road, Brighton, had written to Superintendent Williams of the Brighton CID, on 6 August stating that:

> E. Waite of Preston Road is trying to dispose of cigarettes, Senior Service, 169 cases, 600 [sic] a case, over a million cigarettes, wholesale price £9,000. They are in a 2-ton Bedford

outside town and intend to deliver to purchaser, by-passing
Waite. I think the quantity is too large for any local wholesaler
to handle and I don't think they would buy them as they are
far too respectable. The only chance is to wait for the Bedford
or any other means at their disposal. I don't think anybody
else has been approached, but keep me out of it.

The letter was read by both Heath and Hammersley, and the
contents were passed on to Waite, who declared he was 'amazed' –
but only surprised that it had been written. That didn't stop him.
Nor did it stop the two crooked cops. It didn't stop them even
after Wyatt sent a follow-up letter to Williams, five days later.

Meanwhile, the Transport Commission Police were following
up leads of their own, and on 8 August Moody sent Detective
Sergeant George Spiers to Brighton to make enquiries.

There he met Heath, who asked, 'Yes, would there be
about a million and a half cigarettes involved?'

Told that there were, Heath said, 'Would they be mostly
Senior Service?' and Spiers agreed, adding that a large quantity of
Old Holborn tobacco had been stolen as well.

'I think I can help you', said Heath. 'My superintendent has
received a letter from a friend who has been offered that amount
of cigarettes. My superintendent spoke to me about it this
morning.'

Since Williams was not immediately available, Spiers decided
to return to London, but not before Heath had mentioned
the possibility of a reward; Spiers told him that £50 or more
might be forthcoming.

The following day, Spiers and Detective Inspector Leonard
Wright arrived in Brighton. They saw Heath, and Wright spoke
to Hammersley on the telephone, who told him that according
to his informant, 75 cartons had been sold in London but there
were still 169 cartons in Brighton.

On 14 August, Moody decided to take a personal part in the
investigation and went for lunch to the Caxton public house,
together with Detective Inspectors Wright and Roland Hendy, to
meet Heath, who mentioned that Hammersley was in charge of the
investigation.

At Brighton's CID Headquarters, Superintendent Williams
quoted from Wyatt's letter but told Moody, 'Hammersley has
the enquiry. I know little about how far it has advanced' – which
seeing as how he was Hammersley's senior officer was somewhat
surprising, considering that his junior officer was dealing with
goods which at today's value were worth £308,250.

However, when Hammersley arrived he told Moody:

> I have a reliable contact. A telephone message was received at
> his house at midnight on August 1st. He later received a visit
> and was offered 100 cases of cigarettes for £6 10s 0d a 1,000.
> This was too big for the contact to handle. He offered to find
> someone who would take them. After Inspector Wright's visit,
> I got the contact to go to London to see if he could find out
> where the cigarettes were. He went to the Three Archers public
> house in the East End of London where he met Ackerman and
> another man. They made their way to the Elephant & Castle,
> and the contact knows where the cigarettes are.

Hammersley gave Moody the location where the stolen property
was to be found. He mentioned that his contact was reliable,
adding, 'He'll do anything if you show him a pound.' Moody then
introduced the matter of a reward, saying, 'Well, there is £15,000
involved. I think I can mention the sum of £500 as a reward', at
which Hammersley must have experienced a sexual disturbance.

Moody, accompanied by Detective Inspector Tommy Butler
and Detective Sergeant Peter Vibart of the Flying Squad, went to
the area but found there were so many places similar to the one
described by Hammersley that they had to give up the search.

Moody demanded the name of Hammersley's informant; that
was refused, but help came from an unexpected corner when
Heath suggested to Moody, 'Why don't you knock[3] Hammersley's
informant?'

When Moody said that he was unaware of the informant's
identity, Heath artfully replied, 'You could soon find out.
Why don't you tail-up[4] Hammersley?'

Moody was insistent that something should be done, and there
was a great deal of discussion about how to do it. Moody wanted
the informant to go to London, with Moody following him –
Hammersley vetoed that suggestion and then said, 'Suppose I come
to London with the contact and see the place, and then I can tell
you?' to which Moody agreed. However, Hammersley asked how
they would get there, and Moody suggested two free train tickets;
but Hammersley rejected that as well, saying that his contact
would not travel by train. Moody suggested that the informant
use his own car and he (Moody) would pay the expenses, but
Hammersley said that the gang knew the informant's car. Inspector

---

3 A slang term for 'arrest'.
4 A slang term for 'follow'.

Hendy suggested that they use the car they were all sitting in, but Hammersley refused, saying rather rudely that Moody would pick up the car in London and follow it. Although Moody haughtily repudiated the suggestion, it was clear that Hammersley wanted to follow his own agenda. Finally, Moody suggested that the informant travel in a hire car which Moody would pay for; this was agreed, and they would go on the following Sunday.

Before leaving, Hammersley mentioned that one case of the cigarettes had gone to the Montpelier Hotel, but there were only about 1,000 cigarettes left and they would have been mixed up with the hotel's existing stock, so there was little point in enquiries being made there.

'It's obvious that your contact knows where the cigarettes are, and I want to get my hands on those cartons', said Moody, to which Hammersley replied, 'You'll find out on Sunday.'

CHAPTER 7

A Wild Goose Chase

On Sunday, 18 August, Hammersley saw Moody at his home address in Ewell, Surrey, telling him, 'I've left the contact in a hired car about 70 yards down the road. I've been to the site at the Elephant & Castle and I've made a rough sketch of the place. It's in Meadow Road, it's an old BRS depot.'

He handed over the sketch and then described another location with double brown doors nearby, saying, 'Some of your stolen stuff goes there, but not the cigarettes.' He went on to say:

> I've been to Ham Park Road. I saw Ackerman outside his house, cleaning his car. It's a stone-coloured Ford Consul, OLA 853. We didn't stop – the contact ducked down as we passed. We stopped further down the road by a telephone box. The contact phoned Ackerman and I listened in. The contact asked Ackerman if there were any cigarettes going, and Ackerman said they were all sold on Saturday at a knock-down price. The contact told Ackerman that he wanted some, and Ackerman said he would try to get some back. We went to Adler Engineering Works in Quaker Street, just behind Petticoat Lane. Some of your stolen stuff goes there. I met some of the gang and I posed as a hotel manager, out to buy cheap.

Moody knew the engineering works; it had been visited the day after the theft. But then Hammersley played his trump card: 'They're going to have another load in a fortnight's time. Why not leave everything until then and then you can get the goods and the thieves? My contact is going to have first offer.'

In other words, the goods in which Moody was interested had been disposed of; they could be forgotten about, and instead, he should concentrate on a further theft in two weeks' time – which of course was never going to happen.

Moody was not going to wait for anything else; he was for getting on with the job in hand and that afternoon, back he went; but when he and other officers arrived at the location, it was obvious that no vehicle had been taken into it for a very long time. It was a bomb site, and debris, rubbish and dust were lying undisturbed on the ground; vegetation had grown to a height of four feet. The site with the double brown doors was found; it was locked and bolted, and they were unable to get in. The general consensus was that nobody believed Hammersley's story.

The next day, Moody saw Hammersley in Brighton and told him the result of the search, saying, 'I think we've been taken for a ride.'

'I can't understand it', exclaimed Hammersley. 'Something must have gone wrong, because my informant's never let me down before.'

The same day, Waite telephoned Hammersley to say a man named Richardson – Waite believed he was known as 'Dickie' or 'Rickie' – had brought him cartons of cigarettes, each containing 6,000, to which Hammersley replied, 'Good'.

This had been witnessed by a certain Frank Maher – he had recognized Richardson's shooting brake in Waite's driveway – and Maher, who had worked for Waite as an assistant and a van driver, saw two sacks by the stairs in the passageway, also a lot of Senior Service packets. Maher had often seen money change hands between Hammersley, Heath and Waite. He considered Waite to be trustworthy, and when he committed two office-breakings and stole a quantity of television cable, it was his employer he told about it. He was later arrested by Heath and was lucky to be placed on probation at Sussex Quarter Sessions; obviously not the sharpest knife in the drawer, he was oblivious to the fact that Waite had grassed him up.

Waite later overheard a telephone conversation between Hammersley and Moody. Hammersley said that his contact had been offered thirty cases of cigarettes at £6 10s 0d per thousand and asked if his informant might buy the cigarettes at that price; Moody replied that he wanted to see the cigarettes delivered.

Hammersley suggested that Waite should buy a couple of cartons; he did so and took the empty cartons to Hammersley's house who had told him not to part with the cigarettes until he had the money for them. When Waite told Hammersley that Richardson was bringing down more cigarettes, he replied, 'Oh, my God, I can't have him around!' Heath was present, and Hammersley added, 'I must go up and see Richardson straight away to burn all the cartons.'

The Richardson referred to was Frederick George Richardson of St John's Place, Brighton, a rag and scrap metal dealer nicknamed 'Hicksy'. He had convictions including loitering with intent to commit a felony, and his last had been at Brighton in 1949 for receiving 5cwt of sugar. Hammersley's concern for

Richardson was understandable. During Easter 1957, he and his wife had gone on a four-day trip to Paris with Richardson and his wife.

Moody and Hammersley met up again that evening, and Hammersley told him, 'I was so disturbed by what you said that I went and saw my contact and he now tells me that he didn't actually go into the place but was taken there by the gang and they stood outside. He understood that that was where the cigarettes were.'

But previously Hammersley had told Moody that both he *and* the informant had been to the site.

Confronted by this conspicuous bollocks, Moody hit the roof. 'Do you think I like bringing men out on a fool's errand – being taken for a ride? Because that's what it was!'

Again Moody demanded the name of Hammersley's source, to which he replied, 'I'm not going to tell you. I would not tell the superintendent or the Chief Constable. He's not only my informant, he's also my friend. I visit his home and he visits mine. He has done me many good turns. I'm not going to lose him. If I tell you, you'd be laughing. You'd be 50 miles away, and I live here and have to get my living.'

'For God's sake, Hammersley, let's have a little bit of faith in each other!' expostulated Moody. 'I'm not interested in your contact. I'm only concerned with the people he contacts and tracing back from there to get the thieves in London and the property in Brighton.'

Just as Moody was about to return to London, Hammersley said, 'What about a sweetener for my informant? He's had nothing yet.'

'How much do you suggest?' asked Moody, to be told, 'A tenner.'

It's difficult to say whether Hammersley possessed monumental arrogance, was a serial piss-taker or had a death wish, because later, Waite received about 15,000 more cigarettes and about 40lbs of tobacco.

CHAPTER 8

Undercover Work and Search Warrants

W hat nobody at Brighton police station was aware of – because Moody told no one – was that on 27 August, undercover railway detectives arrived in Brighton, where they kept Waite's address at 155 Preston Road under observation and also Mrs Watson's address at New England Road. One of the officers was Detective Constable Cook, and on 30 August he saw a car draw up at the Preston Road address and two men go into the premises. When they left they were each carrying a cardboard carton tied up with string. These were put into the boot of the car, which then drove off. Cook followed it and saw the man in the passenger seat take the cartons into 37 New England Road, the premises of G. E. Spencer's confectionery and tobacconist's shop.

On 31 August, the premises were searched by a dozen officers of the Railway and Metropolitan Police. At 39 New England Road, 384 ounce packets and 216 small packets of Old Holborn tobacco in two crates, making a total of 30lbs, were found; at Preston Road, 1,360 cigarettes – some in the front room, more in the bedroom – were seized.

Mrs Watson was present, as was Heath, who expressed surprise, saying, 'I thought you'd have had more sense to have had it here.' When it was clear that Waite was going to be arrested, Mrs Watson became worried and asked Heath what could be done. He suggested that she telephone Hammersley (who was on leave) and also Richardson. However, Heath may not have been aware that at 3 o'clock that afternoon, on leave or not, Hammersley had been spotted by Detective Constable Dennis Andrew Ward of the Transport Commission Police driving his Standard Vanguard car into New England Street.

Although the reader may have come to the conclusion that Heath's morals were obviously flawed, he now trumped himself when he told Mrs Watson, 'If Ernie is charged, you can go down and say that it was nothing to do with him; that it was you who received the cigarettes', adding helpfully, 'Probably, as you've got no previous convictions, it won't be so bad for you.'

Hammersley – who said he was most surprised that the shop had been searched – told Mrs Watson that 'he would see what he could do' and later suggested that if she had not heard anything by 8 o'clock she should do as Heath had suggested. She later received a telephone call from Heath telling her that 'Ernie was all right, so far.'

Meanwhile, Heath had accompanied Waite to the police station and taken a statement from him. While Moody was out of the room, Heath told Waite to make the statement as short as he could and, when Moody returned, to carry on for a little while, then finish.

On Monday, 2 September, Waite was seen by Hammersley and told him, 'You made me look like a fool but still, that doesn't matter. I can stand that.'

Peter Vibart, one of the Metropolitan officers who had assisted in the search, told Hammersley, 'This fellow Waite is your informer.'

Hammersley hesitated before replying, 'Is he?'

To this Vibart responded, 'You are a senior officer to me, but if that's your attitude, I've got nothing further to say.'

Referring to Waite, Hammersley said to Moody, 'Let me see him. I might get some more information.'

'No', replied Moody. 'That will not do any good.'

When Moody told Hammersley that Waite had told him it was Hammersley's idea that he should receive the two empty cigarette cartons, he replied, 'He's a liar.'

'You see, Hammersley, I have got you calling your contact a liar', said Moody, 'and he's calling you a liar.' There was nothing the crooked cop could say to that – and he didn't.

At that point, Chief Constable Ridge walked in and asked Moody, 'How's it going?'

'I don't know yet,' replied Moody. 'Waite is Hammersley's informant.'

'Well, good luck to you', replied Ridge nonchalantly. 'I hope you get the bastard.'

Moody later saw Ridge and told him all that had happened. Ridge replied:

> I have something to say to Hammersley. I cannot understand why he wanted to see Waite. I want you, Moody, and all the other officers who come to Brighton to be happy in the knowledge when you leave that you have been speaking to officers of my force in whom you have confidence. If you have not that confidence, then come to me or Mr Williams. I shall always be available. You know, Moody, when you are dealing

with thieves you have got to think their way, and to think their way you have got to know their ways, and to know their ways you have got to mix with them. I was brought up in the CID, but thank God I'm divorced from that now.

It was a lovely, albeit mendacious PR speech and one which was doomed to failure. When Waite discovered that Hammersley intended to prosecute him, he decided like Bennett that he'd had enough and made a statement to Scotland Yard.

But before that happened, Inspector Wright returned to Brighton on 12 September, when he saw Hammersley in the Seven Stars public house; he was extremely nervous (as well he might have been) and was anxious to know details of the conversation which had passed between Moody and Ridge nine days previously.

Wright replied that Moody had said nothing to Hammersley's detriment to the Chief Constable. 'I'm relieved to hear that', remarked Hammersley, although he had nothing to say when Wright commented, 'He could have said a great deal but didn't do so.'

'Our primary job down here in Brighton is to obtain as much information as possible to bring to a successful conclusion a most serious theft', said Wright, adding pointedly, 'if at all possible.'

'That's what we're here for.'

'If that's so, I can't understand why we can't get some real help so we can get cracking', said Wright. 'I've never known a job stand still for so long.'

'I'm doing my best', was Hammersley's helpless reply, but time was now running out for him – and for Heath, too.

The following day, Inspector Hendy and DC Cook carried out an enquiry in Newhaven, and on the return journey they had just driven past Waite's shop when they saw Heath leaving the premises carrying a basket.

In a short space of time the three main sources of illicit income for the two crooked cops had been cut off – Frank Rose, Alan Bennett and now, Ernie Waite, who had not been charged with a sizeable offence and never would be. He was considered to be a not inconsiderably sized sprat to catch a number of tasty mackerel.

Overall, Waite believed he had handed about £200 to Hammersley and probably £50 to Heath.

Stout, loud-mouthed and flashily dressed, Waite cut a louche figure to the man in the street – a scoundrel he certainly was, but he would provide devastating evidence against corrupt cops.

* * *

Quite obviously, Hammersley was severely rattled following his meeting with Inspector Wright but he was completely unstoppable if not downright out of control, because five days later, on 17 September 1957, he arrested Arthur William Kennard and Francisco Paolella for the theft of a car and for breaking into a dairy and stealing a safe containing £679 in cash.

Taking 23-year-old Kennard into the cell passageway at Brighton, Hammersley told him:

> This is off the record, Arthur. You're in a spot of bother and you've been upsetting the mobile squad for some time. However, I've nothing against you personally and I may be able to help you. There's a carve-up over this money and there's some £400 missing. Paolella hasn't got it; you must have it. You can do quite a lot of things with £400. You can buy things . . . freedom for instance . . . In this case, I can't promise you freedom as there are other factors and officers involved, but I could drop this charge or reduce it for a consideration.

Kennard was definitely interested. 'How much would it cost?' he asked, to be told, '£250 would be reasonable.'

'I haven't got £250', protested Kennard, but Hammersley, ever reasonable, told him, 'Think it over. I'll give you an hour.'

No money was forthcoming, and on 28 September both men were committed from the Magistrates' Court to stand their trial at Brighton Quarter Sessions, Paolella on bail but the defaulter, Kennard, in custody; and within a week, nemesis in the form of Scotland Yard would arrive to severely curtail the activities of some crooked coppers.

CHAPTER 9

Call in Scotland Yard!

The feedback from the Folkestone investigation, plus Bennett's revelations, was brought to the attention of Major Sir John Ferguson CBE, QPM, CStJ, DL, the 66-year-old Chief Constable of Kent.

A year after leaving the Army in 1933, Sir John had joined the Metropolitan Police as a Chief Constable and was later promoted to Deputy Assistant Commissioner. One year before his appointment as Kent's Chief Constable in 1946, he had been the Metropolitan Police's Assistant Commissioner 'A' Department, so he knew everything there was to know about administration and discipline; and it was clear that from what he'd heard about the antics of certain members of Brighton's CID office, there was something substantially wrong there.

He immediately wrote to the Home Office and the Director of Public Prosecutions, who just as promptly passed the matter on to the Commissioner of the Metropolitan Police. Naturally, the Assistant Commissioner (Crime) was informed, but Richard Leofric Jackson CBE, who held that position, was not the man to tackle this job. He had been Secretary to the Commissioner in charge of the civil staff since 1946 and, because a vacancy had arisen, he had been inserted into the rank of AC(C) since 1953. He had no investigative background whatsoever and in consequence was unable to differentiate his arse from his elbow. It was an example of maladministration that has been shared by many of his modern-day counterparts.

Fortunately, at the time of this exposé, the Commander of 'C' Department at the Yard – one rank below that of AC(C) – was George Horace Hatherill.

Born in 1898, a heavily built man towering over his colleagues at 6 foot $2^1/_8$ inches, Hatherill had served in both World Wars (being wounded while serving with Queen Victoria's Rifles in the First and attached, as a detective chief inspector, to the British Expeditionary Force during the Second). Speaking six languages, Hatherill had been in Special Branch for the first twelve years of his service, before studying criminal law and being introduced into the CID with rank of detective sergeant (first class).

He had been commended by the commissioner for his actions on twelve occasions in several cases of murder as well as offences of forgery, false pretences and corruption, and his efforts had been rewarded by his being appointed MBE in 1946 and then advanced to OBE seven years later.

Hatherill, a chain-smoker with the ash from his cigarettes tumbling down the front of his waistcoat, was known for glowering at his subordinates; according to Detective Constable John Swain (later Detective Chief Superintendent Swain QPM), he gave the impression 'that he knew the answer to every question he put to you, long before he actually spoke.'

Now, having served in his present rank for two years, he was appointed to head this enquiry.

★　★　★

During his four-year tenure (1931–35) as the Metropolitan Police Commissioner, Lord Trenchard GCB, OM, GCVO, DSO introduced some pretty innovative ideas, including a Wireless Training School, a Detective Training School and a Police Scientific Laboratory, but one of his dottier concepts was the Hendon Police College. This was designed for police officers with public school or university backgrounds, and following a 15-month course (which necessitated the candidates being in possession of a dinner jacket, four dress shirts and a pair of patent leather evening shoes), they were to be released into the force with the rank of Junior Station Inspector or JSI. This was greeted with general derision by the rank and file, who twisted the JSI acronym in order to refer contemptuously to the graduates of Hendon as 'Jessies'. It was felt – with some justification – by the Police Federation (whom Trenchard loathed) and by the Labour Party that the college would produce a kind of military elite of 'officers and gentleman'. Their worst fears were realized when Lieutenant Colonel G. H. R. Halland CIE, OBE was appointed commandant of the college, with the rank of Deputy Assistant Commissioner and an annual salary of £1,000, and a civilian, Mr A. F. Senior, was suddenly transformed into a superintendent in order to become an instructor with a salary of £550 per year.

Like many bonkers ideas, the scheme closed forever with the onset of war in 1939, but by then 197 young Jessies had passed through its doors, one of whom was 22-year-old Ian James Forbes-Leith.

Only just three-quarters of an inch above the (then) minimum height requirement of 5 feet 8 inches, the new candidate was posted initially to the wilds of 'Y' Division, which bordered Hertfordshire Constabulary; one year later, he was transferred to London's rather busier West End, where he received his first commissioner's commendation for the rather ambiguous achievement of 'closing undesirable premises'. Forbes-Leith was promoted to station inspector in 1942, but his career was interrupted by service with the armed forces. As a Captain in the Royal Armoured Corps he was Mentioned in Dispatches, and following his return to the Met, just before Christmas 1945, he was appointed to the CID. In the space of twelve months he was commended by the commissioner on four more occasions for cases of larceny and receiving, plus bringing about 'the arrest of five violent criminals'.

He was promoted three times in the space of as many years, and now, as a detective superintendent, Forbes-Leith was Hatherill's second-in-command. Immaculately dressed, he was known as 'The Guv'nor in the Bowler'; Peter Scott, who was a police constable at Harrow Road police station, described Forbes-Leith to me as being 'One of the ten best-dressed men in England'.

But it appeared that Forbes-Leith was not without his critics. Former Metropolitan Police Sergeant John Kalber was a constable at West End Central police station at the time when this enquiry was being put together. He had, certainly, a jaundiced view of the CID in general at that time, but he later described being in the lift which stopped at the CID floor of the station and hearing the familiar voice of Commander Len Burt CVO, CBE, speaking loudly to a detective superintendent about the Brighton enquiry. Part of what Kalber heard Burt say was:

> Talk about corruption! They [meaning the Yard's hierarchy] have only gone and sent Forbes-Leith down there. Talk about sending a spiral staircase to investigate a corkscrew!

That sounds pretty damning, although it raises more questions than condemnations. After being with MI5 from 19 August 1940, on 1 March 1946 Burt had gone to Special Branch, first as a deputy commander, then commander. It's extremely unlikely that he would have had anything to do with Forbes-Leith, since Special Branch and CID were completely separate departments; in fact, that Burt was at West End Central at all was undoubtedly to liaise with the CID regarding Mayfair hotel security for visiting diplomats. And at that time Forbes-Leith was still on the staff of No. 4 District headquarters, to the south of the Yard. It begs the question, would Hatherill – himself a CID commander and a shrewd judge of men – have selected someone to head a sensitive enquiry, one involving Her Majesty's Inspectorate, the Home Office and the Director of Public Prosecutions, who was considered to be less than trustworthy?

It's more likely that Forbes-Leith, coming from the ranks of the 'Jessies' would have been disapproved of by someone like Burt, who had joined the police in 1912 and come up the hard way, fighting with Whitechapel tearaways; hence his possibly throwaway, albeit cutting remarks.

But whatever the case, Forbes-Leith now had to pick his investigating team. In doing this, he was assisted by Ernie Millen.

★   ★   ★

Following the completion of the Frank Rose case, Millen had been transferred from the Fraud Squad back to the Flying Squad with the rank of detective chief inspector. Nicknamed 'Hooter', either because of his imperious nose or his habit of bellowing orders down the corridors of Scotland Yard, he was famously irascible and a formidable, taciturn character.

'Hooter spoke to me this morning', a newcomer to the Squad would be told.

'What did he say?' the goggle-eyed youngster would ask, only to receive the reply, 'He told me to get out of his fucking way!'

But Millen now had twenty-three years' service behind him and in that time had collected twenty-five commissioner's commendations; he knew detective work inside out, knew his men and knew just who to pick for such a sensitive matter.

The investigation came under the umbrella of Hatherill's COC1 Department at the Yard, and of the ten officers selected just two came from that department; another came from the Fraud Squad, and the rest from the Flying Squad. They included Detective Inspector William Brereton and Detective Sergeant (First Class) William Baldock, the latter having won a BEM for gallantry during the Blitz. In fact, six years previously, both men, under the direction of Forbes-Leith (then a detective inspector), had been responsible for the recapture of the highly dangerous Harold Roy 'Rubber Bones' Webb, who had twice escaped from military custody during the war and also from Dartmoor, having been sentenced in 1946 to eight years' penal servitude and thirty strokes of the birch for robbery with violence.

Also from the Flying Squad came Detective Inspector Tommy Butler and Detective Sergeant (First Class) Peter Vibart, who had worked together since 1955. In the space of nine months, this deadly duo had sown the seeds of discord amongst members of the underworld as they collected six commissioner's commendations apiece for the arrest of safe-blowers, armed robbers and violent and dangerous criminals. They were known as 'The Terrible Twins' and when they were working on a case, the underworld trembled. Anything might happen, and it usually did.

As his own second-in-command Forbes-Leith selected Detective Chief Inspector Richard Alfred Jennings Radford, who had joined the Met in 1930 and, like Forbes-Leith, had initially patrolled the streets of 'Y' Division as Police Constable 563. Soon appointed to the CID, during the next twenty years Radford notched up ten commissioner's commendations ranging from arresting persistent thieves and fraudsmen to shop-breakers and an armed criminal.

Addressing his team, Forbes-Leith told them:

> We have a most unpleasant task. We must forget that the men we are going to investigate are police officers. We must treat this just as we would treat any other criminal enquiry.

The Assistant Commissioner (Crime) had been informed of what was going on, as had the Commissioner, Sir John Nott-Bower KCVO, who in 1923 had been awarded the King's Police Medal for conspicuous gallantry after arresting armed criminals who had shot him in the arm. But nobody else knew. A Scotland Yard secretary, Betty Laskey, who accompanied the team and who would type the most secret documents, was believed by her family and colleagues to be carrying out some extra typing work in the country.

The enquiry team set up their headquarters at Malling House, Lewes police headquarters, some nine miles from Brighton. The reason for this was clear: Lewes was part of the East Sussex Constabulary and had its own Chief Constable, Reginald Breffit OBE, MA. This meant that although the team were in the same county they were completely detached from Brighton; there could therefore be no legitimate reason whatsoever for any officer from that town to come sniffing around the doors of the Scotland Yard investigators.

The team knew what Frank Rose had said; they knew of Bennett's exposés. Their task was to trace everyone and anyone – publicans, club owners, bookmakers –with whom the crooked cops had had dealings and persuade them to talk – not only to talk

but to put their testimony in the form of written statements
and then give evidence at court. Many of the witnesses were
criminals; some had moved to other parts of the country; some
were serving prison sentences. Nevertheless, on 12 August 1957,
this herculean task got underway.

CHAPTER 10

Helping Police with their Enquiries

On 2 October 1957, Sammy Bellson was one of the first to be seen by Tommy Butler and Peter Vibart. They were nodding acquaintances; the previous year, Bellson had appeared as an alibi witness in respect of Francis Davidson 'Mad Frankie' Fraser, one of several defendants accused of a cowardly, vicious attack on gang leader Jack Spot and his wife. This had resulted in Spot requiring seventy-eight stitches in his face and hand, a transfusion of two pints of blood, a pint of plasma substitute and half a pint of blood plasma, as well as several yards of bandages to hold his body together.

Bellson got together with the crooked barrister Patrick Marrinan to manufacture an alibi for Fraser, but it did no good; Fraser was convicted and sent to prison for seven years, and following an enquiry, Marrinan was disbarred and expelled from the Honourable Society of Lincoln's Inn.

Of the five defendants in the Spot case, Butler and Vibart had arrested three: William Edward 'Ginger' Dennis, Robert 'Battles' Rossi and William Patrick 'Billy-Boy' Blythe. The last two had been arrested in Eire, and a vigorous defence had been mounted on their behalf at the Old Bailey, with suggestions of kidnapping and revenge on Vibart's part – for following his arrest as an army deserter, Blythe had previously been responsible for a razor-slashing which required the insertion of twenty stitches in Vibart's face. Sentenced to a total of thirteen years' imprisonment for the attack on Spot, the trio's conviction only added to the two officers' reputation and, with their arrival in Brighton, to general apprehension on the part of a certain dodgy bookmaker.

Bellson nervously told 'The Terrible Twins' that he would meet them outside of Brighton and when he did he told them:

> I could help you a lot. I will help you all I can. One of the worst cases I know about is a woman doing fifteen months . . . Her name is Brabiner. The one who can tell you all about it is Betty Lawrence, who is always in West Street. There's someone else you ought to see. That is old Harry Leach, who lives in Stamford Avenue. They did his son over his jewellery.

Ridge sent me along to do business for him. I went to Leach but he wouldn't pay enough and later, Ridge went himself. You see him and his son and they can help you. Look, Mr Butler, I've been in this town a long time; if I can help you, I will. Keep in touch and as things come to me, I'll let you know.

The officers did just that, on numerous occasions between then and 5 November, and as Tommy Butler would later blandly say, 'I found him most helpful.'

On the same day that Bellson received his ominous visit from Butler and Vibart, Anthony Lyons was seen at Sherry's Bar at 3.30pm by Chief Inspector Radford and Superintendent Forbes-Leith, to whom Lyons said, 'Yes, I know you. I remember you from 1940, when you dealt with my application for the Bagatelle Club in London. What's this all about?'

'You have probably seen in the papers today that there is an enquiry going on respecting certain matters in Brighton, and it's because of this that I've come to see you', said Forbes-Leith. 'In the course of the enquiries I have made so far, your name has been mentioned, and it is only right that I should lay the facts before you, in order that you give me an explanation if you wish to do so.'

'I understand. So what do you want to know?'

Forbes-Leith mentioned the Astor Club in 1955, and Lyons said that he knew the place, which was run by Bennett (whom he referred to as Brown).

'I understand you have known Brown for some years and have been on friendly terms with him', said Forbes-Leith, and Lyons nodded, saying he had known him for quite a number of years, but asked, 'What has this got to do with the Astor Club?'

'Is it to your knowledge that the Astor club was, during 1955, serving after hours?'

'Yes, and so were many others.'

'In fact, it was known as The Bucket of Blood?'

Lyons agreed, but when Forbes-Leith asked if he had visited the Astor Club very much, he replied, 'No, very rarely. How could I? I was a sick man and ill in bed. I couldn't have visited it.'

Upon being asked when precisely he was ill, Lyons replied that he had been ill for eight months and that he did not recover until August of the previous year, whereupon the superintendent pointed out that that meant Lyons had taken to his bed in January 1956, whereas he, Forbes-Leith, was referring to the whole of 1955.

'Well, I must have been down there, I suppose', admitted Lyons, 'but what's all this leading up to?'

'I have evidence to show that you went to the club with Detective Superintendent Ridge for the purpose of effecting an introduction to Brown, the purpose being to make arrangements whereby the club would get protection if it had drinks after the permitted hours.'

'Not me.'

'Now, give this careful consideration. I'm telling you there is evidence to this effect and I'm giving you the opportunity of making some explanation for this introduction.'

'Are you suggesting that I'm a fixer?'

'We're not suggesting that at all', interjected Radford. 'What we're saying to you is that you introduced Superintendent Ridge to Brown for the purpose of effecting some sort of protection to the club.'

'Why should I?' replied Lyons. 'I've got a good business here. I don't want to make money out of things like that.'

'I'm not asking you why you shouldn't', said Forbes-Leith. 'I'm asking you for an explanation for doing so.'

'All I can say is, I didn't.'

'Are you then suggesting that you never took Mr Ridge down to the club?'

'I might have; 1955 is a long time ago.'

'Well, Mr Ridge used to go to your bar?'

'Yes, he's been here hundreds of times, all the CID come here.'

'Well, now you must remember whether or not you did go down to the club with Mr Ridge and whether you did effect this introduction?'

'Well, if I did effect an introduction, I did it here in the bar.'

'All right. If you did effect an introduction, what was the purpose of it and did you ever suggest to Brown that a sum of money would be paid to Mr Ridge for the purpose of giving protection to his clients?'

'No, certainly not. Why me? I've got a good living. I draw my cheque each week and spend it and give it away. I have a good nest egg. All I want is tucked away for an emergency. What do I want with this money?'

The following day, Radford saw Lyons once more, this time in the presence of his solicitor, Mr Cushman, who told Radford that there was no need to caution his client, whereupon Lyons made a statement.

In brief, Lyons stated that he had kept Sherry's Bar for eight and a half years and had first met Brown in 1944–45, when he worked as a chef at a Brighton hotel; and in 1954 Brown told him he had got the Astor Club. He had met Ridge when he first acquired Sherry's, and the officer used to visit once a week, usually on Sundays, although he had stopped doing so several months ago. Lyons had no recollection of introducing Ridge to Brown, and it was quite untrue that he and his friends had frequented the Astor Club after hours.

The newspaper coverage that Forbes-Leith had mentioned to Lyons was the breaking news of the police probe into the activities of certain members of the Brighton police. *The Times* reported, fairly nebulously, that:

> Detective Superintendent Ian Forbes-Leith, assisted by Chief Inspector R. Radford . . . submitted a preliminary report to Commander G. Hatherill, head of the CID, last week . . . Ten Metropolitan Police officers have been taken off other duties to help with the enquiries. This is understood to be the largest team that Scotland Yard have ever sent into the provinces upon a single enquiry. The nature of the enquiry is being kept secret and the officers are reporting directly to Commander Hatherill. Scotland Yard last night confirmed the fact that the enquiry was taking place but refused to discuss details or divulge the police force concerned. It is understood that, while the main enquiries appear to centre on the south of England, some of the officers engaged in the case have made journeys to other parts of the country.

But in the second-floor committee room at the town hall, fourteen members of the Watch Committee listened intently while the town clerk, Mr W. O. Dodd, read out a statement prepared on their behalf to the assembled newsmen:

> We have been informed by the town clerk and the Chief Constable that investigations are being conducted by officers of the Metropolitan Police Force concerning suggested bribery and corruption affecting a member of the Brighton Police Force. Until the results of the investigations are complete and made known to the committee, they do not expect to be in possession of any further information.

The representatives of the press had plenty of questions to ask, the most pertinent one being this: if only one officer was being investigated, why did it necessitate ten Scotland Yard officers being called in? More questions now came in thick and fast. Was it true that a man serving a sentence for fraud had made a statement alleging that for years he had paid bribes to a member of the Brighton police? What was the name and the rank of the officer being investigated?

It was one thing to read from a prepared statement and quite another to battle experienced pressmen voracious for a story, and poor Mr Dodd floundered badly.

The meeting was chaired by Councillor George Baldwin, who now felt impelled to put his two penn'orth into the discussion:

> I have no idea of the identity of the man concerned in the statement. We in Brighton are completely in the dark. It is absolutely true. We have no information or contact with Scotland Yard. I didn't know, and neither did my committee, that these investigations were going on.

If that was the case, Councillor Baldwin must have been hideously misinformed. Tim Sargeant's father ran the Bristol Garage in Kemptown, a small community running along King's Cliff to Black Rock in the east of Brighton, and was certain that when breakdown vehicles other than his own arrived first at the scene of an accident, it was thanks to someone at Brighton police tipping off a rival firm. Before leaving Brighton in May 1957, Mr Sargeant Sr lodged a complaint regarding this practice, and Tim Sargeant believed that it was following this that the enquiry kicked off. It may have done, but that would have been a coincidence, because for months rumours had been circulating around Brighton regarding 'senior officers' accepting bribes, crooked bookmakers, large-scale corruption rackets which were said to involve call-girls and distinctly dodgy clubs.

Two days later, Mr Dodd issued another statement in which he said he knew nothing further about the investigation and that, regarding newspaper reports that businessmen were paying for favours from town officials, if he had had the slightest suspicion that any of his colleagues had been conducting themselves in such an unseemly matter, he would have taken, er, appropriate action. And with regard to allegations of 'land-grabbing', well, Mr Dodd did seem to know something about that, but everything had been conducted openly and legally and it was the subject of a complete statement in the agenda of the council. The decision to sell land privately had been taken following the government's change of policy, and the price of the plots that were sold was based on the advice of the valuer, and it was with the approval of the district valuer that the plots were openly offered for sale. So there.

On a cheering note, on the same day, Councillor Baldwin attended the prize-giving meeting at Wellington Road police station, finishing his speech with these words: 'From my enquiries, I can assure the public that they can repose their full confidence in the police force of Brighton and in the thoroughness of their investigations.'

On 9 October, the Watch Committee held a meeting behind closed doors which lasted for two and a half hours. They later released a statement in which they referred to a letter received from Mr G. R. Paling, Deputy Director of Public Prosecutions, who stated that whoever had released scandalous information to the press concerning the investigations, it had not emanated from their office, nor had it, the commissioner had assured him, from Scotland Yard; but he added that the appearance of any Metropolitan Police officers in any town outside London was 'frequently a matter of interest, comment and speculation by the press'.

The Watch Committee's statement read as follow:

> The committee have not received any further information concerning the criminal investigation being conducted by Scotland Yard . . . It was announced at the last meeting that until the result of the investigations when completed is made known to the committee, they do not expect to be in possession of any further information. The committee wish to add in explanation that the conduct of the investigation is a matter for the police and not the Watch Committee. Furthermore, any prosecution that may follow is the responsibility of the Director of Public Prosecutions with the consent of the Attorney General. Any consequent disciplinary action will be the deep concern of the committee who are determined that at the earliest possible date any defection in the force shall be eradicated, so that the public may continue to hold in full confidence a fine body of men and women of whom they and the Watch Committee are rightly proud.

It did appear that the Watch Committee were aware that something was in the wind and that they were tentatively rowing for the shore, because on 10 October Heath was one of four officers interviewed at the investigating team's headquarters at Lewes.

CHAPTER 11

Questions – Pointed Ones – are Asked

The two interviewing officers were Forbes-Leith and Radford; Heath asked if he might make notes of the conversation, which he was permitted to do.

'We have been asked by the Director of Public Prosecutions to investigate certain matters as to the conduct of Brighton police officers', said Forbes-Leith. 'In the course of our enquiries your name has cropped up, and I am going to give you the opportunity of making any explanation you may wish to give. I want you to cast your mind back to 1955 and to the Astor Hotel and Club. Do you know these premises?'

'Yes.'

Heath stated that he knew Brown but thought that the occasions he had visited the premises had not been recorded in his diary, although when he had visited the hotel for a specific purpose, those visits had been recorded. Neither the casual visits to the Astor Club nor, in fact, to any other clubs he visited, he added, were mentioned in his diary. Heath said he had often met Brown, and then Forbes-Leith said this: 'I'm putting it to you that you visited the Astor Club weekly during 1955 until it closed in September 1955.'

'That is definitely untrue', exclaimed Heath, adding forcefully, 'You have my word on that.'

'The object of your visits was to receive £20 weekly for the protection of this club.'

'That is fantastic', expostulated Heath. 'What protection can I give?'

'You were sent originally by your Detective Superintendent Ridge to collect money for him.'

'Is this coming from Brown?' asked Heath. 'If so, there is a very good reason for him saying this. If they are not coming from Brown, I am only wasting your time, sir.'

Forbes-Leith refused to say who had made the allegations but asked Heath if he wished to make a statement.

'No, sir', replied Heath. 'I have no fear of any investigations that you are making, but if anybody above me has been doing anything they shouldn't – not that I am aware of anything – I have heard rumours that it is possible that some attempt may be possible to shift the blame – if there is any. That is the only thing I am concerned with.'

Later the same day, Commander Hatherill and Superintendent Forbes-Leith interviewed Ridge in his office.

'In the course of the enquiries into the allegations respecting members of the Brighton police force, your name has been mentioned', said Forbes-Leith. 'I consider it proper that the allegations should be laid before you in order that you can give an explanation or make a statement, if you so desire. The matter arises in 1955, when you were a detective superintendent, and in respect of the Astor Club, which operated from March to September this year in the basement of the Astor Hotel at 61 King's Road.'

'I remember it', replied Ridge.

'It was run by a man called Brown. During the period that he ran it, throughout the summer season of 1955, drinks were regularly sold after hours and the club was never raided by police. It is alleged that soon after the club first opened in the spring of 1955, you were taken to the Astor Club by Anthony Lyons, manager of Sherry's Club in West Street, and introduced to Brown. At that meeting a conversation took place when it was agreed that you should be paid the sum of £20 per week as protection money to the club to prevent it being raided by the police if drinks were sold after hours.'

'That is quite untrue', protested Ridge, but there was more.

'On about five occasions from that date, at weekly intervals, you visited the club, saw Brown and received £20 from him, and the last occasion Brown gave you money was in Sherry's Bar one morning before you went on holiday to Spain, when he handed £20 to you in a folded newspaper. Finally, it's alleged that when you went on holiday you arranged for Detective Sergeant Heath, one of your subordinates, to call at the Astor Club and collect the £20 on your behalf. This he did regularly throughout the summer until the club closed in the autumn. I have already put this matter to Detective Sergeant Heath, and he denies it.'

Ridge replied, 'Well, gentlemen, you have certainly come to the point. I can only say that I emphatically deny the allegations.'

Asked if he wished to make a statement to that effect, Ridge replied, 'Yes, I'm willing to do that, but I think it would be better if I had a lawyer present.'

The two Yard officers returned the following day. Forbes-Leith repeated the allegations to the Brighton solicitor, John Bosley, who advised Ridge to make a statement.

In his statement, Ridge said that he recalled walking along King's Road during the spring or summer of 1955 and being invited by Brown to take a look at a room which was being used as a club. He duly looked around it and then left. That was the only time he had visited the club, and to the best of his recollection he did not see Brown again. Regarding the allegation, Ridge denied receiving money from Brown at any time for any purpose and said that he had not authorized or instructed any person to receive money from Brown.

Ridge signed the statement and was told that the matter would be reported to the Director of Public Prosecutions. When Bosley left, the ever-growing number of pressmen not unnaturally wished to know what he was doing there.

'I often call at the Town Hall', replied the solicitor disingenuously.

On 15 October the Attorney General, Sir Reginald Manningham-Buller, received a visit from the Assistant Commissioner (Crime), Richard Leofric Jackson CBE, and Commander Hatherill.

It was mentioned in *The Times* and merited very little news space, but nevertheless it looked rather ominous – and it was.

CHAPTER 12

Arrests

On 17 October 1957, two local magistrates were telephoned at home and asked to be at the Town Hall by 9 o'clock the following morning. Five minutes before they got there, Heath arrived. He was unaware of it, but the reason for their attendance was to sign a warrant for his arrest, alleging that he attempted to obtain £50 from Alan Roy Bennett as a reward for showing favours in affairs relating to the Crown.

At 10.05am a car arrived carrying Commander Hatherill and Superintendent Forbes-Leith, and they were shown into the Chief Constable's office. Other Yard officers arrived, and Tommy Butler also entered the office. Heath, together with his solicitor Mr Cyril Wheeler, was summoned via the internal telephone system, and with the head of the CID, Detective Superintendent Gwyn Williams, in attendance, at 10.10am Forbes-Leith read the warrant out to Heath and cautioned him, to which he replied, 'It is a fantastic allegation. I have said before, he has a reason for making such allegations against me.' After being immediately suspended from duty by the Chief Constable, Heath was then formally charged and replied, 'I am not guilty. I am not guilty of that, sir, but I have nothing else to say at the moment.'

His fingerprints having been taken, he was then taken into the CID office, where his locker was opened and his diaries and pocket books were seized. Also in the locker was an envelope marked 'R vs Mrs Brabiner, exhibit No. 1'. Inside the envelope was a syringe.

'Why haven't you returned this?' asked Butler.

'I forgot I still had it', replied Heath. 'I intended to get rid of it some time.'

Heath was then taken to his home address at 58 Bramble Drive, Withdean, accompanied by his solicitor, Forbes-Leith and Butler. Heath's wife and his two children aged ten and six were not at home when the premises was searched. Butler found four ties in Heath's wardrobe, and the first one bore the seller's name: Christies, Quadrant Arcade.

'Brown bought it for me', said Heath, adding, 'It's the only one.'

It wasn't. Looking through the other ties, Forbes-Leith found another with the same seller's name on it.

'What about this one?' he asked.

'Oh yes', replied Heath. 'He bought me that as well.'

A third tie was found, this one bearing the label 'Hummel, Burlington Arcade', and Heath said that Brown must also have bought that one, since 'I wouldn't go there on my own.' As to where the fourth tie came from, Heath said, 'I really can't remember.'

The possession of four pieces of neckwear, expensive though they were, might appear to be pretty small beer; but the fact remained that the discovery of these ties acted, in part, as corroboration of what Bennett had told the police.

After returning briefly to police headquarters, at 12.18pm Heath stood in the dock of the specially convened Magistrates' Court before the chairman, Mr Harold Vokins, and two other lay magistrates.

Mr Wheeler applied for bail, saying, 'Here is a man with good character, a man with a wife and two children, a man who has lived in Brighton for years.'

That being the case, and given that there was just one charge of attempting to corruptly solicit £50, it might be thought that bail should not have caused any particular difficulty – but it did.

'I oppose bail for four reasons', Forbes-Leith told the bench. 'Firstly because of the gravity of the charge. Secondly, I have strong reason to believe that witnesses may be interfered with. Thirdly, there are still many enquiries to be made. Fourthly, it is anticipated that further charges will be made against this officer.'

There was a short consultation by the Bench, but within thirteen minutes of entering the dock Heath was remanded in custody, and a few moments later, he was starting the eight-mile journey to Lewes prison.

During the next week there were reports of a mysterious woman witness; she was interviewed not at her home in Brighton, or anywhere near that town, but was taken to London by car and interviewed at Scotland Yard. She was then taken to the Cumberland Hotel for the night; the following day, it was back to the Yard for more questioning, before being booked in to the Grosvenor Hotel. She was returned to her home on 23 October, all the while being protected by male and female officers.

'I can't say whether I've been able to help the Yard, or not', the anonymous, attractive, dark-haired woman of thirty told Derek Lambert of the *Daily Mirror*; but the police obviously thought she could, because a watch was kept on the shop where she worked.

The lady in question was understandably being less than frank to the newspaper reporter. Her name was Mrs Joan Watson, she was Ernie Waite's paramour, she and her children had already been threatened and she had been helping police enormously.

Meanwhile, speculation was growing in Brighton. What would happen next? This was national headline news, and it was rumoured that two more warrants had been issued; in fact, an arrest was expected on 24 October, and the crowd of 200 onlookers who surrounded the Town Hall at noon were disappointed when no arrests materialized. But surely something must be happening? Superintendent Forbes-Leith and his men had vacated their incident room at Lewes police station and were seen carrying huge amounts of correspondence into police headquarters. The crowd who started to drift away by 12.30pm had heard of more legal conferences in London, and there was talk of this mysterious woman witness and new evidence that was said to be 'surprising'. And what were these rumours about a tobacco robbery some months ago which had been hampered by a leakage of official information? They would have to wait another 24 hours to find out.

*   *   *

Sir William Johnson CMG, CBE, QPM was one of the most powerful police officers in the United Kingdom. He had joined Portsmouth City Police in 1920 and twelve years later had been appointed Chief Constable of Plymouth City Police. In 1936 he became assistant Chief Constable of Birmingham City Police and five years later, its Chief Constable. Since 1945 he had served with Her Majesty's Inspectorate of Constabularies (HMI), and as the Home Secretary Henry Brooke would later say, he had 'great knowledge and experience'.

It was HMI's job to inspect and report upon how well police did their job; also to monitor police forces and identify areas where improvements were required. And just before 10 o'clock in the morning of 25 October, bowler-hatted Sir William, who stood leaning on the railings opposite the Old Ship Hotel and gazing out to sea from Brighton's seafront, had come to the conclusion that in the matter of the local Borough Police Force quite a lot of improvements were needed – and the sooner the better.

He snapped out of his reverie as he felt a firm hand on his shoulder; turning, he saw a familiar face, Commander George Hatherill, who had just arrived with Forbes-Leith. The men shook hands, exchanged pleasantries, got into the waiting police car and drove up to the Town Hall, where they went to the office of Mr Dodd, the Town Clerk.

At 10.50, Forbes-Leith and Radford went to the Chief Constable's office, where they saw Ridge and Hammersley. 'I have warrants for your arrest', said Forbes-Leith and he read them out:

> That between 1 January 1948 and 18 October 1957 you did conspire together and with other persons unknown corruptly to solicit and obtain rewards for the said Trevor Heath, John Richard Hammersley and Charles Feild Williams Ridge for showing or promising favours contrary to their duty as police officers and thereby to obstruct and defeat the course of public justice. Contrary to Common Law.

Ridge replied, 'I would like to say it is absolutely preposterous', while Hammersley said, 'I would like to say, sir, that I deny the allegation.'

The Chief Constable was immediately suspended by the Watch Committee, who appointed uniformed Superintendent Thomas Hill as the caretaker Chief Constable; he in turn suspended Hammersley.

Fifteen minutes after those arrests, Lyons was arrested by Ernie Millen on an exactly similar warrant and brought to police headquarters, and at 12.15pm he and the others were charged. They had nothing to say.

At Brighton Magistrates' Court, Mr R. L. D. Thomas, Senior Treasury Counsel, appeared on behalf of the Director of Public Prosecutions. Mr A. P. Harris appeared for Ridge and Mr G. V. Hemming for Hammersley. Mr Stanley Cushman, a solicitor, appeared for Lyons, and he and the other legal representatives asked for bail.

Mr Thomas requested a remand in custody, saying, 'Possibly there will be other charges. There are further enquiries to be made', and adding, 'also there has already been an instance of a person who will be a witness in this case having been directly threatened.'

The discussion between the chairman, Mr Harold Vokins, and his fellow magistrates Mrs Elizabeth Dacre and Colonel S. Lynn took no time at all: 'It is the decision of the Bench that all defendants must remain in custody for one week.'

Two vehicles were waiting, their engines running, at the rear of the Town Hall. Ridge got into the first and Lyons, covering his face with his coat, got into the second; Hammersley, not so retiring, paused to shake hands with well-wishers before also getting into the car, and then the three men were whisked away to Lewes Prison.

What had made national headlines a week before now went global. To the west, the fact that a Chief Constable had not only been charged but had also been remanded in custody excited the citizens of Shreveport, Louisiana, as well as being featured in the *Logansport Press*, Indiana. To the north, in Canada, the *Winnipeg Free Press* and the *Vancouver Sun* marvelled at the news; and further south, in Jamaica, the readers of Kingston's *Gleaner* were duly bemused. To the east, according to their dispositions, the readers of the *Straits Times*, the *Singapore Free Press* and the *Singapore Standard* were equally thrilled or appalled, and subscribers to the *Age*, Melbourne, must have wondered what on earth the 'Poms' were up to.

When Heath next appeared at court, to be charged with the same offence as the others, he replied, 'I deny that charge most emphatically', and a spirited application for bail was made once again. Opposing it, Forbes-Leith told the Bench:

> I am opposing bail on these grounds: The two charges against Sergeant Heath are very serious ones. We have still a lot of investigations to make and a number of other witnesses have yet to be seen. We are disturbed that witnesses may be interfered with. Since Sergeant Heath appeared in this court last week one lady witness has been threatened and her children also. It is a position we cannot possibly tolerate. Until we have completed enquiries, it is essential that Sergeant Heath should be kept in custody.

With that type of objection, there was no chance of Heath getting bail; and he didn't.

CHAPTER 13

A New Appointment

Just prior to Heath's appearance, 58-year-old Albert Edward Rowsell OBE, who had been Chief Constable of Exeter since 1941, was appointed temporary Chief Constable of Brighton. He had joined Exeter police as a constable in 1919 and in 1949 had been awarded the King's Police and Fire Service Medal for distinguished conduct.

When Heath was remanded in custody, Mr Rowsell's conduct was more irascible than distinguished. Perhaps he had taken umbrage at being moved from his home in Exeter (even though the Exeter City Watch Committee had given their gracious consent), but in the anteroom of the council chamber, talking to the Mayor of Brighton, Alderman Charles Tyson, the Chairman of the Watch Committee and the Town Clerk, Mr Rowsell suddenly became fed up with the press photographers' bulbs which had been flashing in his face for a good two minutes.

'No more pictures, please', he said, but when some of the photographers complained that they had been unable to obtain their shots, he decided a firmer line should be taken. 'If you want my cooperation, do as I ask and cut it out!' he snapped and walked out of the room, leaving the bemused Chairman to field the reporters' questions as best he could.

The Chairman also stated that Mr Rowsell's task was primarily to boost the morale of the force at a difficult time. It was a cogent point. Jokes were already beginning to circulate about the force: 'Brighton's is the finest police force money can buy!' was one, and another was about a waiter who, handed a banknote in payment, held it up to the light, saying, 'I can't accept this; it has a ridge on it.' And Mr Bosley, Ridge's solicitor, had already written to the BBC's Director General asking for transcripts of *The Alma Cogan Show*; apparently, during its Saturday night transmission, risqué if not downright inappropriate comments had been made about a police force in dire straits.

An application for bail in respect of Charles Ridge was made to Mr Justice Diplock, who was sitting in chambers on 30 October. During the 25-minute hearing, bail was granted in the sum of

£250 in Ridge's own recognizance and a surety of £250, which was provided by his married daughter, Mrs Elizabeth Whiffin. However, further conditions were that he was not to leave his home until the morning of 1 November, when he was due to attend the Magistrates' Court and – something of a first – that his home telephone should be disconnected.

Perhaps the court appearance on 1 November was a bit of an anticlimax for the other three defendants and their legal representatives, believing as they must have done that a further remand in custody would be sought by the prosecution. They were half right – Mr R. L. D. Thomas for the Director of Public Prosecutions did ask for a remand until 25 November, which was granted; but now that police enquiries had been completed, there was no objection to bail being granted, and it was. Ridge had his bail continued, and the other three defendants were each bailed in their own recognizance of £100 and sureties in the same sum: Solomon Rubenstein, a licensee of Cambridge Heath Road, London stood surety for Lyons, Mrs Elsie Astbury of Sussex Square, Brighton for Heath and Mr H. W. Moffatt of Atlingworth Street, Brighton for Hammersley.

'The Bench can only enjoin you not in any way to interfere with any of the witnesses', warned Mr H. Cushnie MBE, the chairman of the Bench, and with that, the four men were released into the 100-strong crowd who had come to witness proceedings.

When the court reconvened on 25 November, the defendants' numbers had increased by one. When Sammy Bellson was seen on 5 November by 'The Terrible Twins' he was told that what he had said to them previously about Harry Leach and his son John had proved to be quite correct, and they had made statements to that effect. Bellson was therefore asked if he would care to commit his testimony to the written word. It is one thing to be a surreptitious grass but quite another to act as one publicly.

'I don't wish to make a written statement or give evidence', he replied. 'Whether the prosecution or the defence call me, I shall deny it.'

Although such a refusal was necessary to uphold Bellson's professional reputation and social standing with the likes of gang leader Billy Hill, it was, of course, quite the wrong thing to say to police officers of The Twins' calibre. The word 'No', coming from a villain, simply did not feature in their vocabulary.

One week later, following a consultation with the Director of Public Prosecutions and a visit to the Magistrates' Court, Forbes-Leith and Ernie Millen turned up at Bellson's front door in The Drive, Hove, with a warrant for his arrest. Taken to the police station and charged, Bellson replied, 'I have nothing to say.'

He later appeared at the Magistrates' Court, and the Mayor of Brighton, Alderman Charles Tyson, who up until then had been one of the Magistrates sitting on the Bench, suddenly (for reasons best known to himself) got up and left; Bellson was remanded on bail.

CHAPTER 14

Court Appearance – and Threats

Now, on 25 November, the prosecution was ready to commence proceedings with a view to having the defendants committed for trial. The witnesses for the prosecution would be called, they would give evidence and they could be cross-examined by the defence; their depositions would be taken by the Clerk of the Court. If defendants wished to give evidence, of course they could, but in most such cases they would plead not guilty and reserve their defence, as they did here. This would give the legal teams the opportunity to evaluate and digest the evidence against their clients and prepare a defence for the forthcoming trial.

The prosecution were heavyweights, led by the Solicitor General, Sir Harry Braustyn Hylton Hylton-Foster QC. Aged fifty-two, Sir Harry had held the post since 1954. During the Second World War he had served with the RAF Volunteer Reserve and had been a Deputy Judge Advocate at courts martial in North Africa.

He was assisted by Mr Gerald Howard QC, a senior prosecuting counsel who had appeared for the Crown in treason cases following the war and in the case of John George Haigh, 'The Acid Bath Murderer'.

Also in the prosecuting team was Mr Maxwell Turner QC; he had prosecuted in the case of the serial killer John Reginald Halliday Christie and would later lead the prosecution in the case of the police murderer Günter Fritz Podola. Acting as backstop was Mr R. L. D. Thomas from the Director of Public Prosecutions' office.

The defendants were represented by their solicitors, with the exception of Lyons, who was represented by Stanley Rees QC; as and when they were committed for trial, they would then be allocated barristers. They appeared on the charge as shown previously; in addition, Heath was charged with attempting to solicit £50 from Bennett.

Queues had formed since 7 o'clock that morning for admittance to the court, which finally opened at 10.40am, when there was a rush for the public gallery; many of the seats were occupied by fleet-footed pressmen. That was not surprising; it was the most important case to be heard in Brighton for many a long year.

The magistrates, led by the chairman Mr Howard Vokins, filed into court, and the defendants entered the dock. Cyril Wheeler, the solicitor acting for Heath, wanted to know how the second charge against his client would be addressed and was told that all of the evidence would be heard together. Wheeler protested that the second charge should either be heard separately or dismissed but was firmly told by Mr Vokins, 'We will hear all the evidence first.'

Opening for the prosecution, Sir Harry told the court:

> The evidence will be of what the accused said and did, which in the prosecution's submission will lead to the prima facie inference that there was a conspiracy. Those involved in a conspiracy are often people who break the criminal law and want to prevent the impact of justice. People who were willing or could be persuaded to bribe the police are not the best people. So some of my evidence does not come from the best people, some of it must come from what may generally be described as tainted sources. Therefore, I submit, it would be unwise for anyone to form a view whether or not the accusations are well-founded until the matter has been tried out before a jury.

The court was informed of Hammersley's threats to the enquiry agent in his desire to protect Bellson, and that was followed by the determined efforts of Bellson, Heath and Hammersley to extort money from Harry and John Leach, the latter being charged with receiving. Ridge's input into the case was also mentioned.

Next came 'The Bucket of Blood' allegations, which the onlookers in the public gallery wanted to hear about in every salacious detail; they would not be disappointed. It was Lyons, Sir Harry told them, who had brought Ridge to the club to introduce him to Bennett, at which time it was agreed that £20 per week, paid to Ridge, would allow Bennett to run the club exactly how he pleased. After a while, it was Heath who collected the payments on Ridge's behalf, and that was followed by a catalogue of payments made by Bennett to Heath and Hammersley to keep him out of a catalogue of trouble with various police forces throughout the country. When Heath was questioned by the Scotland Yard officers he told them that he had visited the Astor Club on two occasions in 1955 and that it was quite untrue that he had visited the club on a weekly basis or that he had gone there to collect money for Ridge.

Ridge, stated the Solicitor General, had said that he had been to the club only once, at Bennett's invitation; he absolutely denied accepting any money or authorizing anyone to collect it for him.

Mentioning that Bennett eventually went to Scotland Yard, Sir Harry said, 'That is probably why we are all here today.'

Mrs Mason was mentioned, with her subsequent running of the Astor Club; Lyons had invited her to make a weekly contribution to permit after-hours drinking. When she refused, she was fined and the club was struck off.

Next, the antecedents of Ernie Waite were introduced to the bench, and calling him 'obviously a scoundrel', Sir Harry added, 'No doubt every word he says will have to be scrutinized with the greatest care.'

Waite's background was appalling; and the way that he received huge amounts of stolen property – coffee, tinned goods and cigarettes – time after time with the connivance of crooked police officers was indefensible. His account was corroborated by a number of people, few of whom, if any, were wholly respectable; their accounts, too, would in the words of the Solicitor General 'have to be scrutinized with the greatest care'.

Then there were the two women, Mrs Brabiner and Mrs Lawrence, one an abortionist, the other her assistant, both of whom had parted with money to Heath, and Swaby the burglar who gave £10 to Heath to drop out details of his previous convictions. Unfortunately, this had been insufficient, and so Heath had tried to induce Swaby's wife to part with £50 – as well as attempting to coerce an honest detective constable into helping him – but without success; and so the burglar went to prison for five years. Heath had also unsuccessfully tried to compel another honest constable to accept payment from Bellson for letting him know when his club was going to be raided.

So that was the litany of crooked behaviour laid out to Brighton Magistrates' Court on that first day of the proceedings. But the criminal behaviour did not stop there; before the day had ended, it would resurface not 100 yards away from the court.

As the 46-year-old witness Betty Lawrence was walking through the town centre that evening, a car pulled up, four men got out and told her, 'We're Billy Howard's boys and we've got a message for you.' She was pushed around, threatened with an open razor and told 'not to say anything about their friends in court, or she'd be cut up'.

Understandably, Mrs Lawrence was terrified and reported this matter to the police. The following day in court, Gerald Howard QC for the prosecution told the bench:

> Before I call any witnesses, there is a matter I should mention to you. You will recollect the very proper warning you gave about any possible attempt at interfering with witnesses. I have been instructed that some such attempts have, in fact, again been made. I am instructed that last night, one of the witnesses in this case, Mrs Lawrence – who has not yet been called – was threatened by persons who said they were Billy Howard's boys. They threatened that she would be cut up if she gave evidence.

Mr Howard then turned to give a withering look at the five defendants in the dock, before adding:

> It is right that I should make it plain that there is no evidence to connect any of the accused with this, but I thought it proper you should know about it in case you might think it right specifically to warn those persons who threatened to interfere with Mrs Lawrence, yesterday.

In response, the Chairman, Harold Vokins, said:

> This is a very serious matter although there is no evidence that any of the defendants had any part in this. If we hear anything of this kind, we shall treat it very seriously. If the press would give publicity to that, it would be a general warning to everybody not to interfere in any form.

So what was behind all this? Although Billy Howard was unknown to Mrs Lawrence, he was well known to the glitterati of the underworld as a South London street fighter (especially handy with a razor) with a certain reputation. He had allegedly beaten gang boss Billy Hill in a fight, the Kray twins were said to be 'terrified' of him (although Reggie Kray would later say that whenever he visited Howard's club, 'He was a genial host and . . . he made me feel very welcome') and unkind members of the criminal classes branded him 'a police informer'.

Was Billy Howard involved in the threats? He owned The Beehive Club in Brixton, but it was in the Spanish Garden Club in Mayfair where he was tracked down, a few days later, by Michael Pilley, a reporter for the *Daily Sketch*. Howard denied any involvement in Mrs Lawrence's intimidation although he obviously gloried in the publicity, but it was quite likely that he was not directly involved. It could have been any number of low-lifes from any number of so-called gangs who had been frightening an already frightened middle-aged woman. So if Billy Howard had just permitted his name to be used, to create a false trail, who was responsible for setting up the incident?

Sammy Bellson was, I suppose, a prime contender, with his connections to London gangs, although I have often wondered about Chief Constable Ridge's unique bail condition, having his telephone disconnected. And there the matter should rest. The Leaches, father and son, gave their evidence, as did the threatened enquiry agent, but now it's time to introduce the most important witness so far into court: Alan Roy Bennett.

CHAPTER 15

Alan Bennett Speaks out . . .

Bennett arrived at court in a Rolls-Royce and was smartly attired in a dark overcoat with a white handkerchief protruding from its breast pocket, and a gold watch chain across his waistcoat. Carrying a tightly furled umbrella, his shoes gleaming with polish, he removed his bowler hat to reveal immaculately trimmed hair. Tall, good-looking and giving a Green Street, Mayfair address, he looked every inch the man about town and he bore a passing resemblance to the Hollywood star, Errol Flynn. He had that actor's habit of touching the ends of his moustache, and when asked a rather awkward question he tended to affect a look of stunned astonishment, in the same way that Flynn had done when in 1943 he was charged with but acquitted of raping Betty Hanson and Peggy Larue Satterlee.

Bennett did not have the actor's gift of projecting his voice (although Mr Vokins agreed that the acoustics in the court were bad), and the defendants were permitted to leave the dock and sit in the well of the court in order to hear him better. However, what Bennett had to say scored considerable points for the prosecution.

Led through his evidence by Gerald Howard, he outlined the approaches that had been made about the running of the Astor Club, as well as other approaches made in respect of the criminal matters of which he had been accused.

One matter in particular raised by Mr Howard was the burglary at the jeweller's in Bournemouth on 30 April 1955.

'Where were you on that day', he asked.

'I was in Brussels', replied Bennett and with that, he took his passport from his pocket and threw it on to the Clerk's table.

'It's not necessary', said Mr Howard, to which Bennett replied, 'It was necessary a few weeks ago.'

The examination-in-chief took the whole of the morning, and by the time the court reconvened after the lunchtime adjournment, more than 100 people were waiting to get in to hear what revelations would appear when Bennett was cross-examined by the defence. Those who did gain admittance were in for a treat.

'You know that Mr Ridge denies your story?' began John Bosley, appearing on behalf of the Chief Constable.

'I would not expect him to admit it, sir', replied Bennett coolly.

'It is a question of seeing who has to be believed, you or Mr Ridge', said Bosley. 'Would you agree with me that their Worships should know a little more about your character?'

If Bosley thought that question would unnerve the main prosecution witness he was mistaken, because Bennett replied, 'My character is bad, I admit that, but let me tell you, I have never resorted to blackmail like your clients have.'

Bennett admitted using five names: Bennett, Brown, Ferguson, Montgomery and, when he was a boy, Poiner, the name of his stepfather; he denied using the name Holt. He also admitted to his previous convictions, saying that he had been out of trouble for ten years and telling the court, 'I have paid money for years to keep these matters out of the court. I do not wish to discuss my past record. You do not think I have given all this money away for years for nothing?'

'You say you have been of good behaviour for ten years?' asked Bosley, incredulously. 'Many people say that. Do you say if the justices or another court have to decide between the word of yourself or Mr Ridge, you should be believed?'

It permitted Bennett to deliver a knockout blow. 'I say Ridge is no better than myself; but I have been convicted and he has not.'

Asked if he agreed that when the Solicitor General spoke of 'tainted sources' in his opening address he could possibly have been referring to him, Bennett cheerfully admitted that he probably had been.

Cross-examined by Cyril Wheeler for Heath, Bennett stated that he did not know that Alan Walker, who complained of missing £1,000 at the Astor Hotel, had a record, adding that on the day in question he had gone to Ascot and only found out about the loss upon his return. 'Walker gave me some money to take to Ascot to put bets on for him. It was £150, and he lost £120, so I returned the £30 to him.'

'Did you find the running of this club a very profitable occupation?' asked Wheeler and was told, 'I earned a decent living.'

Asked if he had a record of the profits for that period, Bennett replied, 'You'd better ask the accountants, old boy'; and when Wheeler enquired whether he had been able to go to the South of France at the end of the season, Bennett replied, 'I had gone to the South of France for many years.'

At this point, David Peck for Hammersley suddenly stood up and, asking the court's permission, said, 'When you came into court today and passed the dock, did you say something to Hammersley?'

'I never spoke to Hammersley.'

'Did you say, "I think you are being framed?"'

Was this a deliberate ploy, to suggest that one of Hammersley's chief accusers was suggesting his innocence, even before giving evidence against him? If it was, it was an innovative ruse – but it didn't work, because Bennett snapped, 'Are you making a joke?' before answering decisively, 'Certainly not.'

Bennett was then asked about statements he had made to Scotland Yard officers. 'I made a longish statement to Superintendent Forbes-Leith and named certain people', replied Bennett, 'but that was much later on.'

Back now to Mr Wheeler, who said, 'It was quite clear to you that you were being accused, rightly or wrongly, of having taken this £1,000 belonging to Walker?'

'Yes, that was clear. I denied it.'

Heath – and two other officers whose names Bennett did not know – had searched his safe, with his permission, and Wheeler asked, 'You say it was on this occasion that Heath said something about giving us our whack of the grand?'

'That is right.'

'In the presence of two other officers?'

'Yes.'

Bennett was asked about the ring he had purchased from Heath 'after a lot of moaning and arguing from him' – he agreed there was no question of blackmail being involved.

Bennett denied that he had been arrested for the Folkestone offence, although it was a moot point. 'I went and gave myself up. I was tried and acquitted', he said, but once again, that was a play on words; the Folkestone magistrates had decided there was insufficient evidence on which to commit him for trial. There was a great deal of difference between being discharged and acquitted, as Bennett well knew; if further evidence was forthcoming after a person had been discharged at the Magistrates' Court, he could be charged all over again; if he had been acquitted at a higher court, he could not.

But Wheeler did not give up. 'There was a genuine enquiry about you by Folkestone?'

'There was a genuine enquiry about a person, but not a Bennett.'

'By any other of your names?'

'When I went to Scotland Yard, there was no warrant out. There was a descriptive warrant, and he' – here Bennett pointed dramatically at Heath – 'put the name to it.'

'Would you be very surprised if you were to learn that it was Folkestone who put your name forward?' asked Wheeler and received the reply, 'Not only would I be surprised but I would be amazed. I walked into Scotland Yard and I walked out again and there was no warrant. If there had been, they would have arrested me then. The name was put on the warrant by Heath.'

'When you were in Brighton on 19 June this year, driving your car', said Wheeler, 'you stopped when you saw Heath.'

'My dear sir', replied Bennett loftily, 'Heath would be the last one I would stop my car and wave to. He stopped me. I do agree I got out and into his car and then got out again.'

'Is it right that when you were interviewed by Hammersley and Heath you adopted a very indignant attitude over the Bournemouth affair?'

'I protested my innocence.'

'Did you threaten you would complain to the Home Office about being accused over the Bournemouth affair?'

'No, but years ago I threatened I would report the matter to a former Home Secretary I knew, which I should have done', replied Bennett, adding once more, 'That was years ago.'

'Did you threaten at any other time you would complain to the Home Office?'

'In the summer of 1955 over one of Heath's blackmailing incidents, namely the photograph.'

'Why had you paid money if you had nothing to fear?'

'I wanted my past to be forgotten. I wanted to be just left alone. By going to Scotland Yard, everybody in the world knows about this and it has stopped me getting a living.'

'You were willing to pay, although you had nothing to fear, because of your past?'

'That is the only answer there can be.'

And that was the end of Bennett's testimony at the Magistrates' Court. Nothing had happened to put a dent in the prosecution's case; his evidence had taken over three hours to recount.

CHAPTER 16

... and so does Wenche Bennett

Now it was the turn of Bennett's wife, who arrived stylishly dressed in a white beret and a beige, fur-trimmed coat.

Mrs Wenche Bennett had never met any Brighton police officers prior to the opening of the Astor Club; but soon after it opened, the first officer she met was Ridge, who had arrived with his co-defendant, Lyons.

'It was arranged that my husband would look after Mr Ridge', she said. 'He would look after him . . . it was for my husband to give him some money, so that the club could be run without interference.'

'Who said that?' asked Maxwell Turner for the prosecution.

'Mr Ridge. I heard him . . . I did not hear any particular sum of money mentioned on that occasion . . . Up to that time the club had closed in the evening at ordinary hours, but after, there was a change in the procedure and it stayed open until everybody had finished drinking and did not want any more – one, two, three o'clock in the morning, it all depended . . . I saw Ridge two or three times when he came to the club. It was closed at the time he called. He came to get money . . . I saw it. It was always £5 notes, because it was white. I do not know how much. My husband handed the money to Ridge, because I have seen him. I remember an occasion when Ridge said he was going to Spain for a holiday; after that, I don't think Ridge came to the club again. At this time I did not know Heath but I first met him a week or ten days after Ridge went to Spain. The meeting was at the club; afterwards, I saw him quite a few times in the club. He also came in the afternoon when the club was shut. I knew he came for money, because I have seen him. He was given white money. When my husband was out he left it in an envelope for him, and then I saw Heath at the club and gave it to him. I had spoken to Heath on the telephone on two occasions and he had said, "I should not open." I took his advice. I know the Astor Club was called "The Bucket of Blood".'

'Why was that?' asked Maxwell Turner.

'Because there was such a lot of fights. The customers were bad customers.'

The prosecution then turned to the time when Mrs Bennett had accompanied Alan Walker to dinner. She told the court that she and Walker had been sitting at the bar having a drink when Heath came in. He left with Walker, telling Mrs Bennett, 'This will only take a few minutes', and suggesting she went home, which she did. Heath later came to the Astor Hotel, and Mrs Bennett overheard a conversation between him and her husband while she was in the adjoining bedroom.

'I heard them saying Mr Walker had lost some money in the hotel and they wanted their share of it', Mrs Bennett told the court. 'They said if my husband would pay them, they would forget all about it. I heard Mr Heath say this. My husband said he would pay nothing because there was nothing to pay.'

That concluded the proceedings for the day; the following day, 27 November, Mrs Bennett was late arriving at court, so the evidence of Mrs Blanche Cherryman was heard who told of her conversation with Ridge about the running of the Astor Club 'because there was no one in the CID I could trust', and of receiving the enigmatic phone call telling her to shut the club for the night and that 'it was Charlie speaking'.

When Mrs Bennett arrived she had just one more question put to her, by Maxwell Turner: 'Was the Astor Club ever raided by the police while you and your husband were there?'

'No,' she replied. 'Never.'

In cross-examination by John Bosley she agreed that she and her husband were a happily married couple.

'You would tell an untruth for him?' he asked, to which Mrs Bennett replied, 'I would not.'

Bosley put it to her that on her own account she had taken part in an attempt to bribe the police, and she replied, 'I did not agree with that. I know it is wrong. I was always telling my husband it is wrong.'

She was then asked, 'Do you know if you are going to be prosecuted or not? . . . Instead of being a witness, you would be put in the dock for taking part in bribery. Do you know if you are going to be prosecuted?'

'I don't know', replied Mrs Bennett, and when she was asked if she expected to be arrested she replied, 'No.'

Bosley pressed her again, and when she replied, 'I haven't thought about it', Gerald Howard QC for the Crown objected, but Bosley ploughed on, asking, 'Is there any arrangement whereby you know you are not going to be prosecuted?'

'There is not', she replied, firmly.

'Have you talked over your evidence with your husband? I mean after he gave his evidence and before you started yours?' asked Bosley.

'There isn't much to talk about', she replied.

'You lunched with your husband yesterday during his evidence, didn't you?'

'I did, and there was present also a police superintendent. He wouldn't let us talk about the case at all.'

With that, John Bosley sat down, having done his best to undermine Wenche Bennett's credibility. In fact, he had made rather an arse of things. Suggesting she should have been in the dock implied that she should be a co-defendant with his client, Ridge.

Mr Stanley Rees QC for Lyons asked if criminals went to the Astor Club; Mrs Bennett replied, 'I have seen some criminals there', and said they had been pointed out to her but denied knowing that Alan Walker was a thief. She was asked about the cars that her husband had owned; she stated that the one Ridge had admired had been a black Jaguar; later, they had had a white Jaguar.

Precisely what any of these trivia had to do with Rees' client Anthony Lyons is not very clear at all. And Cyril Weaver appearing for Heath, against whom she had provided the most damning evidence, had no questions for her at all. Neither had David Peck on behalf of Hammersley.

It appeared that the defence had achieved very little.

CHAPTER 17

More Fuel for the Fire

Mrs Mary Mason, who had reopened the Astor Bar in 1956, told the court that she had never paid any money to the police; and her daughter, Mrs Margaret Elizabeth Newman, stated that after her mother's club was raided, they had gone to Sherry's Bar and told Lyons forcefully that they thought Mrs Mason was being victimized. Mrs Mason could be excitable in drink, and she admitted to having six convictions but said, 'I've only been in prison once.'

The same experience of a single sentence of imprisonment applied to the next witness, Harry Waterman, the odd-job man who lived rent-free at the Astor Hotel. He had seen Bennett pass money wrapped in a newspaper to someone in Sherry's Bar. He was unable to say to whom the money had been passed, but when asked if that person resembled anybody in court he pointed unhesitatingly at Ridge.

Next came police witnesses from different constabularies, all of whom had wanted words with Bennett about a series of peccadilloes and had been obliged to use the CID at Brighton Borough Police Force as the conduit through which to do so.

Detective Sergeant Arthur Broadbent-Speight of Leeds police wanted Brighton police to investigate Bennett in respect of a dishonoured cheque presented in the name of Austin Ferguson. He was asked by John Bosley if he knew that Ferguson operated under a total of seven different names.

'Not to my knowledge', replied the officer. 'Only four: Ferguson, Wood, Brown and Bennett', but added that he had never received a reply to his enquiry.

Detective Sergeant George Richard Dunstan of Brighton police had received the enquiry from Bournemouth police regarding the £8,000 jeweller's shop-breaking for which Bennett was a suspect. But when Heath responded to Bournemouth, stating to Detective Inspector Frederick Tilling that Bennett had denied the offence, saying he was abroad at the time, Heath did not inform Dunstan that he had ever made that telephone call, nor did he tell him that Bennett had been at the CID headquarters on 19 June when the call had been made.

Detective Constable Richard George Crane of Folkestone
CID had investigated an attempted shop-breaking in that area,
and the description of the suspect fitted Bennett. On 24 June
at 9.15pm, Crane telephoned Brighton CID office because he
wanted to speak to an officer who had spoken to Bennett about
some other matter.

'Someone came to the phone and without giving a name said
"I was with Sergeant Heath when he interviewed Bennett"',
Crane told the court and outlined to the anonymous officer the
nature of the enquiry. He described the suspect as being 5 feet
10 to 11 inches tall, thirty-five to forty years of age, of slim
build, with dark hair brushed back and thinning at the temples,
and a thin moustache, and then asked how that compared with
Bennett.

Crane continued, 'He then went on, "He is doing very well for
himself. He is wearing a 50 guinea Savile Row suit and driving a
magnificent Rolls-Royce". I told this officer that Bennett had been
identified by a photograph as a man who committed this job at
Folkestone. He replied, "I know he's been a bad boy but he's done
nothing for ten years". I said to him, "I have a recent photograph
of him here", and he replied, "Oh, you've got him cold, then?"
The conversation ended when I was told that Sergeant Heath
would be on duty the next morning.'

Crane went on to say that he had arrested Bennett on 12 July
and taken him before the court the following day, but that on
10 August the charge was dismissed.

In cross-examination, David Peck for Hammersley admitted it
was his client to whom Crane had spoken on the telephone and
asked what sort of impression he had gleaned from Hammersley's
answer.

'It conveyed to me he was in such good circumstances he
would not do this kind of a job', replied Crane.

The last of the police witnesses (other than the investigating
team) was Detective Sergeant Frederick Powell from Scotland
Yard who said that on 26 June a man named Bennett had called
at the Yard at 5.00pm. He had not been asked to; he had come
of his own accord. Powell knew nothing about him, or about the
attempted breaking at Folkestone.

Mrs Alice Brabiner was an extremely important witness. When
she gave her evidence, a policewoman sat next to her; she had
been accompanied by two women prison officers because she was
serving her fifteen-month sentence for procuring an abortion.
Led through her evidence by Gerald Howard QC, she broke
down frequently as she described the events leading to her arrest

and her payments to Heath, as well as his empty threat that she could be sentenced to fourteen years' corrective training.

She agreed with Cyril Wheeler for Heath that it was she who had initially offered him money, and he immediately said to her, 'You did not say that this morning.'

'I wasn't asked', replied Mrs Brabiner. 'I said it in my statement to the police.'

Reginald Betts and Mrs Brabiner's daughter, Mrs Iris Karrouze, gave compelling evidence of money being procured for Heath and of Mrs Brabiner's distress following Heath's visits.

Betty Lawrence was next, and the press and public gallery were most eager to hear her testimony, since the approach by 'Billy Howard's Boys' had been the subject of not only local newspaper headlines, but national ones too.

Maxwell Turner led her through her evidence, of assisting Mrs Brabiner with the illegal abortion and supplying the necessary syringe, and of the accusation of her involvement by Heath. There was Lyons' involvement, demanding 'a ton' for her exculpation from the crime, and then Heath's reduction of the payment to £50, which he eventually received from her.

At the completion of her evidence in chief, Mrs Lawrence appeared to turn pale, and a glass of water and smelling salts were brought to her. Although it was a bitterly cold day, doors in the courtroom were opened, and the chairman asked her if she wanted a five-minute adjournment before continuing; Mrs Lawrence replied that she was willing to carry on.

Cross-examination started with Mr Purchas for Lyons, and Mrs Lawrence agreed that she did not believe that she had ever spoken to Lyons and Heath together.

'It is to your credit that on occasions you have been of considerable assistance to the police?' he asked.

'I have tried to be', replied Mrs Lawrence.

'You have given them information which you thought it was proper to pass on?'

'If any police officer asked me and I knew about something, I would pass it on.'

'They would properly resort to you if they wanted assistance?'

'That is right.'

Next, Cyril Wheeler for Heath asked, 'Regarding the occasion of the charge against Mrs Brabiner, did you give Sergeant Heath some important information?'

'I tried to help him', replied Mrs Lawrence. 'He asked me questions and he told me he knew it had occurred at my flat.'

'Is it right that Sergeant Heath explained to you that the syringe was an important piece of evidence in what I may call the Brabiner case?'

'Yes.'

'So you made a special journey to the CID office with the syringe?'

'Sergeant Heath told me he knew the syringe was in my flat. He said he would get a search warrant, so I took it down because I did not want him to search the flat on the Sunday, because my husband was at home that day.'

Mrs Lawrence stated that she had known Heath for two or three years and had been of assistance to him once or twice.

'Giving him information that had come to you about offences that had been committed?'

'Yes.'

'Did you give him any assistance about a woman called "Big May"?'

'I was approached about it but I did not know anything about it. I did know her but I did not know on that occasion what she had done.'

Wheeler asked her, 'Do you say that any information you have given to the police as an informer was before the Brabiner case?'

'I have been questioned by the police about other matters, before the Brabiner case.'

And that concluded Mrs Lawrence's evidence, which had lasted for two hours; little had been achieved in cross-examination except branding her as a grass. However, it may not have been lost on the Bench that police informants are supposed to receive money, not hand it over, which was what Arthur Thorn, Mrs Lawrence's benefactor to the tune of Heath's payment of £50, was able to inform the court about.

Now came one of the highlights of the proceedings.

CHAPTER 18

The Receiver's Version

The public had now heard from the super-smooth Alan Bennett and his exotic Norwegian wife with her enchanting accent, although few of the honest burghers of Brighton had personally experienced the spills and thrills of the Bucket of Blood.

They had witnessed the woman abortionist and her assistant – the one who had been threatened and terrified by the London gangsters – and these two had been portrayed as rather tragic figures, forced (if the prosecution was to be believed) to hand over what were to them substantial amounts of largesse to some corrupt cops.

And there were other witnesses; some interesting, others less so. But now it was the turn of Ernie Waite, and just about everybody in Brighton had had dealings with Ernie, with legitimate purchases from his shop and others that . . . well, they didn't care to say too much about. Yes, everyone knew Ernie. Was he a lovable rogue . . . or something else?

★ ★ ★

The wet wind beat against the walls of the Town Hall on Friday, 29 November 1957 as the crowds gathered to witness – if they could – the fifth day's proceedings against five allegedly very crooked defendants.

When Ernie Waite arrived he did not disappoint those who viewed him as 'a character'; he wore a smartly cut grey suit, it's true, but the sober effect was spoilt by the addition of a vivid blue waistcoat and a maroon bow tie.

Gerald Howard QC led him through his evidence, and pretty tawdry it was, too. There was the grisly business of the meat which had been sold to customers when fit only for consumption by cats and dogs. He spoke about the arrangement he had with the detectives to accept only stolen goods from outside the area; when he heard of properties within the area being broken into, he had offered up those responsible for arrest. When Waite received an enormous amount of stolen goods, it was Hammersley's friend who supplied the lorry to transport them. There was the case involving cigarettes and tobacco worth £15,000 in which the crooked officers were deeply involved – and all the while, money changed hands, and investigating officers – straight ones – were led on a wild goose chase.

There were ripples of laughter from the public throughout Waite's testimony, especially when he described how he had beaten a hasty retreat when the police constable walked up his driveway as the dodgy gear was being unloaded from the stolen lorry.

The best laugh of all came when John Bosley, cross-examining Waite, asked if he agreed with Sir Harry's somewhat scathing description of him during his opening address and added, 'Is it right you are an undischarged bankrupt?'

'You should know that, Mr Bosley', replied Waite. 'You're acting for the trustees. We've had litigation for years, have we not? You were once my solicitor.'

'Just answer the question', directed the Chairman frostily.

Asked if he thought the Solicitor General's description of him as 'a scoundrel' was correct, Waite replied 'I don't think I'm as bad as that; that's why my feelings were hurt', but he made those remarks with a grin and nobody really believed him.

Waite said that he thought proceedings were going to be brought against him in respect of the cigarettes and tobacco he had received but added, 'I wasn't charged. Mr Hammersley wanted me prosecuted.'

David Peck for Hammersley asked when he had been given permission to buy stolen property outside the Brighton area.

'When I was charged with the Nescafé', replied Waite. 'I kept my mouth quiet and seemed to come into favour.'

He went on to say that it was in 1952 or 1953 that he was told about 'certain commodities' that he could get through a friend of Hammersley's.

Waite denied giving information to the police but added, 'I have only given information to Mr Hammersley because he more or less put me on to good things.'

However, Peck persisted, saying, 'Over what period have you been giving information to the police?'

'Since Hammersley and I have been tied up together, about three or four years.'

In answer to Cyril Wheeler in cross-examination as to how many times he had disposed of goods which Waite had said were the proceeds of an organized London gang in contact with a friend of Hammersley's, he replied, 'Only two', and went on to add, 'I was made their "golliwog" to dispose of the goods for them.'

Nobody asked Waite to elucidate this curious expression; possibly he was referring to the popular children's stuffed toy of the time, the inference being that he was attempting to distance himself from the illegal transaction by suggesting that he had been made the gang's dummy or dupe. If that was his intention, it really didn't have a ring of authenticity about it.

Waite agreed that he had provided the information as to the identity of the thieves who broke into the Brighton jeweller's shop, but when he was asked if he had received an informant's fee of £25 from the insurance company, Waite replied, 'Sorry, sir', and requested a glass of water, which he drank down in one go, immediately followed by another.

After his previous convictions were read out – he stated he could not remember one and disputed another – he told Mr Turner for the prosecution, 'If you say I'm a villain, I will accept that.'

When he stepped down from the witness box after three hours and fifteen minutes, having admitted conniving with bent police officers to receive and dispose of stolen goods as well as being a police informer, there were few who would have queried that description. 'A lovable rogue?' 'A bit of a character?'

Well, maybe not.

CHAPTER 19

Stolen Consignments

The weekend intervened, and then it was the turn of Waite's paramour, Mrs Joan Watson, who was clearly nervous; Maxwell Turner for the prosecution had to tell her to 'speak up' as he led her through her evidence. She described her and Waite's association with Ridge, Hammersley and Heath and how the latter two would offer ten shillings or a pound for groceries costing three or four times that amount and then expect change. There was the matter of the Co-operative Society being broken into and how Waite had paid Hammersley to keep her out of it, followed by the trip to London, during which stolen groceries were loaded into a lorry which she accompanied on the drive to Brighton. Then there was the lorry full of tinned peaches and tomatoes which was unloaded on Waite's driveway, and finally the large consignment of cigarettes and tobacco for which Heath suggested she should take the blame.

It was when the searching of her premises was mentioned that Mrs Watson became unwell. She swayed, became pale and accepted a glass of water. She had been giving evidence for an hour and a half, and it was almost another two hours before she could resume.

She was cross-examined by David Peck for Hammersley and told him that when Ackerman had first brought items to the house she did not know that he was a thief, although she knew the goods were stolen.

'You knew Waite was a receiver of stolen goods?'

'Well, that's a matter of opinion, isn't it? I knew he received goods, but if I may say so, he received them because most of the time he was made to receive them.'

There was a pause while Peck removed his spectacles and shot a look of shocked incredulity to the Bench before returning to Mrs Watson. 'And you knew the goods he received were stolen goods. Ackerman had produced those goods?'

'Some of the time I knew they were stolen.'

'You knew that the goods that you brought down with you in the lorry from Petticoat Lane were stolen goods?'

'Yes.'

'And you were disposing of the goods, or some of them, for Waite through your shop?'

'Yes, some of them.'

Mrs Watson was then escorted from the court and driven off by a Flying Squad driver. Since she and her child had been threatened while out shopping, the investigating team were taking no chances; her evidence was dynamite.

On Tuesday, 3 December, the bombastic bookmaker William Albert Page arrived to give evidence regarding his conversation with Ridge in the Chief Constable's office and immediately attempted to take over the proceedings by making himself the centre of attention. Asked if he could recall a certain passage during the meeting with Ridge, he replied, 'Just a second – I recall every word', then paused and raised his eyes heavenwards, as if seeking inspiration from some higher being before answering the question.

When Gerald Howard started to ask a question, Page interrupted him, saying, 'Just a moment, sir'; and when Howard finished his examination in chief and sat down, Page told the Bench, 'There is one special question the gentleman hasn't asked me.'

By now Howard must have been as fed up with this pompous bully as anybody else; rising to his feet he replied, 'I have asked such questions as I desire to ask you' and sat down again.

John Bosley for Ridge, in a rare moment of agreement with his opposite number, stated, 'I should have thought the matter was concluded', and Page, sensing that the curtain was coming down, albeit prematurely, on his performance, gave a poisonous look at the Bench before flouncing out of the witness box.

The next few witnesses were necessary for the prosecution because they proved the continuity of events, although they really pointed the finger of guilt at Ernie Waite for being the thoroughgoing crook that he was; and in some cases they were actually helpful to the defence.

Mrs Olive Tarff, who received the butter from the stolen consignment at 155 Preston Road and rewrapped it, said nothing to implicate any of the accused; and Frederick Ketley, who had made a statement to Brighton CID about Waite's stolen consignment, agreed with Cyril Wheeler that when Ketley had spoken to Heath later on about the consignment, Heath had told him, 'I wish I had known; if you had phoned me before, I could have caught him at it.' In fact, Ketley told the court, Heath stated that he was most anxious to receive any information he could about Waite.

Then there was Detective Sergeant Robert Johnson, to whom Hammersley had handed Ketley's statement and who, with Heath, had interviewed William Watson. 'Did he tell you to investigate

Waite and pursue the enquiries as hard as you could, or words to that effect?' asked David Peck, to which Johnson replied, 'Yes, he did.'

'When you saw Watson that evening with Heath, were you able to take a statement from Watson?'

'Yes.'

'As a result of your enquiries, did you establish that the goods, the peaches, were stolen or not?'

'I could not.'

'Could you find any report that peaches had been stolen at about that time?'

'No.'

'Or that a lorry had been stolen about that time?'

'No.'

'Or indeed that a lorry had been abandoned at Redhill about that time?'

'No.'

'As far as the police could discover, there were no stolen peaches?'

'As far as I could discover, there were no stolen peaches.'

Cyril Wheeler for Heath hammered home the point with Johnson that he was unable to determine the origin of the peaches, and having received his agreement on this, asked whether Waite, who had received them, had paid anybody for them, to which Johnson replied, 'No.'

He was followed into the witness box by Police Constable Harold Kerry, who had seen Waite and observed the unloading of the lorry in the middle of the night but had simply wandered off – or, as he put it, 'continued on my beat'.

So the sum total of this testimony was that Hammersley and Heath were credited with being intrepid crime-busters, dedicated to nailing Waite for receiving some very dodgy goods, whereas Johnson (who went on to be promoted to detective chief inspector) had been unable to discover their origin, and Kerry, who could have asked questions, hadn't done so.

Fortunately, Waite and Mrs Watson had been on hand to inform the court that those goods were very crooked indeed, and that far from wanting to feel their collars, all Hammersley and Heath desired was to help themselves to some of the items and relieve Waite of some of his ill-gotten cash.

But matters were about to change.

CHAPTER 20

Dynamite Evidence

After the lunchtime adjournment, the first witness was the newsagent and tobacconist Edward George Wyatt, who had sent the first of two letters to Detective Superintendent Williams of Brighton CID, informing him of details of a large quantity of cigarettes and tobacco which Waite was attempting to distribute. Not too many questions there; Wyatt could not implicate any of the defendants, only Waite, and by now nobody was in any doubt that Waite was a big-time receiver.

He was followed by Detective Superintendent Edwin Moody of the Transport Commission Police, who had assumed personal charge of the theft of the cigarettes and tobacco, valued at £15,000, and who outlined the whole of his investigation at Brighton and elsewhere and described his conversations with Ridge, Hammersley and Heath. It was an impressive performance, presented by a very experienced police officer, and a straight one.

Cross-examining, David Peck asked, 'Did you receive a statement from Inspector Hammersley on 4 or 5 September? Did that set out in outline what had transpired between you and him regarding Waite?'

Moody examined the three-page document and then said, 'There is one part of this statement that is not accurate. It says the officer required some empty cartons. I did not require empty cartons. I wanted two full cartons.'

Pointing out that Hammersley had made the statement on 3 September at Brighton, Peck then asked, 'The object of the statement was with a view to prosecuting Waite, wasn't it?'

'No, not to my knowledge, sir', replied Moody, and Peck then read the statement aloud. At its conclusion Moody said, 'It is also inaccurate when it referred to Hammersley's journey of the 18th. In that statement, Hammersley said that he supplied me with the name of the Montpelier Hotel in Brighton; in fact, he gave me the name before that.'

Moody had mentioned in his evidence in chief Hammersley's refusal to identify his informant. 'It did not surprise you that Inspector Hammersley was unwilling to disclose his contact?' asked Peck.

'Not at the very initial stages.'

'In your experience, it is not unusual, is it, for the CID to use a contact in a case like this?'

'No.'

Moody agreed, in cross-examination by Cyril Wheeler, that Heath had accompanied him to 39 New England Road after three search warrants had been obtained, and that about a dozen police officers were deployed.

'Is it right to say that Sergeant Heath made a suggestion to you?' asked Wheeler. 'Did he say that was where you were most likely to find Waite?'

'He didn't tell me that', replied Moody. 'Someone did, but he didn't.'

Moody went on to say that it was Heath who had pointed out the stolen tobacco at that address and it was Heath who had arrested and obtained a statement from Waite.

Wheeler then asked Moody if a decision had been made whether or not to prosecute Waite for receiving the cigarettes and tobacco; Moody replied that Waite would not be charged.

'As we know, you tried to find out the name of the informer and did not succeed', said Wheeler. 'Did Sergeant Heath tell you that he didn't know the name of the informant?'

'He told me he didn't know', confirmed Moody.

'Do you remember on one occasion Sergeant Heath suggesting to you or saying that some effort should be made to find the informant's name and if necessary, to follow him?'

'What he said was this: "Why don't you knock Hammersley's informant?"'

'I don't find that very illuminating', replied Wheeler.

'It means "Why don't you arrest him?" My reply to him was, "I don't know him." He then said, "You can soon find out." I asked, "How?" He answered me by saying, "Tail up Hammersley".'

The next witness from the Transport Commission Police was Detective Sergeant George Spiers, who described his encounters with Heath when he first made enquiries at Brighton; in cross-examination he agreed that Heath had 'given him all the help he could', which was a mistake; it would have been better if Spiers had replied that Heath had 'appeared' to do so.

Spiers was followed into the witness box by Detective Inspector Leonard Wright, who like the previous witness described his enquiries in Brighton regarding the stolen tobacco and his conversations with Hammersley and Heath. David Peck crossly cross-examined him regarding apparent discrepancies in his notebook which were easily explained away, and the next witness was Detective Inspector Roland Hendy of Brighton's Railway Police, who on 20 August saw Hammersley and Heath in his office. Hammersley had handed Hendy two empty cartons of Senior Service cigarettes, and when Heath asked, 'What about the other twenty-eight cartons?' Hammersley replied, 'I don't want to know. I'm on leave.' After they left, Hendy had telephoned Superintendent Moody.

Detective Constables Cook and Ward gave evidence of their observations which led up to the three search warrants being executed, all of which was compelling evidence against the accused, but the next three witnesses would give utterly damning evidence against Heath.

* * *

The first was Mrs Sheila Swaby, who was able to tell the court what happened after her husband had been arrested for housebreaking: that when she asked Heath what he thought her husband's chances were, he had wanted to know how she was fixed for £50. She was unable to raise the money, and after her husband was sentenced to five years' imprisonment and Heath told her that he hadn't looked after her because she hadn't looked after him, she had told him that 'he was no good'. However, since she was a prostitute with fifty previous convictions, it is possible that she uttered her condemnation of him in more graphic terms.

James Thomas Swaby described handing Heath the two £5 notes he had concealed in his raincoat in consideration of Heath's leaving out a couple of his convictions, especially the latest pertaining to living on immoral earnings.

Answering Cyril Wheeler for Heath, Swaby agreed with various details of his convictions: 'I don't suppose that's wrong or you wouldn't have it.'

Regarding the search made at Paddington police station, Swaby said, 'He went through my pockets if you call that searching. He didn't examine my raincoat minutely, only the pockets.'

The prosecution now called Detective Constable Raymond Hovey, who had brought Swaby from London to Brighton, and he described the demands made by Heath to both Mrs and Mrs Swaby. It was obvious that in cross-examination by Cyril Wheeler he was going to get a battering.

Wheeler suggested that little of the property that Swaby had stolen had been recovered, and Hovey agreed. And when an officer said to a prisoner, 'Well, it's up to you' (as Heath had said to Swaby), this implied, suggested Wheeler, that the prisoner should cooperate with the police to recover the stolen property. However, the inference in this case was that Heath was suggesting a corrupt payment.

He next asked if Hovey had searched Swaby, who had explained that it had been the Metropolitan Police who had searched him and that Hovey had simply 'rubbed him down'; but what Wheeler was keen to confirm was that the two £5 notes had not been found by Hovey, as indeed they had not. The implication in the question was that they had never existed at all.

There was then the matter of the preparation of the prisoner's antecedents, and Hovey agreed that he had prepared them and handed them to Heath for verification.

Now came the all-important questions.

'Officer, I want to ask you about the occasion when reference was made to a "pony". That, I think was at Lewes prison?'

'That's right.'

'Do you keep a notebook?'

'Yes.'

'I would like to know the date of that visit to Lewes Prison. Can you give me that?'

'I can give it by reference to my diary. I made no entry in my notebook.'

'A conversation of this nature you thought too insignificant to record in your notebook?'

'I was alarmed. I was disgusted, in fact; but I think it is a case of misplaced loyalty.'

'When did you report it?'

'I did not report it.'

'When did you first make a statement about it?'

'It was on 31 October. I received an anonymous letter.'

'The 31st was after the "probe", if I can call it that, had started?'

'Yes.'

'Turning to the conversation of 20 June in the court, when did you report that?'

'When I made the statement on 31 October.'

'Did you make a note in your notebook?'

'No.'

'Who was the Chief Constable of Brighton at this time?' interjected Gerald Howard for the prosecution.

'Mr Ridge.'

'You have been asked why you didn't report this matter. Just tell us why?'

This was definitely an answer that neither of the legal representatives for Messrs Heath and Ridge wanted disclosed, with Wheeler saying that Hovey had already answered the question, explaining that it was a case of misplaced loyalty, and Howard replying that he was entitled to ask that particular question.

Next, Bosley said, 'I don't know whether the second question has any reference to the first. In this case, we are troubled with the fact that so much has been given in evidence which should not be evidence if the prosecution had not charged with conspiracy but with individual cases of crime. Nearly all the evidence so far would not be evidence against the defendants.'

There was a consultation between the Bench and the Clerk of the Court, after which the chairman, Mr Vokins, ruled that the question was permissible.

'Why did you not report this matter?' asked Howard.

'I didn't, sir, because I thought to do so might have had unpleasant effects on my career', replied Hovey, adding, 'I knew that Mr Ridge held Sergeant Heath in very high esteem as a CID officer.'

One honest police officer was followed into the witness box by another, Police Constable Frank Knight, who had been keeping observation of Sammy Bellson's club and who was asked by Heath if he wanted 'to earn a tenner a week'.

As he was led to this part of the conversation, Cyril Chapman for Bellson leapt to his feet, saying that anything the witness said should not be regarded as evidence against his client; he was overruled and that evidence was heard. What Hovey had to say to Police Constable Vernon Tullett, who had been waiting outside the CID office and had heard none of the conversation, was not, of course, evidence. However, Tullett was called to confirm that when Hovey left the CID office where he had been speaking to Heath, Hovey had indeed spoken to him.

Detective Sergeant Peter Vibart gave evidence of his (and Tommy Butler's) illuminating conversations with Bellson, and in answer to Bellson's lawyer told him that his client had been 'most helpful'.

Superintendent Thomas Hill, the newly appointed deputy Chief Constable of Brighton, gave evidence of the composition of the force and detailed the three accused police officers' records. He also produced diaries and pocket books belonging to Hammersley and Heath; pocket books written by Heath numbered 1–45, but No. 27 was missing. And amongst the documentation produced there was no record of the message from Detective Constable Richard Crane of Folkestone CID on 24 June, when he telephoned the CID office at Brighton and spoke to an unnamed CID officer – later identified as Hammersley.

It appeared that the superintendent was not a fan of Heath's; Cyril Wheeler tried repeatedly to get Hill to admit that Heath's record number of arrests as a detective constable was indeed greater than any of his colleagues, and eventually Hill admitted that Heath had carried out a large number of arrests, ending with the words, 'As far as I am aware, his character in the police force is good.'

Chief Inspector Radford stated that he had been present on 26 November when Mr and Mrs Bennett, who were both giving evidence, had lunched together. Asked if the evidence in the case had been discussed, Radford backed up Mrs Bennett's denial by saying, 'Not at all.' Cross-examined by Stanley Rees for Lyons, Radford said that when Lyons had asked 'Are you suggesting I'm a fixer?' he interpreted this to mean 'In the course of crime investigation . . . a person who promises a service for another in trouble, on more than one occasion.'

The final (and 64th) witness to give evidence was Superintendent Forbes-Leith.

CHAPTER 21

Committal

The superintendent was led through the interviews with Lyons, Heath and Ridge – oddly, Hammersley was never interviewed, and one wonders why – and he mentioned Heath's financial circumstances. Heath had purchased his house, valued at £2,468, on 16 March 1957 with a deposit of £220 and was currently paying mortgage repayments of £15 0s 4d per month. The 1955 Standard 10 car which he had purchased second-hand in 1955 for £530 had been paid for with a deposit of £330; the balance of £200 had been paid by January 1957. The car had been sold to provide the deposit for the house. His £90 television set and washing machine had been obtained on hire purchase, which had been paid off; the gas oven was still being paid for. His independent source of income amounted to £4 in the Post Office.

There was some desultory cross-examination, Forbes-Leith stood down, and that completed the two-week case for the prosecution. Gerald Howard then asked the Bench to commit the five accused for trial at the Old Bailey.

John Bosley submitted that Ridge had no case to answer, suggesting that the charges against his client were based on 'rotten foundations'. He described as 'silly' the suggestion that an allegedly crooked detective sergeant working with an allegedly criminal Chief Constable would tell a junior policeman about his rackets and suggest a payment of £10 per week to give a club information. That, he said, was just as silly as the evidence from Bennett, whom he described as 'picturesque'.

'All there has been is a dreary procession of people who have spoken of alleged corroboration', said Bosley, adding, 'If you are going to allow citizens to stand their trial on evidence like that, nobody would be really safe.'

David Peck for Hammersley conceded that there was evidence upon which his client could be committed for trial, but Hammersley had not been asked to give any explanation for those matters. 'The defence case is that the evidence is wrong', he said.

It would not be right for the magistrates to commit Lyons for trial, said Stanley Rees QC, describing the case against his client as being 'exceptionally thin'.

The second charge against Heath, said Cyril Wheeler, stood or fell on a single sentence alleged by Bennett: 'Half a ton will put it right, down here'. He asked the Bench, 'Coming as it does from the lips of Alan Roy Bennett, is it conceivable that any jury would be prepared to convict a police officer on the uncorroborated evidence of this man?'

Mr C. Chapman for Bellson said the vaguely worded conspiracy charge extended over ten years, and had there been any offences committed by his client in 1953 or 1954, he should have been charged separately.

After rejecting an application for the case to be heard at the Lewes Assizes and committing the five defendants to stand their trial at the Old Bailey, the Bench was informed that all of the accused pleaded not guilty, reserved their defence and did not wish to give evidence or call witnesses at the Magistrates' Court. They were then released on bail, on the same terms as before.

On 17 December 1957 an application was made at the Divisional Court in London by the five defendants to have the venue of their trial changed to Lewes Assizes. This was before the Lord Chief Justice, Lord Goddard, who had held that post for almost twelve years; he was one of the sternest judges to sit at the Old Bailey, and it was difficult to say which was the most severe – his constant interruptions, his pro-prosecution views or his sentencing. Sitting with him were Mr Justice Pearson and Mr Justice Devlin, the latter appearing astonished that Hammersley and Heath had been granted certificates under the Poor Prisoners' Defence Act 1939. 'Are they not lucky to have been granted legal aid?' he asked.

But eventually it was decided that the case would be heard more speedily at the Old Bailey than at Lewes, and the application was refused.

Before that trial got underway, several other matters were going on behind the scenes.

*　*　*

First, there was the matter of Detective Superintendent Gwyn Williams, head of Brighton's CID. It was Williams who had received the letter from Wyatt warning him of Waite's activities with the stolen cigarettes, the letter he had shown to Hammersley and Heath, and who had told Superintendent Moody that he had no idea how far the stolen cigarettes case had advanced.

Ridge, Hammersley and Heath had been arrested and banged up, then on 12 November 1957, Bellson was arrested and joined the others in the dock. The following day, Williams was replaced.

Apparently he was seriously ill, suffering from mental exhaustion, and was now on sick leave in his native south Wales and would not be returning, either to work or to give evidence. His place had been taken by Bill Cavey who, like the new Chief Constable, was from Exeter Constabulary. As a detective inspector, his rank did not quite fit the bill for the head of CID, so the Watch Committee provided him with two instant promotions to become a detective superintendent. The Town Clerk, Mr W. O. Dodd, was questioned regarding the appointment of an officer to a post which was still officially held by another. It was not unusual, protested Mr Dodd . . . under the circumstances.

Then there was the case of Kennard and Paolella. Kennard, remember, following his arrest on 17 September, had been approached by Hammersley, who told him that for £250 the charges he was facing, including stealing a safe, could be watered down. The two men had been committed to Brighton Quarter Sessions to stand their trial, Hammersley's arrest and suspension had followed, and since he would not be called by the prosecution in those circumstances, one would have thought that would have been the end of the prosecution's case. Kennard had twice petitioned the Home Secretary complaining of Hammersley's conduct, and the matter had been investigated by the Scotland Yard team.

But even though Hammersley was not called, there must have been compelling evidence, although not necessarily in the shape of the ballast from the safe which was found on Kennard's clothing and in his holdall.

Mr Anthony Harmsworth, prosecuting, told the jury:

> It is well known that there is domestic trouble in the police force at Brighton. We know that there has been an investigation and a trial is about to take place. That may encourage any number of accused persons to come here and say what they like about one or other of the police officers involved. Quite obviously, the prosecution cannot call these police officers while they are awaiting trial, so these things can be said with impunity.

It looked as though the Recorder of Brighton endorsed those comments when he said:

> Suppose that, in fact, Detective Inspector Hammersley did say he would drop or reduce the charges for £250? It certainly would appear that it has no relevance to this case.

The jury found both men guilty of breaking into a dairy and stealing a safe containing £679, as well as taking and driving away a car without the owner's consent. Kennard was sentenced to three years' imprisonment and disqualified from driving for four years, while Paolella received a twelve-month prison sentence and was disqualified from driving for two years.

Following the sentencing, it was revealed that the private secretary to the Home Office had received a letter from the acting Chief Constable of Brighton to say that 'No evidence has been found to support the allegations of corruption.'

There was one other matter. On the morning that the committal proceedings finished at Brighton Magistrates' Court there was a mysterious fire at the Castle Club, Castle Street, Brighton. Its owner was William Page, who had previously given evidence at the court. Four men had been playing rummy in the first-floor card room, which was where the fire had started.

It had been discovered by a patrolling police officer, who had summoned the Fire Brigade, and six appliances had arrived. Within an hour, the fire was under control but not before it had spread to the second floor and also to the furniture store next door.

Surveying the smoking, burnt-out shell of his club, later that morning, 'Pagey' stated, 'I'm not going to cry about this. I'll just look for another place.'

He did not appear to be too concerned about the fate of 58-year-old Miss Hilda Mary Skelbeck, who had been the top floor's resident. When firemen gained access to her floor through a window, Miss Skelbeck was found in her nightclothes, collapsed on the floor near the stairs. She was carried to safety and conveyed by ambulance to the local hospital, where she recovered.

The cause of the fire? Inconclusive.

An insurance job? Perhaps.

A revenge attack? Possibly.

However, if this was some form of rough justice which had been meted out to 'Pagey', justice of a more conservative kind was coming his way – but that can wait.

Now it's time to concentrate on the Old Bailey trial.

CHAPTER 22

The Trial Commences

The Old Bailey's correct title is the Central Criminal Court; the Old Bailey is the street in the City of London where it resides, but the court building is inevitably referred to (as it will be here) as 'The Old Bailey' and by the police officers who attend it simply as 'The Bailey'. If an East End CID officer was complimented on his natty attire, his response would inevitably be, 'It's me Bailey suit, ain't it?' When a criminal mentioned to his contemporaries that he was 'going up the steps', no further elucidation was needed; it was accepted that he was about to stand trial at the Bailey.

First mentioned in 1585, the present building dates from 1902, and above the entrance are the words, 'Defend the Children of the Poor and Punish the Wrongdoer'; worrying words indeed for the wrongdoer who goes up those steps beneath them. At the top of the building is a dome, upon which is placed F. W. Pomeroy's bronze statue of Lady Justice.

It was a Court of Assize where the most noteworthy trials are held, mainly murders; the Stratton Brothers were convicted of murder in 1905, the first conviction on the testimony of a fingerprint being found at the scene, and other notable defendants included Dr Hawley Harvey Crippen for the murder of his wife and Florence Ransom, a wartime triple murderess.

Court No. 1 was the most famous of all the courts in that building, and it was there that the trial got underway on 3 February 1958.

★   ★   ★

The Judge was 59-year-old Mr Justice Donovan – Terence Norbert Donovan as was – who had served during the First World War with the Bedfordshire Regiment and later with the Royal Air Force. Called to the Bar by the Middle Temple in 1924, he was appointed a High Court Judge in 1950.

The prosecution team was the same as that which had appeared at Brighton Magistrates' Court: the Solicitor General Sir Harry

Hilton-Foster QC, MP, Gerald Howard QC, MP and Mr Maxwell Turner QC.

Ridge was represented by Geoffrey Lawrence QC; although *Time* magazine had described him as 'a relative stranger in a criminal court', ten months earlier at the same court he had obtained the stunning acquittal of Dr John Bodkin Adams who, it was believed, had been responsible for the deaths of 163 of his patients. Lawrence was assisted by Mr J. MacManus, and Hammersley was represented by Mr Donald McIntyre QC, assisted by David Peck, who had appeared at the lower court for his client.

Edward Clarke had assisted Lawrence during the Bodkin Adams trial and now he, assisted by Mr O. Martin, appeared for Heath.

Lyons was once more defended by Mr Stanley Rees QC and Mr F. B. Purchas, and Bellson by Victor Durand QC and Mr J. W. Harkess. Bellson needed a tricky barrister and probably would have sought the services of Patrick Marrinan, had he not been disbarred six months earlier. Nevertheless, Durand was a great favourite in defending the criminal classes; a little later in his career, he would be suspended from practising after concealing evidence at a trial.

The day began with Geoffrey Lawrence arguing for 153 minutes that the charge was not sufficiently specific and should be quashed; the other counsel wished to be associated with his remarks, all without success, the Judge telling them, 'Whilst I appreciate the difficulties of the matter, I do not think I ought to quash the indictment on any of the grounds suggested and I dismiss the motion.'

That had been discussed in the absence of the jury, to whom the Judge had said that the case might last four weeks, which was longer than most trials. He added, 'If that is going to mean to any one of you that some calamity is going to occur in your private affairs – as distinct from inconvenience – mention it now and we will see what can be done.'

None of the ten men and two women spoke up, and the Judge told them, 'That being so – that none of you is anticipating being overtaken by some calamity in the next four weeks – we can proceed.'

There was little time left for Sir Harry Hilton-Foster's opening speech to get underway when he started at 3.30pm, but before the court adjourned at four o'clock, the Judge warned the jury, 'Be extremely careful not to speak about this case to anybody until it is all over. Some stranger, when you leave the court, might try to get into conversation with you. If that is reported, that juror will be taken off whatever stage the case may have reached and we would have to begin all over again.'

After the court was adjourned, the defendants were kept waiting for 25 minutes; when Mr McIntyre for Hammersley asked why, the Judge (who had obviously been apprised of the witnesses who had been threatened at the lower court) replied, 'So that the jurors can get clear of the building.'

*　*　*

The following day, Sir Harry explained to the jury:

> I feel sure you readily understand how police officers can obstruct the course of public justice by acting contrary to their public duty in the administration of the law. If, for instance, they deliberately refrained from making proper police enquiries when enquiries ought properly to be made, or refrained from making a charge when a charge ought to be made or if they, to use a slang phrase were to 'tip off' wrongdoers and give them warning when police action was afoot, or if they took money for doing that, that would be an instance of the obstruction of the course of public justice . . . The evidence of one class of witness which the Crown must call – either people with a criminal past . . . people intending to break the law for their own profit . . . or people who had already broken the law and wanted to soften, if they could the impact of justice upon them . . . then I suggest you consider that evidence with very great care. The Crown's case can best be told in chapter form.

The Solicitor General then set out, in chronological order, the circumstances of the cases and the details of the witnesses and took all of the hearing's second day and some of the third in doing so.

The first prosecution witness to be called was John Robert Leach, part-owner of the Burlesque Club, who had been convicted, sentenced to imprisonment, then subsequently cleared of receiving stolen jewellery.

Leach stated that the first person (outside of his family) whom he had informed of the approach by Hammersley and Heath to 'make the evidence disappear' was Brighton's Councillor Field. Asked by Edward Clarke for Heath 'Did he advise you to go and make a complaint about it?' Leach replied, 'He didn't believe me.'

'He thought you were lying?'

'It appeared that way, sir.'

This was a perfect opportunity for Mr McIntyre for Hammersley to ask, 'Would it be fair to say that no one believes a word you say?'

'No', he replied and told Victor Durand that he had not heard his father say to Bellson, 'If you know anybody friendly with the police, offer them something on behalf of my son.'

John Leach's father, the 65-year-old fishmonger Henry Leach, gave evidence that having given Bellson £100 he had told him that 'they could do their worst' when the offer was rejected. Asked by the Judge, 'The only people who could do their worst in this matter would be the police?' Leach agreed.

He was cross-examined by Edward Clarke for Heath who asked in relation to the meeting with Heath and Hammersley, 'Did you not, in fact, say to the police officers who were doing their duty, "Come now, we are men of the world, can't we settle this here and now?"'

'Not at all.'

'Do you usually carry £100 with you, in your fob pocket?'

'I have to, for business.'

'Is it not right that after you put your hand to your fob pocket, Hammersley said, "Harry, you had better put that away before you make a bloody fool of yourself?"'

'No, that is not true, no money was ever mentioned.'

The only time that money was mentioned, Henry Leach told Mr McIntyre, was between himself and Bellson; was it possible, asked Mr Durand, that Leach had got the two occasions mixed up? He had not, replied Henry Leach.

The next witness was the one everybody had been waiting to see and hear: Alan Roy Bennett.

CHAPTER 23

'Brighton Police Were Crooked'

It was almost as though a film star had arrived to give evidence. Bennett was described as being the owner of a Rolls-Royce, a man who had a Mayfair flat and a lease on a flat in Paddington, as well as shares in offices in Albemarle Street and an interest in a metal business and lately, ownership of the Astor Club. He was, to quote the words used by the Solicitor General, 'a man who had prospered'.

Now living at 20 Wimpole Mews, W1, Bennett was led through his evidence of issuing bribes to Ridge, Heath and Hammersley, and when Maxwell Turner asked if the customers at the Astor Club behaved themselves, Bennett replied, 'I'm afraid not. They got drunk and they wanted to fight somebody. They usually wanted to fight me so there was a lot of blood flying about; the club was known as "The Bucket of Blood".'

There was the discussion of Alan Walker's 'missing grand', the dishonoured cheque at Leeds, the 'screwing job at Bournemouth' and the offence at Folkestone. All this the public in the gallery already knew about from the newspaper reports at the committal proceedings; now they waited to hear what Bennett would have to say to the challenges which were to come.

He cheerfully agreed with Edward Clarke for Heath that he had used multiple names in the past: 'I admit I have had a bad record in my young days', he said, and when Clarke said, 'I'm not asking you about that', Bennett replied, 'Well, I admit it before you ask me.' He also admitted his many prison sentences and that he had posed as a RAF pilot 'to get out of the Air Force'.

But when Clarke asked him, 'Do you swear on oath that you had never been known in your life as Alan Roy Holt?' and Bennett replied, 'I swear that I have never been convicted in that name', there was clearly a difference between using and being convicted in that name. Bennett was later obliged to tell the court, 'I may have used it in my criminal activities and forgotten about it.'

'In your criminal activities, for the purpose of defrauding people?'

'It may have been.'

Asked to produce the roll of banknotes that he had in his hip pocket, Bennett ostentatiously placed it on the edge of the witness box, stating that it contained about £500. 'I got that from my bank', he told the jury. 'I've got a lot more than £500.' That was just one example of his affected behaviour – another was to flick his shirt cuffs to reveal gold, platinum or diamond cufflinks, a manoeuvre he performed often.

Bennett denied Edward Clarke's assertions that he did not pay his debts, did not make an honest living and now, did not carry on a respectable business. He stated that he was the director of about eight companies; however, he was not receiving any remuneration from any of them and at the moment he was not working.

When Mr Clarke asked, 'Did it surprise you very much when it was first suggested by anybody that by paying the police money, you could...', that was as far as he got, because Bennett interrupted him, saying, 'It did not surprise me – it was known the Brighton police had been crooked all their lives. I had heard that from many people.' This denunciation was delivered in a raised voice and it had a telling effect, as Bennett had known it must do. Asked who had told him, Bennett wrote a name ('Lyons') on a piece of paper which was passed to counsel; Bennett later qualified his remarks by saying it was known that 'some of the Brighton police were crooked.'

Bennett said that he had about fifty shirts and sixteen or seventeen suits (on this occasion he was wearing a dark pinstripe). 'All paid for with money that has been honestly acquired?' facetiously asked Mr Clarke, and Bennett concurred: 'All paid for with money that has been honestly acquired.'

On the matter of Heath showing Bennett his police photograph, Mr Clarke suggested that once the police knew that he was a man of bad character and he had better be careful, 'You realized you might not be so welcome in Brighton?'

'I was more than welcome in Brighton', riposted Bennett, and when Mr Clarke asked, 'More than welcome to the police because you were providing them with money?' it appeared that Clarke had done his client no favours, since Bennett was able to answer honestly, 'Quite.'

But after Bennett had said, 'I did what I wanted. I kept the club open all night', Edward Clarke really shot himself in the foot when he asked, 'You did what you wanted? Could you have done housebreaking?'

'Do you really want me to answer that question?' asked Bennett, and despite all the danger signals that were flashing, Mr Clarke – who was still some way from becoming His Honour Judge Edward Clarke QC – answered, 'Yes.'

'It was suggested by Heath that I do housebreaking. He knew a manager of Woolworth's personally, and it was suggested I take the keys and open the safe and Heath would look after it. He suggested I should open it at Christmas when there was plenty of money in it.'

Edward Clarke was learning the hard way that barristers should not ask questions unless they know the answers, because now he was wading in some very murky waters indeed. In fact, the questions that he asked elicited replies that were downright injurious to his client.

'Have you told the police about this?' asked Clarke and received the reply, 'No. I did not want to mention it at all.'

'You kept it up your sleeve until you got into the witness box?'

'I could mention a lot of other things as well.'

More warning signals, but Clarke blundered on. 'What advantage would Heath have out of this?' he asked and then incredibly provided Bennett with the answer: 'He would share in the proceeds?'

'That's right', replied Bennett – it would have been nonsensical for him to have delivered any other answer.

'You told him that you were a reformed character and not prepared to do any housebreaking?'

'I had enough money of my own; I did not want to do housebreaking.'

When Clarke suggested to Bennett that he was 'making up stories', it must have been clear to the jury that in answer to the type of questions posed by Clarke, Bennett didn't need to.

'Is it fair to describe you as one of a "number of rather shady witnesses who might be called by the prosecution"?' asked Donald McIntyre QC for Hammersley.

'I should not say I was a shady character now', replied Bennett.

'What about all these bribes which, according to your story, you have paid?' said McIntyre. 'Do you agree that was honest?'

'I admit it', replied Bennett, adding, 'but it is not so dishonest compared with the things I used to do.'

Bennett had a rather rougher ride with Stanley Rees QC for Lyons, whom Bennett had known since 1945. They had been friends, and Bennett told the court, 'I would give every penny I possess not to see Lyons in the dock.' His response was rather bad-tempered when asked if the conversation regarding the £20 per week had been heard by Ridge. 'He could have heard it', he replied. 'He was standing there. That was what the man was there for. We were all together at the bar. How do I know if he heard it? The man might be deaf. The answer could be "yes" or it could be "no".'

Rees then took Bennett through his cash book, which revealed that for the whole of April 1957 the takings amounted to £45; then there was nothing in May, £50 in June, £214 in July, £222 in August, £92 in September and £160 in October; a total of £783.

However, this did not tally with the £914 10s 0d which had been taken out for spirits, and Bennett said that £60 had been taken out of the club takings and not shown in the books. After Bennett said, 'I don't think that was dishonest; plenty of people do that', a spirited exchange ensued between him and Rees.

'The takings have got to be false to account for £60 for five months?'

'Could I declare £20 a week to Ridge on the books? Could I put down: "Chief Constable – £20 a week"?'

'What about the £40?'

'I put it in my pocket.'

'And you did not want to pay tax on it?'

'I did not want to pay tax on it.'

Bennett stated that he had submitted income tax returns prior to 1955 but not since.

'During 1954–1955, when in your own words you were going straight and honest, you bribed and were swindling the income tax?' asked Rees.

'Yes, sir', replied Bennett.

'And you have come in this witness box to lie about these events of those years, have you not?'

'No, sir.'

Geoffrey Lawrence QC, a very clever exponent of the art of cross-examination, was next and suggested that his client Ridge was simply shown round the Astor Club by Bennett, had never returned and had never received any money from him, assertions with which Bennett disagreed. Lawrence further suggested that the whole gist of his evidence was that the conversation 'at which this plot was hatched' was between Bennett and Lyons and not in the hearing of Ridge at all.

'That conversation, according to you – if it ever took place at all – settled the terms on which you were to be given what you called yesterday "the freedom of the city",' said Lawrence.

'Yes.'

'The whole thing is a lie, is it not?'

'No.'

Saying that the jury had to make up their minds about Bennett and Ridge, Lawrence then detailed Bennett's previous convictions between 1931 and 1948. 'Tell them over ten years what I have been, don't tell them about twenty years ago when I was a boy', snapped Bennett.

'You do not scruple to come in this witness box and tell lies for your own purpose, do you?'

'I am gaining nothing; I have lost plenty.'

And with that, Bennett stood down; he had been in the witness box for in excess of six hours.

CHAPTER 24

'£5 Notes in a Newspaper'

Mrs Wenche Bennett was up next. She described meeting her husband when she was working as a waitress in Shanklin; they had worked together and bought a hotel and restaurant in the Isle of Wight, but she denied knowing that there was a dispute over £400 regarding that business.

Dealing with the goings-on at the Astor Club, Mrs Bennett stated that she had seen her husband hand Ridge £5 notes wrapped up in a newspaper, but said that she was against bribing the police and that the time at the club was the unhappiest of her life.

'Did you suggest to your husband that he should give up the club?' asked Edward Clarke and received the reply, 'I would have loved it; he would not have listened to me.'

'I suggest that you never saw any money pass to Sergeant Heath?'

'I saw it many times.'

'Did that seem to you something that was completely dishonest?'

'Yes, it did.'

'Were people carried out with bleeding noses and drunk and things of that sort?'

'It happened . . . there was always trouble.'

'You had on your hands a club which you say was thoroughly disorderly over a period of months?'

'Yes.'

'Did your husband's income increase considerably after his arrival in Brighton so that he was able to buy much more expensive things?'

'He has always been extravagant. This might sound very silly, but I am not all that interested in money.'

Cross-examined by Geoffrey Lawrence, who asked, 'Is this what you say, that on to the Brighton front, night after night, these drunken, fighting people were either carried out or staggered out?' Mrs Bennett replied, 'Yes.'

'Either you are the sort of woman to whom that is all in the day's work or you are the sort of woman who would be revolted and nauseated by it?'

'I can assure you, I did not like it . . . I know it is wrong and I know I should not have done it, but I did it.'

Mrs Bennett had spent half the time in the witness box that her husband had, and her place was taken by Mrs Blanche Cherryman. Certainly, she was one of the more honest witnesses and she described her meeting with Ridge in his office when she complained of the misbehaviour at the Astor Bar, of the telephone call to close the club 'and to say it was Charlie', and that she had also seen Lyons taking people to the club after hours. Geoffrey Lawrence's cross-examination was cut down to a minimum when, in answer to the Judge, she stated that she had never seen Ridge at the club.

She had, however, seen Heath there, and Edward Clarke (who many might have thought was secretly working for the prosecution) gloriously shot himself in the foot once more when he asked her, 'Were you shocked and worried about Sergeant Heath going down into the club after hours?'

That was bad enough but it was nothing compared to Mrs Cherryman's answer:

'Yes, but not only that, sir. I was worried over the money they paid him . . . I was worried because I knew what he was going in for.'

Mrs Mary Mason appealed to the Judge to stop Stanley Rees QC enquiring about her past, but as Mr Justice Donovan pointed out, 'They want to know your character.'

This was after Rees had alleged, 'In fact, not only are you a drunken woman but many times . . . ' Here 60-year-old Mrs Mason interrupted, saying, 'I am not a drunken woman!' but Rees continued, saying '. . . but many times a convicted woman, too?'

She was obliged to admit to seven convictions and added, 'But I've been in prison only once, and that was more than twenty years ago.'

The reason for the questions raised about Mrs Mason's apparent lack of sobriety was because when she had refused to pay money to anybody after taking over the Astor Club and it was raided in August 1956, she had confronted Lyons at Sherry's Club and had told him that she had had to pay the penalty for what other people had done.

She admitted going to several public houses in Brighton and blaming Lyons for her misfortunes, but denied being ejected from any of them. Asked if she had said, 'I have fixed that bastard', Mrs Mason replied, 'Oh, no', adding, 'It is lies. I have never fixed anyone in my life.'

Mr Rees asked her, 'Perjury was a cheap price to pay to punish Lyons, wasn't it?'

'Perjury would be a dreadful price to pay, a terrible thing', replied Mrs Mason.

Detective Inspector George Richard Dunstan of Brighton CID was asked about raiding clubs, rather an odd line of questioning to a CID officer, since irregularities at clubs were dealt with by uniformed police; therefore, when a club was due to be raided, he believed that just the Chief Constable, the uniformed superintendent and perhaps his deputy would be aware of it. However, Inspector Dunstan was also questioned about the jewellery burglary in Bournemouth and stated that at the suggestion of Detective Superintendent Williams (currently sick) he had carried out the preliminary enquiries. He said that there was nothing improper in Heath interviewing Bennett and taking a statement from him.

'The only matter you were criticising was that you were not told afterwards that Brown [i.e. Bennett] had been interviewed?' asked Edward Clarke, to which Dunstan replied, 'Correct, sir.'

'Do you agree that that omission to report to you was something which might quite easily have arisen by a completely innocent oversight?'

'Quite, sir.'

Not quite so easily assured was Detective Inspector Frederick Tilling of Bournemouth police, who stated that he had received a message from Brighton CID saying that Bennett could not have committed the burglary because he was out of the country.

The Judge asked, 'Were you satisfied with the report you had got from Brighton as exculpating Brown?'

'Not completely', replied the inspector.

'Supposing someone had said, "We haven't seen any passports or any documents", what would you have done?'

'Taken steps to see that that was done', was his answer.

Where it Started . . . and Where it Ended

Above: Brighton Pavilion

Right: Brighton Town Hall, 'A' Division of Brighton's Police Headquarters

Below: The Old Bailey

The Defendants

Above left: Detective Inspector John Hammersley

Above right: Detective Sergeant Trevor Heath

Below left: Chief Constable Charles Ridge

Below right: Samuel Bellson

The Prosecution Witnesses

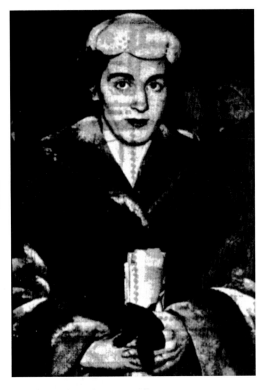

Above left: Ernest Waite

Above right: William 'Bookie' Page

Right: Joan Watson

Below left: Alan Roy Bennett

Below right: Wenche Bennett

The Good Guys

Left: Detective Sergeant Ray Hovey

Below left: Police Sergeant Frank Knight

Below right: Superintendent Edwin Moody

The Lawyers and Senior Officers

Above left: The Solicitor General, Sir Harry Hylton-Foster

Above right: Geoffrey Lawrence QC

Above left: Assistant Commissioner (Crime), Sir Richard Jackson

Above right: Commander George Hatherill

The Investigators

Deputy Assistant
Commissioner Ernest
Millen

Above: Detective Superintendent Ian
Forbes-Leith

Left: Deputy Assistant Commissioner
Ernest Bond

Above left: Detective Superintendent Peter Vibart

Above right: Detective Chief Superintendent Thomas Butler

Below left: Detective Superintendent Richard Radford

Below right: Detective Superintendent William Baldock

The Men Who Started the Enquiry . . . and Finished it

Alan Roy Bennett

Detective Superintendent
Ian Forbes-Leith

CHAPTER 25

An Unwelcome Visitor

The trial now entered its second week, and one of the first witnesses was Mrs Alice Brabiner, recently released from her fifteen-month sentence for performing an abortion. Having outlined the circumstances of how Heath had obtained money from her in the lead-up to her trial, Edward Clarke asked her, 'So that after the Magistrates' Court proceedings you knew nothing could save you from being prosecuted?'

'Yes', she replied.

'And that whatever Heath did, you were bound to be sentenced?'

'No. I knew I would be sentenced, but I did not want fourteen years.'

'What did he tell you he was going to do, to stop you getting fourteen years?'

'He said that what he told the Judge in court would go a long way.'

'After Heath, according to you, had refused the £25, do you say the second time you proffered the £25, he accepted it?'

'Yes, sir. He knows he did.'

'Sometimes you say something which is one way and sometimes the other?'

'No, sir. It's you that does that. I'm telling the truth.'

Referring to the abortion she had carried out, Clarke asked her, 'You have done it more than twice, haven't you?' and Mrs Brabiner, after replying, 'I have just paid for what I have done', left the witness box in tears.

The next witness, Mrs Brabiner's daughter, Mrs Iris Karrouze, described her mother's distress on each of the numerous occasions that Heath visited. Never once did she see money change hands, never once did she overhear any conversation that might have incriminated Heath. It might therefore have made sense for Edward Clarke not to cross-examine Mrs Karrouze at all. Unfortunately, he did.

'So often did he come that it became quite clear to you he was there for an improper purpose?' he asked; and if Heath failed to actually bury his face in his hands at the question he must have felt like doing so when Mrs Karrouze answered, 'Yes.'

'Did you ever face him with an allegation that he was there for an improper purpose?'

'No. My mother always told me to keep quiet.'

'Do you know from what your mother told you that Heath was alleged to be taking money from your mother?'

'Yes.'

'You knew not only that she was being terrified, but that he was doing something that was about the worst thing a police officer could do, and any complaint you made to the station which could be justified would have stopped the visits?'

'Yes.'

'But you say you did not do that because your mother told you not to?'

'Yes.'

Next was Mrs Betty Lawrence, the threatened witness. Describing how she had paid Heath £50 to prevent her being prosecuted as an aider and abettor of Mrs Brabiner's illegal operation, she said her statement about the syringe was altered. She said the second page was re-written and she signed it.

'Did you say that Sergeant Heath said that the alteration would help you?' asked Mr Clarke.

'He did say that', replied Mrs Lawrence.

'Do you say he was taking money from you because he was threatening you would be prosecuted for this offence, even after you had given evidence at the Magistrates' Court?'

'He said he would try.'

Stanley Rees QC, whose client, Lyons, Mrs Lawrence had initially approached for illicit assistance, asked her why she had not previously paid the £50 in full; Mrs Lawrence replied that she had not previously been sure that she would not be prosecuted.

Of all the witnesses previously called by the prosecution, Alan Roy Bennett – he of the fifty expensive shirts, the flamboyant lifestyle and the unpaid bills – had been an excellent media attraction. The way in which he had sidestepped the allegations of his misdeeds levelled at him by the bent coppers at Brighton (of which he was undoubtedly guilty) and had fielded off the illicit payments, the cooking of the Astor Club's book and the defrauding of the Inland Revenue were all eminently newsworthy.

But Bennett's snook-cocking at the law was one thing; now it was the turn of probably the most important of the prosecution witnesses. Ernie Waite would not only unveil the defendants' venality in accepting bribes, he would also set out the crooked cops' complicity in wide-scale criminality, including not just receiving stolen goods, but also setting up the thefts to start with; and then, when honest police officers investigated a huge theft involving thousands of pounds, leading them on a wild goose chase.

CHAPTER 26

'A Gentlemen's Agreement'

Waite described how he had known Ridge for about seven years and how Ridge accepted 'presents' of black-market goods and other items, never paying for them. The same applied to Hammersley and Heath, with Waite estimating that he had paid Heath something in the region of £50 and Hammersley over £200.

When Waite agreed with Gerald Howard for the prosecution that between 1949 and September 1957 he had dealt in stolen goods, Mr Justice Donovan intervened to warn him that he need not incriminate himself; nevertheless, he did.

Waite said that he and Hammersley had a 'gentlemen's agreement'; Hammersley did not wish Waite to receive anything that was stolen in Brighton, 'but I was given the sort of freedom of the town with regard to things outside Brighton', and he went on to describe the lorry-load of goods he had received from Richardson and the cigarettes from Ackerman.

'I think we'll be on a good thing there if we can get the cigarettes. We should get about £1,500 from the insurance company', Hammersley had told Waite, but when Hammersley discovered that it was Richardson who had brought more cigarettes, he exclaimed, 'My God, I can't get Freddie [*sic*] into trouble.'

Cross-examined by Edward Clarke, Waite said that from 1953 he had supplied information which helped Hammersley to arrest thieves and that he gave Heath money on about seven occasions. Heath, he said, did not directly ask for money but 'threw hints'. When Heath told him he had to get enough money to buy a new suit, Waite gave him £5, which Waite regarded as 'a form of blackmail'.

'Do you mean to say that when a friend who is not so well off says, "I find it difficult to rake up the money to get a new suit", you would be inclined to regard that as blackmail?' asked Mr Clarke.

'No one else would have the cheek to ask you', replied Waite.

He added that when Heath visited his shop he would order groceries worth £2 to £3, offer a 10 shilling note – and wait for change.

'Do you mean Heath waited his place in the queue with other people who might know him?' asked Mr Clarke.

'I don't know whether the customers knew who he was', replied Waite. 'He came in his best clothes, looking like a gentleman.'

'Are you trying to be offensive?' snapped Clarke and was innocently told, 'No.'

Waite described to Mr Peck for Hammersley that his client called at the shop 'as regularly as clockwork at 8.30 every Saturday morning' and had two or three pounds of pears, grapes or bananas, tinned fruit, a tin of cream, pineapples and maybe some bacon and chicken, after which he would offer one pound or ten shillings – and like Heath, wait for change.

Even better was Christmas – in 1953, 1954, 1955 and 1956, Waite had provided Hammersley with a free turkey, plus a £10 note.

The following day, Waite's cross-examination continued, but not before he had informed the court that due to his answers in cross-examination the previous day he had received two threatening telephone calls.

Referring to Waite's evidence that Ridge had collected his black-market meat from a shop run by a man named Matheson, Geoffrey Lawrence stated, 'I put it to you, Waite, it is absolutely untrue to say that Ridge had any meat for human consumption from that shop?'

'No, that's quite untrue', replied Waite.

He appeared rattled when questioned about his past; he denied failing to obey a notice of call-up for army service but agreed that he was picked up as an absentee and admitted he was tried by court martial. As details of his previous convictions were put to him, Waite agreed with them, although he drew the line at the suggestion that he had given 'lying and perjured evidence' in the case of the stolen coffee at West Sussex Assizes; and when it came to the theft of oranges in 1936, Waite said, 'I was unlucky. Had I known your client at the time, I should have been an honest citizen; perhaps the Lord Mayor of Brighton with no convictions against me.'

'To your dishonesty and perjury you do not hesitate to add cheekiness?' asked Lawrence and received the reply, 'I'm just telling the truth.'

The next witness was Mrs Joan Watson, and she received the same warning as Ernie Waite from the Judge that she need not reply to questions that might incriminate her. But like Waite, she disregarded the warning and provided some pretty sharp answers in cross-examination, especially from Edward Clarke, as shown in the following exchange.

'You have been associated with Mr Waite in running a dishonest business, haven't you?'

'I did not know it was a dishonest business and what I have done I was forced to do, by your client, for one.'

'Do you say that you were forced, as a woman of twenty-nine, to receive stolen property by Sergeant Heath?'

'Yes, he was one of them.'

'And was the man you were living with forced to receive stolen property?'

'On some occasions, from what I saw, yes.'

'Did he ever receive stolen property without being forced?'

'Not while I was with him.'

Asked if she knew she was living in a house with a man who owed £16,000 as an undischarged bankrupt, Mrs Watson stated that she was not now living in the same house as Waite. She employed him at £7 10s 0d per week to work in her fruit shop and she had also paid his doctor's bills in respect of a recent operation. He lived in one room at a house in Preston Road which belonged to her.

'Why do you think Heath and Hammersley were getting free goods from the shop, and what were they doing in return?'

'They were telling Mr Waite what stuff was going around as stolen and telling him to take it.'

'They were telling Waite to receive stolen property?'

'That's right.'

Asked about re-wrapping the butter, part of the consignment stolen from Kearney & Tongue, Edward Clarke asked, 'Who forced you to do that?'

'Nobody.'

'Did you realize you were taking part in a dishonest transaction?'

'Well, the whole lot was dishonest.'

Mrs Watson now became distressed, and the Judge suggested that she leave the court while evidence was taken from two police witnesses. When she returned she agreed that she knew the property belonging to Kearney & Tongue which she had bought was stolen, and Edward Clarke pursued the point:

'Immediately Ackerman rang up, you knew it was dishonest?'

'Yes. I also knew he was a friend of Hammersley, and he was told to contact me.'

'And because he was a friend of Hammersley and told to contact you, you were prepared to be a receiver of stolen property?'

'I had no alternative. There was nobody I could turn to.'

'You have not, up to today, been prosecuted for any of this property you have received . . . you are quite clearly in no danger of it?'

'If you say so. You have relieved my mind a lot.'

And with that, the day's proceedings ended. The following day, Mrs Watson came up against David Peck for Hammersley.

Saying that Hammersley had received foodstuffs including tins of peaches that he had taken to his house, Mrs Watson was asked, 'How many?'

'I don't know', she replied.

'Isn't that because it is not true?' asked Peck.

'If you persist in saying I'm lying, there is no point in my being here, is there?' responded Mrs Watson, and that was one of several barbed little exchanges between the two of them.

She had already given evidence that when the several premises had been raided by police and the stolen cigarettes and tobacco were found, she was willing to take the blame, rather than Waite.

She agreed that she was frightened about her part in the matter, and when asked if she was frightened of what might happen to Waite, she replied, 'Yes. I would not like to see anything happen to him.'

'And you are willing to say anything if necessary on oath that you think will help him?'

'I am not willing to say anything on oath that is not the truth', replied Mrs Watson firmly, adding somewhat caustically, 'One can get into trouble for that, I believe.'

CHAPTER 27

The Close of the Prosecution

The 27th witness for the prosecution was Roy John Mitchell, who was currently serving a term of three years' corrective training and was accompanied by a warder. Having broken into the Co-operative Stores at Brighton, he had sold cigarettes and tobacco to Waite; when he next broke into Davis the Jeweller's he was arrested before he could dispose of the watches and jewellery. When Heath and Hammersley visited him in Lewes prison whilst he was awaiting trial and told him, 'You can help yourself', Mitchell, knowing full well that they were referring to a bribe, replied, 'It's no good talking about that, because I'm skint.'

Just to ram the point home, the Judge asked, 'What does "skint" mean?'

'I did not have any money at the time.'

Cross-examined by Edward Clarke, Mitchell was asked, 'You, Mitchell, for most of your life, have not been at all friendly with the police?'

'No, sir.'

'They have been your enemies?'

'Not my enemies, just on the other side of the fence.'

'Is it right to say you are a young man who is set on living a life of dishonesty?' Clarke asked, and with disarming candour Mitchell replied, 'It looks like it, sir.'

'You are now putting an interpretation on an innocent conversation that you and Heath had about helping yourself which you hope will at least do Heath harm after he had done you harm?'

'No, sir, I don't get anything for coming up here. If you think I've come up here to do harm to Heath or Hammersley, you're wrong, sir', replied Mitchell and he denied that if his evidence was believed and Heath was convicted, he might get his sentence reduced. He had made no complaint to anybody regarding the attempt to extort money from him, until he was seen by the investigating team from the Yard.

'Do you say the words immediately indicated to you that Sergeant Heath was asking for money?'

'Yes. I knew Sergeant Heath and Sergeant [*sic*] Hammersley.'

'Why should you think Heath was asking for a bribe?' asked Mr Justice Donovan, to be told, 'Because I've known for years that certain members of the Brighton police force were what we call bent.'

'How could they have helped you?' asked the Judge, and Mitchell replied, 'There are plenty of ways in which bents could help; one way was by not opposing bail.'

Superintendent Edwin Moody of the British Transport Commission Police, who investigated the £15,000 theft of cigarettes and tobacco, told the Solicitor General that with regard to the enquiries conducted by the Brighton police he had never known a case where progress was so slow. He said that he had sent a man down to Brighton, undercover, on 27 August with certain instructions, and as a result had obtained search warrants without telling Brighton police what he was doing.

The Solicitor General asked, 'I suppose it is – to say the least – unusual for one police force to send a police officer into the area of another force to make enquiries without informing the force?'

'Most discourteous and most unusual', replied Moody.

'Why did you take that step?'

'I no longer trusted the Brighton CID. I began to lose confidence on 16 August and lost it on the 19th.'

Asked the reason for his distrust by Mr Justice Donovan, Moody replied, 'I got the impression that Inspector Hammersley was stalling . . . that he was putting me off . . . It seemed Hammersley was merely acting as a Post Office between me and the contact . . . some more practical help, I thought, might have been forthcoming.'

The superintendent mentioned that when they met in the Caxton public house, he was taken aback by the company Heath was keeping and that a round of drinks came to 15s 0d – money that Moody thought could not be spared out of a sergeant's pay. 'I was not suspicious of his honesty', he replied in response to a question from Edward Clarke, 'but I did note that . . . Heath told me, "My wife takes in foreign students at £8 per week. I get roughly £20 a week coming into the household and my police pay represents a very minor part of the total."'

Moody thought that £8 was 'an extraordinary amount to charge', believing that a more probable figure would have been £2–£3 per week, and he assumed Heath's statement was a lie.

Detective Sergeant Robert Johnson, who had eleven years service, seven of them spent in Brighton's CID, was now called by Edward Clarke.

'As regards Heath, you knew him as an officer and a sergeant in the CID who had a high reputation for his efforts to arrest criminals in Brighton?' asked Clarke, to which Johnson replied, 'Yes.'

'As a detective constable, he had a record during the year of making more arrests than any other?'

'Yes.'

'And he carried out his duty against criminals perfectly properly and honestly?'

'Yes.'

And with that, the officer who had been unable to determine whether or not a lorry-load of tinned peaches had been stolen was the last witness of 13 February.

Blustering, burly bookmaker William Page burst into court to inform the jury that he had not remonstrated with Ridge in his office because he believed he was being victimized: 'I was not being persecuted. I was breaking the law every day and if I was caught I was entitled to pay. But Ridge was going to victimize an innocent man.'

It was a self-centred, bombastic performance of how Page was going to 'clean up Brighton', although when it was put to him that he had been convicted on a number of occasions for betting offences, this simply caused him to sneer, 'How trivial.'

Rather than being an evangelical knight on a white charger, Page seemed rather keener on publicizing his daughter, singer Jill Day, because he mentioned that Ridge had said to him, 'Remember when you leave here and speak to your friends that you don't put your neck out to embarrass your daughter.'

'I immediately jumped out of the chair', roared Page, 'and said to him, "For your information, I have gone all through this with my daughter before I came to see you, and she said to me, "Daddy..."' but what Miss Day had had to say to her father was clearly inadmissible, and that completed Page's testimony.

Precisely why this bellowing braggart had been called in the first place by the prosecution is questionable. Perhaps in the course of his ranting it was thought that he might blurt out something to thoroughly compromise Ridge, but the fact remained that he didn't, and as far as the thoroughly unpleasant bookmaker was concerned, it appeared nothing more than a noisy exercise in self-aggrandisement.

James Swaby, currently serving his five-year sentence of preventative detention for housebreaking, told the court of passing the two £5 notes secreted in his raincoat to Heath in part-recompense for the officer hopefully not disclosing his last conviction for living off immoral earnings. He added that his wife would take the £50 demanded by Heath to the Town Hall and that DC Hovey was present whilst this was going on.

'I suggest that Heath never mentioned any money at all', protested Edward Clarke, only to be told, 'He did'; and then Mr Justice Donovan ordered that Swaby's raincoat be produced. Swaby described how he had hidden the money, explaining how he had rolled the notes round a pen 'and just shoved them in'.

'How did you get it out of the coat – with your fingers, or what?' asked the Judge, and Swaby, warming to his task replied, 'Yes, my Lord. It was pretty easy. It comes out. If I can demonstrate?'

'I have not got two £5 notes', replied the Judge politely but firmly, and with that, the case was adjourned until Monday, 17 February.

But before that date there occurred what appeared to be an exciting blip in the proceedings, when on the Saturday afternoon Joan Watson went shopping in the London Road shopping centre, Brighton with a friend, Mrs Rose Hancock – and disappeared.

Saying that they had been threatened, Ernie Waite frantically phoned the police, but when it was discovered that Mrs Watson's mother, Mrs M. Parsons, had seen her daughter at her Basingstoke Road, Reading address and that she would be returning to Preston Road the following day, large sighs of relief were expelled. A police search had been proposed, since right from the beginning of the proceedings Mrs Watson and her children had been threatened, but with her reappearance – it appeared that the stress of the court proceedings had temporarily affected her – the police operation was cancelled.

Back now to the Old Bailey, where 26-year-old Sheila Swaby, the wife of the accomplished thief James Swaby, admitted that she had been married for nearly two years and had been a prostitute for three; and when it was suggested to her that Heath had never asked her for money, she replied that he had.

Asked what work she was doing now, Mrs Swaby replied frankly, 'Soliciting.'

The two honest police officers, Detective Constable Hovey and Police Constable Knight, on-the-spot witnesses to corruption, had their evidence attacked, with Edward Clarke telling Knight, 'I suggest to you, officer, that in point of fact that conversation did not take place at all?' but the officer responded firmly, 'It definitely did.'

Two other honest police officers – Peter Vibart and Tommy Butler – were similarly accused of being less than frank regarding their dealings with Sammy Bellson. Vibart gave evidence of first meeting with Bellson when he and Butler had received information that he had been paying money to certain police officers in connection with the running of the Burlesque Club.

Vibart told the jury, 'Bellson said, "I half expected to see someone about this. We can't talk here. Let's go outside the town."'

They went by car to the outskirts of Brighton racetrack, and Butler asked, 'Would you tell us about it? Have you paid any money to any officer for any purpose?'

It was then that Bellson made his expansive and fulsome statement that he would help the officers 'any way I can', before changing his mind and joining the other four defendants in the dock.

But between the initial meeting and the refusal to give evidence, there were apparently quite harmonious meetings between the three men, one of which took place at Bellson's home on 4 October 1957.

'Did one of you say that if Bellson told you anything about the police, nothing would happen to him?' Victor Durand QC asked Peter Vibart, who denied it.

He also denied staying at Bellson's house as late as 2.00am, that consumption of liquor led to 'a little bit of trouble that night' (Durand added, 'I am not suggesting any impropriety by Butler or you'), or that 'one of you officers unfortunately had a drink on an empty stomach'; if Bellson had said, 'Much as I dislike Ridge, I would not swear an innocent man's life away', Vibart did not remember him saying anything like that.

Tommy Butler was next and he described the initial meeting with Bellson by the Brighton racetrack as lasting two hours. Asked if there was an occasion at Bellson's house when there was 'a great deal of drinking', Butler replied, 'On one occasion, he did give us a drink.'

'On one occasion?' gasped an incredulous Durand. 'Did that occasion last from 8.30pm to 2.00am?'

'I was never there as late as 2.00am', replied Butler frostily, adding, 'On one occasion, we left there at midnight.'

The newspaper reports containing the imputation that Butler was sloshed caused huge merriment back in the Flying Squad office, because it was known that he was practically teetotal. On the rare occasions that he accompanied his team to the Red Lion in Derby Gate he would sip one small glass of Tio Pepe sherry before hurrying back to his office, there to continue typing reports until 3 o'clock in the morning.

And that closed the case for the prosecution.

CHAPTER 28

Heath's Defence

The proceedings on Tuesday, 18 February opened in the absence of the jury, with Edward Clarke making a submission to the Judge that there was no case to answer. It was much the same argument that had been used at the commencement of the trial, it lasted for almost an hour and a half and the other defence barristers once more wished to associate themselves with the submission, but again the Judge kicked it into touch, telling them, 'I consider the case must go on.'

The jurors filed back into court, and Edward Clarke commenced his opening address to them, saying:

> You are not here trying the Brighton police or having to decide whether or not any general police force is corrupt or any criminal or private individual has been corrupt. The words 'Brighton Police' have almost become a music-hall joke. That is what is called pre-judging and that is one thing you must not do . . . Never can it be for a very long time that so many honest men were in the dock and so many dishonest men were in the witness box . . . Heath is a man who has more commendations than most of the witnesses for the prosecution have convictions.

Heath's eleven commendations were certainly praiseworthy, but Clarke was either unaware or had conveniently forgotten that the Scotland Yard team between them possessed a total of 131. Now it was more important to introduce Heath into the witness box, to give evidence on oath.

Dealing first with the Leaches, father and son, Heath agreed that as soon as the incriminating rustle of paper currency was heard coming from Leach Senior's fob pocket, Hammersley had swiftly and virtuously exclaimed, 'Harry, you had better put that away before you make a bloody fool of yourself.'

'Is there any truth in the suggestion that either you or Hammersley said anything about £250 being wanted for the purpose of evidence being thrown in the sea?' asked Clarke.

'No truth whatever, sir', replied Heath.

Heath stated that he had first met Bennett either at the end of 1954 or in early 1955, when he knew him as Alan Roy

Brown; he had no idea at the time that Bennett had a criminal record.

Edward Clarke then referred to what he called 'The London Episode'. Heath told the court that when he had a day off, Bennett asked if he would care to go to London, where he had business to attend to. They drove up in Bennett's Jaguar, lunched at an Indian restaurant and Bennett paid the bill. Afterwards, Bennett said he wanted to buy some ties and they went to a shop in the Burlington Arcade.

'When you got into that shop had you any intention at that stage of buying any ties?' asked Clarke.

'No', replied Heath.

Bennett chose some ties which Heath thought were rather nice and also selected another three or four, all of which were expensive.

'Did you intend yourself to pay for those ties?' asked Clarke, to which Heath replied, 'I fully intended to do so.'

But Bennett had produced a £5 note, telling the assistant, 'Take for the lot', whereupon Heath protested, 'I don't want you to pay for mine', but Bennett repeated to the assistant, 'Take for the lot.'

'Apart from those ties, have you ever accepted any clothing or presents from Bennett?' asked Clarke, to be told, 'No, sir.'

Replying to a question from the Judge, Heath confirmed, 'I have never had any money from Bennett.'

Speaking of the time when Heath arrested Alan Walker in the presence of Mrs Bennett and told him that Walker alleged that money had been stolen from his room at the Astor Hotel, Clarke said, 'It is suggested by Bennett in his evidence that you, in the presence of two other officers, said to him, "Give us our whack of the grand."'

'That is not so, sir', replied Heath.

He then said that he had sent to Scotland Yard to see if Bennett had a criminal record, and when he discovered that he had he stated that he had shown Bennett his police 'mugshot' in the hope – and this is difficult to understand – that doing so would keep him 'inactive'. In other words, it would jolt him into living a crime-free and industrious life. Right.

'Is there any truth in the suggestion that the reason you showed him that photograph was to try to get money out of him?'

'Certainly not, sir.'

Heath went on to say that there was no truth in the suggestion that he went to the Astor Club to collect £20 a week so that it would not be raided; nor did he have any arrangement with Bennett or Superintendent Ridge that the money should be paid. He did not

see Bennett screw up two £5 notes and throw them on the floor
for Hammersley when Bennett was interviewed about the offence
at Bournemouth, and when he was contacted by Folkestone
police about the offence on their patch he telephoned Bennett
in London to come down to Brighton but not to bring his car.

Heath said he had been to the Astor Club on two or three
occasions but never after hours; indeed, he was unaware that
the club was being kept open after hours.

He denied altering a statement made by Mrs Lawrence in
the abortion case and when he was asked, 'Did you ever receive
any money from Mrs Lawrence?' he replied, 'No, sir. She never
offered me any money and I never asked for any money.'

Asked if at any stage he had asked Mrs Brabiner for money,
Heath replied, 'No, sir. She offered to give me some at the first
interview I had with her. She said words to the effect of "Can't
you take a few pounds and forget about it?", and I said to her
words to the effect of "Look Alice, if you won the football pools,
you would not get out of trouble this time."'

Heath stated that he knew Ernest Waite had a criminal record
before first meeting him in 1954 but was unaware that he was
a paid informer. When in 1956 he had purchased greengroceries
from Waite's shop he had always paid the full price.

He denied taking the two £5 notes from Swaby; there had
never been a conversation about 'a pony', nor had there ever
been a conversation with Mrs Swaby about how she was fixed
for £50. However, he *had* asked her if she could assist in getting
any of the money back that had been stolen by her husband, and
if the money, about £75, had been returned, he would certainly
have mentioned it in court prior to Swaby being sentenced. And
that was the reason why he had sent DC Hovey out of court
twice, to see if Mrs Swaby had any money for him. 'I wanted
the £75 from her before I went into the witness box', he told the
jury. 'I would then have been able to tell the Recorder the money
had been repaid.' It was a novel defence.

Regarding PC Knight's assertion that Heath had approached
him with the offer of 'a tenner a week' to keep Bellson informed
about when his club was going to be raided, Heath's response was
that he had never had any fiddles to the extent of corruption, nor
had he received any bribes; and in answer to Edward Clarke's
question whether from 1949 to 1957 he had conspired with
any of the defendants to obstruct the course of justice in any
way, his answer was an emphatic, 'Never.'

And after Clarke had called two police officers who had been
with Heath when he quizzed Bennett regarding the missing £1,000

from Alan Walker's bedroom, and they told the court that there was never any indication that Bennett was going to give any money to Heath or that Heath was going to get any money from Bennett, it was time for Heath to be cross-examined by the prosecution.

When the Solicitor General asked Heath why he had not reported Mr Leach Senior's attempt to offer a bribe, Heath's reply was that he was not the officer in charge of the case (which was understandable) and that the matter was 'insignificant' (which it was not).

Sir Harry pointed out that despite his denials, Mrs Cherryman said she had seen him in the Astor Bar after hours, but Heath replied that she was either lying or mistaken.

He denied telephoning Mrs Bennett telling her not to open the Astor Club; nor did he say to anyone there that Ridge had sent him.

With regard to showing Bennett his police photograph, the Solicitor General asked, 'Are you saying now you regarded that as a proper thing for a police officer to do?'

'Possibly not proper, sir', replied Heath.

'Why did you sell your wife's ring to Bennett, a man who was not a jeweller and who had a bad criminal record?'

'I wanted to sell the ring. There was nothing improper in the transaction at all. He paid a fair price for it.'

'Looking back on it, do you think it was a wise thing for a detective officer to do?'

'I should say it was a little indiscreet, sir.'

Asked why he wanted Bennett at Brighton about an offence committed at Folkestone, Heath replied, 'I would like to have arrested him personally for Folkestone, sir.' He went on to say that he told Bennett to ring him on his private line because he did not want anybody to know he was using this means to get Bennett to Brighton to arrest him: 'I just wanted to arrest him out of the blue.'

Questioned by Mr Justice Donovan, Heath agreed that when Mrs Brabiner tried to bribe him he was with another officer, but on the second occasion the officer had left. 'On reflection, it was most imprudent to be left alone with a woman who had tried to bribe me on the last occasion', he said, and then he was asked why he had never charged the people who had tried to bribe him. 'Most of them were in trouble already', replied Heath, 'and it would have been a bit hard to put them further in trouble.'

It was not really a believable answer, and Heath, who had spent five and a half hours in the witness box, had not given an impressive performance.

CHAPTER 29

Three More Defences

When Hammersley was examined by his counsel, Donald McIntyre QC, he was asked whether he and Heath had tried to extort the sum of £250 from John Leach to prevent his prosecution.

'No, sir, the boot was on the other foot', replied Hammersley.

Ernie Waite was an informant but certainly not a friend, stated Hammersley, and there was no truth in the suggestion that Waite had given him money. 'Until August 1957, I was able to rely on the information he gave me', he said. 'Everything he told me had been right until the cigarettes incident, last year.'

Hammersley denied there had ever been 'a gentlemen's agreement' in respect of property stolen in or outside of Brighton, and when he was asked about Waite's behaviour regarding the theft of the cigarettes he replied, 'He completely double-crossed me.'

He had 'not the slightest inkling' that Waite was a receiver of stolen goods but was obliged to admit that Frederick George Richardson, with whom he and his wife, together with Richardson's wife, had travelled to Paris for four days during Easter 1957 ('sharing the expenses') was to his own knowledge a receiver of stolen goods.

Richardson, who had apparently supplied huge quantities of stolen cigarettes and tobacco to Waite with Hammersley's connivance, declined to be called as a prosecution witness. It was, of course, up to the defence to call Richardson to dispute those matters; something they had not the slightest intention of doing.

'Is there any truth whatever that you failed to make any proper investigations into the Bournemouth matter?' asked Mr McIntyre, to be told, 'No.'

'Does the same apply to the Folkestone matter?'

'Yes.'

Denying that Bennett had thrown two £5 notes on the floor, Hammersley stated that there was 'not a word of truth' in the allegations against him.

Mr Justice Donovan asked him if it was unusual for an officer to go alone to arrest a man, and Hammersley replied, 'I have always worked as a lone wolf.'

'Didn't you always have someone with you in case of resistance?' asked the Judge, to which Hammersley replied, 'If I thought there was danger of resistance I would have taken somebody.'

Now Sir Harry Hylton-Foster QC rose to commence cross-examination, asking, 'And if you thought someone was going to offer you a bribe?'

'I would have taken someone.'

'Had you known Ernest Waite was the person alleged to be disposing of cigarettes, would you have sought to make use of his services as an informer?'

'Certainly not, sir.'

'Would you have taken steps at once to have his premises watched?'

'Certainly, sir.'

'The only reason these things were not done was because from the beginning to the end your detective superintendent concealed from you the only piece of information he had got of who was dealing with these things?'

'He never told me.'

Hammersley knew he was on safe ground, here, knowing that Williams would never be called from his Welsh sickbed to state, quite categorically, that he had certainly shown Hammersley and Heath Wyatt's letter. Consequently, it was easy to deny that he had taken the letter and shown it to Waite in the presence of Joan Watson; nor did he have a conversation condemning the writer of the letter, Mr Wyatt, as an informer; and nor had Waite told him that it was Richardson who had the cigarettes.

'All this has gone sadly wrong', said the Solicitor General, 'because your superintendent, who put you in charge of the enquiry, never let you know – at any stage – who it was who was supposed to be dealing with the cigarettes?'

'In fact', replied Hammersley, 'that is a big part of the cause.'

The Judge asked about Wyatt's letter, saying, 'You did not know Waite's name was mentioned in it until Waite came to court?'

'No.'

'Waite came to court and said that on 3 December last?'

'Yes.'

'But Mrs Watson gave evidence on the 2nd. How would she know of that letter and of Waite's name being in it when you did not know?'

'I cannot answer that, I do not know.'

'It's a mystery, isn't it?'

'An absolute mystery.'

With that, Hammersley stepped down from the witness box. His testimony had arguably been even less impressive than Heath's.

★   ★   ★

Next up was Anthony John Lyons, the proprietor of Sherry's Bar since 1950. His barrister, Stanley Rees QC, asked, 'You understand, it is being said in relation to Bennett that you made an arrangement with Bennett in which he was going to pay money to Ridge in April 1955. Did you ever make any such arrangement?'

'Not at any time', replied Lyons. 'I had never been to the Astor Club with Ridge. I visited it myself several times but never after hours. I was an honorary member. I knew Ridge very well as a customer.'

Lyons also denied that he attempted to induce Mrs Mason, the next owner of the Astor Club, into an arrangement about the conduct of the club. He knew a Mrs Lawrence. He had barred her from Sherry's Bar on a number of occasions, once for trying to solicit, at other times for fighting with her husband, for being drunk and for fighting with a woman.

Lyons told the court that he had first met Bennett in 1945 who was then working as a chef. He knew nothing of Bennett's criminal background and had helped him since he was in a financial difficulty. Lyons next saw Bennett ten years later, in Sherry's Bar, 'looking very prosperous'.

'Bennett was talking sort of high finance', said Lyons. 'He told me he had property all over Brighton and if he could continue with his mortgages for another eight or ten years he would be a very rich man.'

Cross-examined by the Solicitor General, who asked, 'Do you know of any reason why Bennett should have involved you in a tale of corruption which was false?' Lyons replied, 'No, sir, I can't. I can't think of any reason why Bennett should have involved me except he may have been pressed or forced into it.'

'Have you anywhere introduced the accused Ridge to Bennett?'

'I could have introduced him in the bar, in the ordinary course of my business as a host.'

Sammy Bellson was next and through his counsel, Victor Durand, denied that he had taken a total of £100 from the Leaches and handed it to Ridge, or that when he had met 'The Terrible

Twins' at Brighton racecourse, they asked if he had ever given money to a police officer, which he denied. He agreed that he was raided by police about a dozen times between 1952 and 1957.

The Solicitor General asked, 'Did you ever ask Hammersley to arrange that you should be tipped off if your place was going to be done?'

'Definitely not, sir', replied Bellson and went on to say that the two Yard officers said that he was the most persecuted man in Brighton and asked what he knew about Ridge; Bellson told them what he thought of him. However, nobody had referred to jewellery, and Leach was never mentioned.

'Did you say Ridge had been to see old Harry Leach?' asked the Solicitor General, and Bellson replied, 'No, sir.'

Mr Justice Donovan pointed out that the police officers had stated that he had said that Ridge sent him to do some business with the Leaches. Was there a possibility of a mistaken recollection? Bellson replied that there was not.

Finally, Charles Ridge took the stand. It was the first time in British policing history that a Chief Constable had been placed on trial at the Old Bailey. Public interest was enormous.

CHAPTER 30

Ridge's Defence

Having taken the oath in a firm voice, Ridge was taken through his home circumstances and his career by his counsel, Geoffrey Lawrence QC; he said that when he took up his appointment as Chief Constable, one of the first matters he addressed was the question of clubs.

'Rumours had reached me', he said, 'that certain clubs were failing to observe the licensing regulations and that others concerned with betting were indulging in ready money betting.'

He described the action he took and produced documents and charts which showed a comparison of police activity over six or seven years. He also mentioned introducing a radical change in the way that bookmakers' pitches at Brighton racecourse were allocated and agreed with his counsel that he had 'trodden on the toes' of many people in the district.

His progressive work in the force itself revealed that he had launched a vigorous policy for better housing, and his force was one of the few in the country that was up to full strength. This had nothing to do with the case, but everything to do with Ridge's credibility.

Ridge said that on 17 December Hammersley had told him that Harry Leach had put his hand in his pocket, made some remark and had then broken down and cried. The following day, Ridge had seen Leach privately and had told him to consult a solicitor and 'keep within the law'.

Asked if he had confronted Leach regarding his putting his hand in his pocket the previous day, Ridge replied that he had not; he did not want to increase Leach's embarrassment.

'Did you utilize the services of Bellson or anybody else to get money out of Harry Leach to show favour to his son?' asked Lawrence.

'No, sir.'

'Or have any improper purpose, whatsoever?'

'No, sir.'

Lawrence then remarked that there seemed to be a suggestion that Sherry's Bar was a conspirators' den. Ridge replied that he had never received a complaint about Lyons or the conduct at

Sherry's Bar; he went there about once a week in summer, less often in winter, and to other licensed premises as part of his duties as a CID officer, 'keeping his ears open'. He admitted that it was possible that he had first met Bennett there; in fact, at Easter 1955 he had been walking past the Astor Hotel when Bennett had asked him if he would like to see his club. After being introduced to Bennett's wife, he looked around the club but never went there again.

'Is there any truth in the allegation that you were party to an arrangement that you should be paid money as a consideration for seeing that Bennett was not prosecuted for breaches of the licensing laws?' asked Lawrence.

'No, sir', replied Ridge.

'Did you ever receive any money at all from Bennett?'

'No, sir.'

'Do you have any recollection of meeting a man called Harry Waterman?'

'No.'

'Did you at any time in your professional career take any steps to see that Bennett was not prosecuted, or to influence in any way the course of justice in relation to him?'

'No, sir.'

Ridge stated that the first time he had heard the Astor Club being referred to as 'The Bucket of Blood' was at the Magistrates' Court, when he was committed for trial. He described the authentic financial arrangements he had made to fund holidays for him and his wife.

Ridge described the visit to his office by Mrs Cherryman but said the burden of her remarks was regarding the £2,000 she had lent to Bennett. Regarding her remarks about not knowing whom she could trust in the CID, Ridge said that she did not give him a satisfactory explanation, and the following day, he had reported to his Chief Constable her remarks about the telephone call she had received about closing the club that night and 'to say it was Charlie'. The Chief Constable, said Ridge, told him that 'he would look into it'.

Ridge said that he had known Ernest Waite for 10–12 years and denied ever receiving anything from him improperly. He first learnt that Waite was Hammersley's informant on 3 September 1957; he was annoyed when he heard about it, he told Lawrence, and he had told Hammersley he was extremely distressed that the enquiry with the railway police officers about stolen cigarettes had not yielded more expeditious and profitable results.

Questioned about Page's visit to his office, Ridge said he had complained that a bookmaker named Ki-Ki had not been prosecuted; in fact, said Ridge, he had made enquiries and Ki-Ki had been prosecuted and convicted.[1]

'Is there any truth in the allegations that you have at any time conspired to obstruct the course of justice by failing to do your duty?' asked Lawrence.

'No, sir', replied Ridge.

'Is there any truth in any suggestion you have ever accepted or attempted to take bribes from any individual as a means of influencing you in the conduct of your duty?'

'No, sir' – and with that, Sir Harry Hylton-Foster got to his feet.

'It is very important that policemen should not be unaccompanied if there is a risk of their being offered bribes?' he asked.

Ridge agreed and was then asked, 'From the point of view of their own protection?' and Ridge agreed once more.

'Is that what you teach your subordinates?'

'Yes.'

When Ridge had gone to see Harry Leach he asked to see him alone, and John Leach – accused of receiving stolen jewellery – had 'made himself scarce'.

'When you went to see the elder Leach', asked Sir Harry, 'his son was there, and you knew that one of your officers had reported that he [Harry Leach] had done something near being unwise, like offering a bribe?'

'No, sir', replied Ridge, 'but I felt Harry Leach needed legal advice.'

'Why did you wish to see him in private and say, "Keep within the law"?' asked the Solicitor General.

'I thought he was getting a little desperate', replied Ridge.

'Don't you agree that if there had been the slightest effort at bribery', asked Sir Harry, 'it was not the duty of any unaccompanied officer to be in the exact position that you were in when you went to see Harry Leach?'

'Harry Leach was not the subject of the enquiry', replied Ridge.

---

1 Ki-Ki, also known as 'Syd Kye-Kye' was the nickname of Nathan Mercado, who had been sentenced to twelve months' imprisonment at Hampshire Assizes in 1952 for conspiracy to evade customs duty on 16,500 pairs of nylons. Having his finger in any number of dodgy pies, he was accused in court of setting up the gang leader, Jack Spot, to be savagely attacked in 1956. Mercado was also a prolific informant.

'Do you mean to say there was not the risk of him trying to bribe you because it was his son who was involved?'

'Yes.'

Ridge agreed that he had requested another officer to leave the room when Page entered his office, 'because I thought he had some information which he was only prepared to give to me, alone.'

'Was that just another instance of what you would recommend your detective officers not to do?' asked Sir Harry.

'In my capacity as Chief Constable, when a person requests to see me privately, and that person is a reasonable person, I agree to that request', replied Ridge. It was an unfortunate response, because it enabled Sir Harry to come straight back at him.

'Was he a reasonable person? He was a man convicted of doping dogs?'

'Yes.'

'And he was a man who had tried to slip Alderman Cullen a fiver behind a clock?'

'He could be.'

'Is that the right person for your young officers to see alone?'

'No.'

There was a great deal of smoke and mirrors about the Alderman Cullen incident. Prior to the incident at Ridge's office, Page had gone to see Cullen at his home address to complain of Ridge 'victimizing' him; and after Page left, Cullen found a £5 note behind a clock on his mantelpiece. Cullen, who had previously served in the Metropolitan Police as a detective sergeant, reported the matter, and Ridge passed it on to the deputy town clerk and the Watch Committee. Ridge stated that he had warned Page about leaving the money on the mantelpiece, something that Page denied doing.

If Page had left the £5 note there, it begs the question, why? Was it an inducement for Cullen to make mischief with the Watch Committee against Ridge? Yes, possibly, and it would give the domineering bookie a sense of power to believe that he had an alderman (and a member of the Watch Committee to boot) in his pocket.

But the waters became really muddied fifty-eight years later.

On a police blog it was stated that 'most of the prosecution witnesses were professional liars', which was quite accurate; many of them were. This attracted the ire of Desmond P. Cullen, Tom Cullen's grandson, who stated that his grandfather 'was a prosecution witness and not a professional liar'. He went on to say that his grandfather had served for many years on Brighton Council, was not a freemason and was well-respected. But then, he said this:

> On the eve of the trial, Ridge visited my grandfather and tried to leave an envelope containing money on the mantelpiece, hoping my grandfather would have a lapse of memory. My grandfather gave the envelope back and refused to back down. Tom Cullen was sure the jury had been nobbled, but Brighton Police would not investigate . . .

Tom Cullen's mantelpiece appears to feature large in this matter. What was Cullen supposed to have a lapse of memory about in respect of Ridge? Why would Ridge do this at all – and especially on the eve of the trial – when he was in London anyway? Or was the reference in fact to the committal proceedings, when it was part of Ridge's bail conditions that he was not to leave his house – which, had he done so, would have rendered him liable to arrest? If this – or anything like this – actually happened, did Cullen report it to the investigating officers? If not, why not? One thing's for sure; while accepting Mr Cullen Jr's assertion that his grandfather was not 'a professional liar', he was certainly not a prosecution witness; he never gave evidence at the Old Bailey.

Perhaps the memory of what actually happened became a little confused over the passage of years; now, over sixty years after the trial, the whole incident raises more questions than answers.

Back to Ridge in the witness box, who said that he had heard of a man named Richardson by reputation and that he would not have approved if he had known that one of his detective inspectors had spent an Easter holiday with him abroad. Additionally, he was not aware that Matheson was a black market trader and he had never purchased meat for human consumption from his shop, where he had only obtained meat for his cat and dogs. He was unaware that his officers had seen Bennett about either the Bournemouth or Folkestone enquiries.

'Has there ever been, at any time in any circumstances, any occasion when you, Lyons, Bennett and Mrs Bennett were together in that small room, the Astor Club?' asked the Solicitor General, and Ridge replied, 'No, sir.'

Ridge said that he could find no reason for Mrs Cherryman's statement, when she came to see him, that she did not know who to trust in the CID. He did not ask her which officers she doubted, because she did not give him any indication of personal misgivings. He did not ask her if she was prepared to make a statement about her distrust. He agreed that the matter of the telephone message of which Mrs Cherryman spoke, about closing the club that night and 'to say it was Charlie', was a matter of the utmost gravity, because that was exactly the kind of 'tip-off' which was probably associated with corruption.

'You reported the matter to your then Chief Constable and after that, as far as you were concerned as head of the CID, you were prepared to leave the matter?' asked Sir Harry.

'No, sir.'

'What did you do about it?'

'I did nothing, pending further observations by my Chief Constable, sir.'

Re-examined by his counsel, Geoffrey Lawrence, Ridge said that he would not have expected the 'tipping-off' to be done over a public telephone in such completely intelligible language.

That was Ridge's defence. Would it be enough? After he stepped down from the witness box, Edward Clark QC for Heath made a submission to the Judge in the absence of the jury; Mr Justice Donovan rejected it.

But when the jury returned, so did 'The Terrible Twins', at the direction of the judge.

CHAPTER 31

Final Speeches

The Judge's decision appeared to be an odd one. After all, the case for the prosecution had closed; and if it came to that, so had the case for the defence.

But while the majority of the investigating team from the Yard had simply recorded the defendants' denials, the testimony of 'The Terrible Twins' had attracted a number of challenges; and what was more, it had been attacked when Bellson had given evidence.

Addressing the jury, Mr Justice Donovan said:

> Inspector Butler had given evidence that when he and Vibart saw Bellson near Brighton racecourse, Bellson suggested that they see 'old Harry Leach' and something about the money not being enough and Ridge going to see them himself. Bellson in the witness box had said that that was an invention. Inspector Butler replied that the evidence he gave was perfectly correct and true and the instances which he recorded in his pocket book were recorded more or less word for word. Sergeant Vibart said that Bellson had said the things that he had previously given evidence about. Mr Victor Durand for Bellson suggested over and over again Sergeant Vibart had asked Bellson to make a statement implicating Ridge; Sergeant Vibart denied it.

The Solicitor General now got to his feet for his closing address to the jury:

> People do not bribe policemen for nothing, so you would expect to find in such a case as this that there would be some reason for bribing them, and among those who sought to give bribes, one would expect to find people with a criminal record. It was the record that made them willing to bribe, to dodge publicity and which made them 'blackmailable' by the dishonest policeman.
>
> It is your duty to look at the evidence of such persons with the greatest care. No one in the country doubts that you will get the right answer to this case ... but I hope it will not be based on the proposition that the person with a criminal record can never be

telling the truth and a police officer can never be lying, because I would submit that would not be a sound way of approaching the problem at this time. If the Leaches' account was invented, surely it was a most elaborate invention? What good was it to the Leach family, when it involved saying that this respectable old gentleman, Harry Leach, had been trying to bribe the Brighton police? It might be one of the sad things in this case that where these things happened in the presence of the members of the Brighton CID, they were not reported. When Leach was asked why he did not report the matter of the police trying to bribe him, he answered that he did tell a councillor but he was not believed and he did not persist because he did not think it would be any use. Perhaps in Brighton in the last few years, it might not have been any use to report that CID officers were trying to get bribes.

Once again, the Crown will ask why, unless it was true, had the witness Alan Roy Bennett come to tell the rather disparaging facts. After all, I do not suppose you think he is a fool, in the sense of failing to know what it meant for him after he went to Scotland Yard and revealed what he did, that he had been bribing police officers – not something that he would be likely to bring to the attention of the police gratuitously – the public revelations of his public record which meant ruin for him in whatever business he was trying to live, and of defrauding the Inland Revenue persistently. He has got all that to deal with now. If he had decided to do all this to get rid of Heath, why involve Ridge – unless it was true? Why involve Lyons, for there was no trouble between them? There is no point unless, as the Crown submits, it is the obvious, naked – though ugly – truth.

The Crown would say that Mrs Bennett was a wholly convincing witness of truth. How had the Bennetts contrived to remember and recall that Ridge did go on holiday to Spain in May, for if you, the jury, looked at his passport they would find that was true in fact?

Dealing with the arrest of a man called Walker and a subsequent conversation between Heath and Bennett, Mr Edward Clarke in his submission for Heath had implied that the prosecution had kept the evidence of the two police officers who were present under their hat. But that was not so, for the Crown gave their names to the defence. I do not run away from the fact that you will have to hear whose version of that interview you prefer – Bennett and Mrs Bennett on the one hand and the two Brighton CID officers and Heath on the other . . . but I would submit that the only safe view to take is that it is quite impossible to think that the demands described by Bennett for 'a whack of the grand' could have passed unknown to the other two police officers seated in the lounge, and you will have to decide which is the truth.

Why did Mrs Brabiner say she had paid Heath money while he was enquiring into an illegal operation which she performed? She had finished her gaol sentence before this hearing . . . it was all behind her. Unless she spoke the truth, what good was it to her to come forward and reveal herself as guilty of bribing the police?

If I refer to rumour, it is not to invite you to act on rumour to convict, but rumour . . . has its significance here. Supposing you were to be told what seemed to you to be a rather naked approach to a policeman about a bribe with a build-up to it, it might be so odd and unconvincing to you that you might say it did not happen; but if on the other hand the circumstances showed it was regularly accepted that certain officers would accept bribes then, of course, the circumstances might be quite different and you might think that no preparatory work would be required before you reached that point. Regarding the sale of a ring by Heath to Bennett, what a revelation that is of the relationship which existed between a detective sergeant and this criminal that such a thing could happen . . . The complicity of Ridge about the Astor Club was abundantly proved by the evidence of Mrs Cherryman.

I know, because we have so much good, faithful, honourable and honest service from the police officers in this country, how painful it must be to you to have to face up to the proposition that here you are finding three policemen and some outside persons engaged in a criminal conspiracy to obstruct the path of justice; and the picture, I appreciate, is a gloomy one and one that one would be reluctant to accept as true. But it is my duty to you on behalf of the Crown that on this evidence the conclusion is inescapable that this charge is proved beyond peradventure against each and all of the accused.

The first of the closing speeches for the defence came from Edward Clarke QC:

You are not trying the issue of whether the Brighton police were corrupt. I say this at once – it is possible that some Brighton police officers have been corrupt during those nine years and those police officers are not in the dock and it may be one of the reasons why the prosecution have not called some of those officers. They have been selective not only in their witnesses but in their defendants. There has been a big investigation down at Brighton. You have heard Superintendent Forbes-Leith say he had interviewed more than 200 people and had taken statements from more than 150 witnesses. The prosecution called 64 . . .

Out of those pieces of evidence and witnesses statements and documents, the prosecution put in what they think is important.

Important for what? Important to establish the guilt of these men.

There is a horrifying danger that with such an indictment, something is bound to stick and therefore, the prosecution will have attained what they had set out to prove. I suggest you should find Heath not guilty of this charge, unless you are satisfied beyond any reasonable doubt that he is in this corruption racket, right up to his neck.

There has been a contest between the crooks and the honest men. The crooks' team was Bennett, Brabiner, Waite, Lawrence, Mr and Mrs Swaby, Mitchell and Betts – eight or nine people. Never can there have been such a procession of crooks through the witness box. Would any of you like to keep company with any of these people? Are you not much more impressed with the evidence of Heath than these other people, nearly a cricket team with their convictions? If Heath, before this case, had come to see any of you members of the jury, was he not the sort of person you would believe on oath, quite apart from the others? They start off as people with a bad character who, if called for an alibi for a defendant and if cross-examined by the Solicitor General, would be blown sky-high, and rude remarks would probably be made about their insolence in coming into the witness box and trying to swear falsely.

It is oath against oath, oaths against oaths. You just don't count heads in a case of this sort. You have seen certain witnesses for the prosecution who, you may think have the motive, the character and all the other attributes of liars.

The second thing was that they were accomplices. What will probably be running round your minds for a long time this week is why should these people tell this story?

I am going to suggest to you – and I hope I shall not leave anyone out – that in each one of these cases, there is a motive. In some cases, it is a motive which is as clear as daylight. In other cases, it is a motive which is a possible motive and a reason why they might have done it. It is suggested by the Solicitor General that Bennett must have had courage to come forward. I shall suggest he had a good reason and considerable advantage. Bennett is forty and during those forty years he has managed to amass thirteen or fourteen convictions. He was an expert housebreaker, and if you believe that he is now carrying on an honest living, anything can be believed. Here was a man who ran companies from passages in estate agents' offices, a man who put MHCI after his name to impress people when it was something to do with cooking and a man who produced £500 in £5 notes from his hip pocket and said he always had to deal in cash. The oath did not mean anything to him.

I challenge the Solicitor General. Both Bennett and Mrs Bennett had given evidence about an occasion when Heath had told Bennett he wanted 'his whack of the grand'. He denied this. Two other policemen were there who were called by the defence. If they were telling the truth, that it did not happen, Bennett and his wife lied. My challenge to the Solicitor General is that if he had cross-examined the two policemen on the basis that what they were saying was not true, the matter would be in issue. But he never suggested to either of them that their evidence was other than true. Once there was a wedge driven into Bennett's evidence to show he was lying, did not that make a crack right across the whole of his evidence?

Regarding the evidence of constables Hovey and Knight, have you any doubt that everybody in the Brighton force now is doing his best to keep, not out of the dock, but in the police force? I suggest there is no evidence of conspiracy between Heath and any of the other defendants in the case concerning Swaby. The conversation between Heath and Police Constable Knight, in which it was alleged Heath asked if he was interested in earning 'a tenner a week', was not Knight just trying to make it worse for Heath, by leaving out all the innocent part of the conversation and putting in the guilty part?

In this case, you have been taken into a world of criminal detection by police officers – by plain clothes police officers – in a small and crook-infested area, where they carry on a ceaseless war against these criminals for the benefit of the ordinary members of the public. There are certain rules and regulations about that – general principles – but you do not, as a detective sergeant, when dealing with people like Bennett, Waite and Swaby, if you are trying to catch them, follow the Queensberry Rules. You use what methods you can for the purpose, for getting these people arrested and punished. There are twenty-seven members of the Brighton CID, of whom only three are in the dock. That means there are tywenty-four out of the dock and some are still in the force. What I ask you to say is that on this evidence, and not on rumour or on prejudice, you are not satisfied that Heath was a party to these dishonesties.

* * *

David McIntyre QC for Hammersley was next and he promptly steamed straight into the Solicitor General; what the jury might think one of the most powerful speeches ever made in a court of law was in fact

> Two and a half hours of studied, calm and calculated vituperation – and I use those words advisedly – having regard

to what we have heard this morning, you may wonder, is there a single good word that can be said for any of these men?

You would have thought as from this morning certainly, that you were not trying three police officers and two civilians but the whole of Brighton's CID, and by implication, possibly other police officers who do not happen to be in the CID and possibly – for one never knows the length to which a barbed sting may go – local officials, councillors and people living in the county and the town. Are people all either black or white? I would suggest that the case had changed its whole aspect in the course of the morning; so thin and tenuous apparently is the case now thought to be by the prosecution that the prosecuting counsel had to descend to the level he did this morning. What the prosecution was saying was that this 'canker of corruption' had spread throughout the whole of the force. If the Solicitor General is to be given any attention at all to all he says, you cannot trust a single member of the Brighton CID.

No other person than Waite and Mrs Watson has come to court to refer to any criminal conspiracy between Hammersley and Waite up to 1956. The allegation that Hammersley had allowed himself to be tempted by Bennett, 'this lordly gentleman' who screwed up two £5 notes and threw them on the floor, was a stupid story. Do you imagine that a fly-boy as Bennett would choose that place, that moment and that manner of bribing an almost complete stranger? Isn't he exactly the sort of criminal, crooked with the twisted type of mind, who would glory in the position in which he now stood in the witness box, day after day, scoring points off us in our ignorance – and not realizing all the time that he was giving himself away? Bennett has said in evidence that he bribed people – so why isn't he in the dock? There can be only one answer. If he is guilty of the crimes he himself swears he committed, he has bought his way to freedom or he is morally certain he will never be prosecuted. He knows his onions all right, you may think. He illustrates the utter recklessness which some blackguardly people like himself and Waite level charges against decent, honest men. On Waite's story, he should be the sixth man in the dock. He is one of the biggest conspirators there, if his story is true.

Don't go away with the idea that the whole of Brighton CID is corrupt. What reliance can you place on the word of perjurers, thieves and burglars? Every bit of mud that can be raked up has been produced. I ask you to say that Hammersley is not guilty of the one crime with which he is charged.

*   *   *

Stanley Rees QC for Lyons said his client had come into a mass trial 'with mud and darts flying about all over the place'. He described Mrs Mason as 'a vicious, spiteful, drunken, criminal woman' and Mrs Lawrence as 'an abortionist's mate' but saved his real venom for the Bennetts, saying:

> You must be very careful with Bennett's evidence. It has been said that his story must be true because it could not have been invented, but Bennett's stock in trade is lies. Look out, members of the jury for the Bennetts of this world! This snake was saying at one stage that £20 was paid over to Ridge on the night when Ridge and Lyons were together. Not a word of that came from him in this court. He ran out of that. Just think of the strength of that. Think of the vicious jab it would be if you could be satisfied that £20 was paid over when Ridge and Lyons were together. It would kill them both. He was going about with that story on October 2 last year and then it disappeared.
>
> Members of the jury, if you don't know what sort of man Bennett is by now, there is nothing I can say to help you. I am not dedicated to the proposition that Bennett can never tell the truth, but I am dedicated to the proposition that nobody can tell when he is – least of all him.
>
> I venture to suggest that the ladies amongst you may be the best judges of Mrs Bennett. She was the lady who liked the quiet life and wanted to get home to mother in Norway for quiet little holidays and found it a tremendous burden sitting in the back seat of the Rolls-Royce bathed in Chanel No. 5, given to her by Walker. She also served in 'The Bucket of Blood' and she lived in daily contact with Bennett. If you do not believe Bennett, you do not believe Wenche Bennett.
>
> You are going to see no Bennetts convict anybody. If that is so, that is the end of the case against Lyons. If it comes to a question of whether the guilt of Lyons depends on the evidence of Bennett, waste not a minute in acquitting him. If there is anything left worth a rag, use it by all means but be slow in the case of Lyons lest you do an injustice to the dreadful task placed upon you and I ask for an acquittal.

Victor Durand QC was next and waxed lyrical in his closing speech for Bellson:

> If I had the power and right to preach at you, I could not do any better than take as my text a quotation from the third paragraph of the 53rd page of the 18th book in the address of the Solicitor-General in which he said, referring directly to you, the jury, 'Your answer to this trial will not be based on the

principal that a person with a record can never can never tell the truth and the police can never tell a lie.'

That is particularly apt in dealing with Bellson on the one hand and Sergeant Vibart and Inspector Butler on the other. You would not go very far wrong in applying that text as far as Bellson is concerned and the two police officers. According to the evidence of Inspector Butler and Sergeant Vibart, Bellson told them something that put the noose right round Ridge's neck and right round his own neck. These two Metropolitan Police Officers are probably not telling the truth when they had said that Bellson told them Ridge had sent him to the Leaches to extort money. Their evidence is not to be preferred to that of Bellson's. There might be suspicion but certainty is seriously lacking.

You might think the covering afforded by the large number of people interviewed by police from Scotland Yard was twisted, re-cut, stretched here and there and comes before you in the end as a rather odd-looking garment. It has been described as a cloak of corruption covering these unfortunate policemen in Brighton. A mantle was erected over each of these persons held up by the Chief Constable. Where does Bellson come in? When the hem is lifted up, out pops this tiny little man, Bellson. I suggest to you, if you find it in your hearts to say, 'We do not accept the evidence of the two policemen', that is an end of the case against Bellson.

Lastly, Geoffrey Lawrence QC rose to address the matter of the Chief Constable in his closing speech:

It has been a long case. In the annals of this court, it will be an historic case. All those who have been called upon to play their part in it will live with their consciences for the rest of their lives.

There are two questions in the case against Ridge. The first is, are you satisfied that there ever was one single conspiracy over the years, as the prosecution allege? If you are not satisfied about that, all these defendants are entitled to be acquitted. If you are, the second question is, was Ridge a member of it or has it been proved to your satisfaction that Ridge was a member of that conspiracy? Suspicion or probability is not enough.

You may think that Ridge is a man who, in spite of a life's work in the CID, has retained the instincts of humanity and has paid for it by being criticised. There is a great unbridgeable gulf between the dictates of humanity and the results of corruption.

I submit that Bennett is not only a criminal but a very dangerous criminal. It is on that man's word that you are asked primarily to convict Ridge, who has thirty-four years' service in the Brighton police. The amount of gossip and rumour that went about the clubs and the bars of Brighton that has found its way into the case under the guise of evidence is something you may care to ponder. In a case like this, so far as Ridge is concerned, it would be utterly wrong to brand him with a conviction. You are not sitting there to make Ridge or any of the other defendants a sacrificial victim on the altar of rectitude in public affairs, so to speak, to encourage the others, up and down the country; that would be a shocking thing.

Your decision means for Ridge, on the one hand, the dust and ashes of over thirty years' service in the police force; and in the other hand, the release from a nightmare.

The speeches for the prosecution and the defence – sometimes flowery, often damning, always compelling – were over. Now it was the turn of the Judge's summing-up, the most important for the jury to address.

CHAPTER 32

The Judge's Summing-Up

It was the fourth week of the trial – in 1958, when murder trials might be dealt with in two to three days, this was a long one – and in addressing the jury, Mr Justice Donovan told them:

One must allow for frayed nerves towards the end of a long trial and that, perhaps, might be the reason why the court heard the Solicitor General's closing speech described as a 'sustained vituperation', a comment I cannot endorse. The duty of prosecuting counsel is to be fair and just and temperate and not to be extreme, and I desire to say that in my opinion, that duty has been faithfully performed in this case. You may think that the Solicitor General has been of the greatest help to all of us, as indeed have other counsel, and in my view, the conduct of it has been beyond reproach.

Four of the men in the dock are of exemplary character and you are entitled to take that account in their favour. The court has been told that Heath was an extremely zealous police officer. In one year, there were competitive lists put up to see which detective could make the most arrests in Brighton and he headed the list. You may think it a wholly revolting idea to put up such lists in police stations; I do not know whether they got a prize at the end of the competition. If these championship lists are still put up in police stations, you might think it is time they are taken down or authority in Whitehall should take steps to see they are taken down.

The ordinary criminal is a problem enough to society, but if those who are paid to protect us against them instead join forces with them, then a much more deadly enemy appears on the scene. Because as far as these guardians who turn criminal are concerned, the community's guard is, for the moment, down, and until the difficult task of detection and conviction is accomplished, much harm may be done . . . That is why this case is important, because the charge against Heath and Hammersley and Ridge is that they have betrayed their trust by conspiring against the community to do these criminal things.

Conspiracy is an agreement of mind and not an agreement on paper and it constitutes an offence, even if nothing is done to implement the agreement. You have to decide: was there such a common purpose and was each of the accused persons a party to it? Such a conspiracy is usually uncovered only if one of the conspirators, for one reason or another, comes forward and confesses; so the principal witness or witnesses is almost certain to be someone who is himself in the conspiracy, and therefore that person could be described as an accomplice. I will endorse the warning that it is dangerous to act on the evidence of accomplices unless you find it corroborated by untainted evidence on which you can rely. But if, bearing that warranty in mind, you think that the accomplice is telling the truth, then you might believe him, even if there is no corroboration. This is highly important, for otherwise, if law officers joined with law breakers, how is one going to convict them, if it were going to be said that the evidence against the accused is evidence of an accomplice?

It is oath against oath with one side clearly lying and the question is, which is it? How are you to defeat the lies and ascertain the truth? Since it is oath against oath, very largely you will keep in mind the character of the man Bennett and remember he was an accomplice to the bribing, and so the warning I have given you applies.

The undisputed evidence is that the Astor Club kept open regularly and blatantly after hours. How did Bennett, a man known from May onwards to be an ex-convict, manage to do it? Was it just bad luck on the part of the police or was it something worse? That is where the evidence of Mrs Cherryman assumes such importance when she says that Heath went twice to the club after hours and Lyons, several times. You have to ask yourselves, would a detective sergeant and a local licensee risk being found in such circumstances by the police raiding unless they knew it was quite safe? And how could it be safe in such circumstances unless on the basis that the police would be inactive? If one wanted to describe the episode in one sentence, it is a case of power without plenty, being opposed by money without morals and losing the contest through weakness of will . . .

If you believe Bennett and his wife in their story of Heath asking for 'a whack of the grand', it goes into the scale against Heath, but if you cannot make up your mind with any confidence you should disregard it altogether.

Heath denied receiving the two £5 notes from a man called Swaby, and you might think you cannot accept Swaby's story concerning it. Heath also denied asking him for a 'pony' for leaving out Swaby's last conviction for living on immoral earnings, and here Swaby was corroborated by Detective Constable Hovey, who said he was disgusted. You might ask yourselves – why should Hovey invent this story? Police

Constable Knight alleged that Heath had asked him if he would like to earn £10 a week to let Bellson know when his club was to be raided. Heath denied it. Did Knight invent this conversation? If you think his evidence is not trustworthy, you will dismiss it; if you think he is telling the truth so far as Heath is concerned, you will act upon it. You may well wonder, if his evidence is true, at the sheer brazenness of the suggestion and the frankness, if it was said . . . and wonder if that indicated the sort of conduct which the Solicitor General hinted might have become commonplace in the Brighton CID, at this time . . .

You can dismiss from your minds an allegation that Ridge had received illegal meat. There is no evidence that any of the men in the dock conspired with Ridge over the illegal meat business, even if it happened – and Ridge denied it.

You can also rid yourself of the matter of some coffee which Waite had said he received in 1949 or 1950. This only concerns Hammersley and Waite, and even if Waite's evidence is true, it does not support the charge, nor should any adverse influence be drawn from it against Hammersley.

Heath and Hammersley have both denied that £250 was asked for as the price for disposing of evidence against John Leach on a receiving charge and have said that both John and his father had tried to bribe them. You will first ask yourselves if you accept the story that Leach senior entrusted Bellson with £100 as he has said he did. If you are not satisfied of that first step, you will dismiss the whole matter entirely from your minds. If you reach the conclusion that it was entrusted to Bellson, the next question will be, 'What for?' If you reach the conclusion it was entrusted to Bellson for the police, the last question is, 'Who for?' I remind you of the evidence that when Bellson was subsequently interviewed by two Scotland Yard officers, he said, 'Ridge sent me along.' If – as I think it is probable – you prefer Scotland Yard evidence to Bellson's, you will conclude that Bellson did refer to and name Ridge to the Scotland Yard officers. But the only evidence in support of Ridge's complicity at this stage is Bellson's word to those police officers, and I dare say, having seen Bellson in the witness box, you would not hang a cat on his evidence – let alone a Chief Constable. In law, what Bellson had said to the police officers is not evidence against Ridge because it was something said by Bellson when Ridge was not present. According to Ridge, Bellson never came to him with the first £100 and never at any time did he try to get money out of Leach senior and he simply told Leach senior to see a solicitor and to keep within the law. If you are not satisfied Leach senior sent Bellson off with £100 at all, then you will dismiss this matter from your mind straightaway. If you are satisfied he did, and Bellson went to the police with it ,and are satisfied he did not go to Ridge, then dismiss the matter from your mind. And if you think it is all suspicion and grave doubt, it is also your duty to forget it. But if, after considering all the evidence, the conclusion you come to is that Bellson did go to Ridge with the money, who said it was not enough, and Ridge did go back to the father to give him the opportunity of increasing the offer, then you have evidence implicating Ridge and Bellson in a common design to obstruct justice, because justice requires a due investigation of suspected crimes . . .

The questions for you are: does the evidence show a conspiracy as alleged in the indictment? If not, there is no case against any of the accused. But if the evidence does show such a conspiracy, the second question is: are each of the accused a party to it? It does not matter whether he joined it, soon or late . . .

The Judge's summing-up had taken four hours and twenty-nine minutes, and now the jury filed out of court into the jury room to deliberate on their findings . . .

CHAPTER 33

The Verdicts and Sentences

On Thursday, 27 February 1958, preceded by Mr Leslie Boyd, the Clerk of the Court, and the shorthand writer, the jury returned to Court No. 1 at the Old Bailey, having – initially – taken slightly less time over their deliberations than the Judge had with his summing-up. After nineteen days of evidence, the jury had taken four hours and twenty minutes to partially arrive at a conclusion; they also arrived with a note.

Counsel and solicitors also filed into court, and amongst them was Sir Theobald Mathew KBE, MC. Now aged fifty-nine, Sir Theobald had been Director of Public Prosecutions since 1944, and as he had authorized the enquiry he certainly had a vested interest in its outcome. It was now 7.28pm.

Mr Justice Donovan entered the court and Mr Boyd had a quiet word with him. Turning to the jury, the Judge said:

> I am obliged to you for your note. I have to bring you back into court because that is the procedure. These questions are asked and answered in open court. The note I have is: 'The jury are agreed on three of the accused and disagree on two. May we have guidance, please? We are agreed on Heath, Hammersley and Lyons, and we are disagreed on Bellson and Ridge. Can Police Constable Knight's evidence and Barnard's evidence be accepted against Bellson? Can we have a transcript of the summing-up against Ridge?'

'If you are agreed on three', remarked the Judge, 'it would be better to take that verdict as regards those three.'

Holding the indictment, the Clerk of the Court asked the jury foreman, 'Do you find Heath guilty or not guilty?'

'Guilty', was the reply.

'Do you find Hammersley guilty or not guilty?'

'Guilty.'

'Do you find Lyons guilty or not guilty?'

'Not guilty.'

'Heath and Hammersley will be taken below and Lyons discharged', ordered the Judge, and whilst the first two showed no emotion, Lyons was pale and shaking and appeared on the point of collapse.

The jury were then told that they could accept the evidence against Bellson, and he was duly found guilty.

Once more the jury left, to consider Ridge's fate; it was now 7.35pm. One hour and ten minutes later, they rang the bell to inform the usher that they had reached a verdict.

'Are you agreed upon your verdict?' asked the Clerk of the Court, to be told, 'We are. We find Ridge not guilty.' There was a long drawn-out cry of, 'O-h-h-h!' in court.

Bowing to the Judge, Ridge said, 'Thank you, my Lord', and at the foot of the dock steps he was handed his hat and coat by the dock warder; in a most un-Chief Constable-like display of emotion, Ridge flung his arms around him and kissed him on the cheek.

Thereafter he appeared to be in shock; outside the court, his face covered in perspiration, he appeared not to comprehend the questions or the congratulations shouted to him and was unable to find his car.

Mind you, there were quite a number of others who were bemused by the verdict, possibly for the same reasons as Ridge.

His wife, who for some time had suffered from heart trouble, was confined to her bed at the Ridges' detached home at Burntleigh, Bavant Road, Brighton. Upon hearing the news, a neighbour reported that Mrs Ridge 'had always been confident'.

Hammersley's wife Vera had been stoic throughout the trial, saying, 'My place is here with my son', although when the verdict was announced, she sobbed, 'What can I say?'

Gina Heath, the wife of a convicted man, had nothing to say.

Although Ridge and Lyons had been acquitted, there still remained other indictments in which they (as well as the convicted men) featured. The two acquitted men were therefore released on bail.

The following day, 28 February, the three convicted men appeared for sentencing. Superintendent Forbes-Leith was able to tell the court that both Heath and Hammersley had excellent characters and he mentioned Bellson's numerous convictions for betting and gaming as well as his two previous sentences of hard labour.

Pleas for mitigation were made by the convicted men's barristers, Edward Clarke suggesting that 'there were many people outside the dock who probably knew as much about the case as those inside the dock' and asking that the sentence on Heath should be 'as merciful as well as just'. Mr McIntyre believed that there was no large-scale gain for Hammersley, saying, 'If ever there was a case where a man threw his whole career away for a whole mess of pottage, it is this', whereas Victor Durand stated that Bellson's participation had lasted only two or three days at most and that his client 'did not bestir himself about the matter very much'.

Mr Justice Donovan had not been enamoured of Bellson at all, something that he had made plain in his summing-up. His disgust with the bookmaker was plain to see and hear when he sentenced him in just ten words: 'You, Bellson, the sentence is three years' imprisonment – get below.'

The two former detectives were sentenced together:

> I now have a duty to perform which I would rather have been spared because I know your punishment does not end here, and that there are others who are going to suffer as much as you. I am going to take into account all that has been urged on your behalf. I am not going to prolong your ordeal, but this also has to be said – and it is not based on disputed evidence but on facts admitted in the course of this trial – those facts establish that neither of you had that professional and moral leadership which both of you should have had, and were entitled to expect from the Chief Constable of Brighton, now acquitted. That he had contrived, as he did, to go to a suspected briber of police in private and alone, it is small wonder that you, Heath, followed that example in the case of Mrs Brabiner. And if he could admit – as he did – to his private room a much convicted and hectoring bookmaker and there discuss with him, almost as a colleague, the policy of the police in certain matters, then it is small wonder that you, Hammersley, saw little or no wrong in going off on holiday with a local man with a serious criminal record.
>
> Reflecting on that, just as much as I have been reflecting on other matters since urged on me, I have reached the conclusion that the sentences which I originally felt would be my duty to put on you, can properly be reduced, and accordingly I sentence each of you to imprisonment for a term of five years.

The two white-faced officers were led off to a prison van to commence their sentences at Wormwood Scrubs; their counsel asked the Judge for certificates to appeal, which were refused.

The Judge thanked the jury for their duty, then turned to the police officers in the case; tribute was paid to Superintendent Forbes-Leith and his officers for their work, which had been carried on with 'efficiency and integrity'; and to Superintendent Moody and the British Transport Commission Police for 'their defeat of the discreditable obstruction which, I regret to say, they encountered at the hands of certain members of the Brighton CID, in the matter of the £15,000 theft of cigarettes'.

Lastly, the Judge said, 'I also desire to say a word of praise in favour of Detective Constable Hovey and Police Constables Knight and Tullett of the Brighton police for the integrity they showed in coming forward and giving evidence here.'

With that, the court rose for the day; but that was not quite the end of the matter.

*   *   *

On 6 March 1958, both Ridge and Lyons stood once more in the dock at the Old Bailey before a jury and Mr Justice Donovan. There were further indictments against them: Lyons was accused of inciting Alan Roy Bennett to give a reward to Ridge for showing favour and also inciting a woman named Gwladys May Lawrence to give a reward to Heath for showing favour, and Ridge was accused of corruptly obtaining a gift from Bennett for showing favour. To these indictments, both men pleaded not guilty.

The Solicitor General told the Judge that after consultation with the Director of Public Prosecutions it was felt that the evidence to put before a jury in these matters was substantially the same as that given in the previous trial, and therefore he offered no evidence; and since similar charges of showing favour existed in respect of the three imprisoned defendants, they should remain on the file, not to be proceeded with without leave of the court or the Court of Appeal (Criminal Division).

The Judge agreed, and after the jury had delivered their formal verdicts of not guilty, Mr Justice Donovan gave one of his withering looks at the two men in the dock and told them, 'You are discharged.'

But as they left the dock, Mr Justice Donovan spoke of certain incidents mentioned in the case and of unfortunate results which might occur, saying:

> This prospect and this risk will remain until a leader is given to that force who will be a new influence and who will set a different example from that which has lately obtained. I realize that this is a matter which is about to engage the attention of those persons whose responsibility it is, and I have no desire to trespass upon their domain, but since the matter will also affect the administration of justice in the courts, I felt it right to make these observations.

And those stinging words were passed straight on to Brighton's Town Hall and the Watch Committee; they would lead to far-reaching consequences for police forces throughout England and Wales.

PART II

LEAVING

'You may give him good advice, but who can give him the wit to take it?'

Thomas Fuller (1608–1661)

CHAPTER 34

The Aftermath

Brighton's Town Clerk, Mr W.O. Dodd, confirmed on 2 March 1958 that he had received an application from Ridge for his reinstatement as Chief Constable; this had arrived, rather cheekily, while Ridge was still on bail in respect of the outstanding indictments.

But the day following Ridge's second official acquittal, Councillor George Bernard Baldwin and eleven members of the Watch Committee decided that Ridge had been 'negligent in the discharge of his duties and was unfit for the same', and he was dismissed. The aggregate amount of his pension contributions would be repaid to him.

There was talk of appointing a new Chief Constable to replace the temporary one, Albert Rowsell, but in the event it was Rowsell who became permanent on 11 July 1958, and he remained in the post until 1963.

On 18 March 1958, Ridge appealed against the committee's decision, saying it was unlawful; the appeal was rejected. Next, the Home Office rejected Ridge's appeal, and the Attorney General refused leave to appeal to the House of Lords.

However, in April 1961, the case was heard at the Queen's Bench Division at the High Court of Justice with Mr Justice Streatfeild presiding. After a seven-day hearing, on 19 April judgement was given against Ridge; his solicitors immediately appealed.

The matter was heard at the Court of Appeal on 22 January 1962 before Lord Justice Holroyd-Pearce, Lord Justice Harman and Lord Justice Davies. Eight days later, the appeal was dismissed.

The Appeal Committee of the House of Lords granted Ridge leave to appeal against the decision of the Court of Appeal on 7 March 1962.

A year went by. On 14 March 1963, the House of Lords allowed – by a majority – Ridge's appeal. On 24 July 1963, the Divisional Court granted an application that the order of the House of Lords in Ridge v Baldwin should be remitted to the Queen's Bench Division to make an order that Ridge had succeeded in his action against the Brighton Watch Committee. It had been held that the committee had not informed Ridge of the charges he was to face before them, nor had he been invited to attend the disciplinary proceedings.

At the Queen's Bench Division on 29 July 1963, Mr Justice Mocatta made an order disposing of the action. With that, Ridge gave notice of his resignation, and the Judge granted an application that he be repaid his salary of £6,424 6s 8d over the period of his suspension, that he be paid his pension as from 1 August 1963 and that all the costs of the case be paid by Brighton Watch Committee.

This had taken over five years. His solicitors, Bosley & Co. of Brighton, were now very well off. Ridge, who was now sixty-four years of age, disappeared from view; he died a month before his seventy-ninth birthday in Newtown, Powys, some 65 miles from the place of his birth.

* * *

In fact, Ridge was not the first Chief Constable to stand trial for dishonesty; as long ago as December 1894, the Chief Constable of Bradford, Philip John Woodman, appeared at Bradford Police Court and, after admitting embezzling over £200 during the period of a year, was sentenced to five months' imprisonment. The most surprising aspect of this case was that it attracted no more than a few lines in the national press.

But hot on the heels of Ridge's acquittal came news of the court appearance of the Chief Constable of Worcester, Glyn Davies, accused of fraudulently converting £1,147 from his force.

'I'm carrying the can for somebody else', he told the investigating officer and pointed the finger of blame at the force's previous Chief Constable, but he wasn't believed and in May 1958 at Worcester Assizes he was sent down for eighteen months and forfeited his pension.

If it wasn't quite open season on erring Chief Constables, Her Majesty's Inspectorate was certainly viewing allegations of misconduct with a more jaundiced eye.

When William McConnach MBE, who had been the Chief Constable of Southend-on-Sea since 1953, claimed expenses for his daughter's twenty-first birthday party (which was held at police headquarters) he was found guilty of seventeen charges of fraud and false pretences, jailed for two years in November 1966 – and lost his pension.

Stanley Parr CBE, QPM, Blackpool's Chief Constable, was somewhat more fortunate than his fellow Chief Constables, inasmuch as he did not stand trial. Nevertheless, he was accused of twenty-four cases of breaches of discipline which included showing favours, improper use of police vehicles and falsification of records. In 1977 he offered his resignation, but it was not accepted and he was sacked instead.

* * *

Something was quite clearly wrong with the relationships between the Chief Constables and the watch committees of various boroughs. Brighton had, of course, kicked the whole matter off, but following that smarting rebuke from Mr Justice Donovan they fought back, saying they could not properly supervise the force since they had no access to the annual report of Her Majesty's Inspectorate of Constabulary, which was sent direct to the Home Secretary.

But before the glowing embers from Brighton could cool, just one year later came the matter of the Chief Constable of Nottingham City Police, Captain Athelstan Horn Popkess CBE, who in 1930, aged just thirty-seven, was the youngest Chief Constable ever to be appointed.

Apart from his rather unusual name, the future Chief Constable exhibited some odd behaviour as well, as was evidenced in 1936, when as a member of the Auxiliary Division of the Royal Irish Constabulary (as well as having been an officer in army intelligence, he had also been a member of the infamous Black and Tans), he was seen to be giving a Nazi salute at a boxing ring in Stuttgart. Precisely what he was doing in Nazi Germany, six years into his Chief Constableship, as an auxiliary member of another police force, is rather difficult to comprehend; nevertheless, back in Nottingham City during his reign of almost thirty years he was a pretty innovative Chief Constable.

He opened an advanced driving school, introduced traffic wardens and promoted wireless communications with his fleet of cars and motorcycles. He also introduced police dogs into the force and opened a forensic science laboratory. But he came rather unstuck when, in 1959, he clashed with the city's Watch Committee. There were certain members of the city council who had come under scrutiny for corruption and financial irregularities; they were also members of the Watch Committee. His enquiries complete, Popkess refused – quite justifiably – to hand over his findings to the Watch Committee, who promptly suspended him. However, details of this investigation were mysteriously leaked to the press on the eve of the municipal elections. The Home Secretary of the day, Richard Austin ('Rab') Butler KG, CH, PC, DL, stepped in and saw Popkess reinstated in 1960, after threatening to withdraw central government funding – to the surprise of many, given Butler's views on appeasement, both prior to the Second World War and in the Suez crisis. Nevertheless, Popkess resigned the same year.

★   ★   ★

What was needed was a Royal Commission – and this was much to the liking of the Home Office. They had wanted borough police forces to come under their control for the past hundred years, but the attempt to pass a police bill in 1854 failed after it was defeated by the boroughs, although the Police (Counties and Boroughs) Bill 1856 did come into force the following year, after the Home Office agreed to pay a quarter of the boroughs' policing running costs. However, it was stipulated that those forces would now be subject to the eyes and ears of Her Majesty's Inspectors of Constabulary, thereby giving the Home Office feedback on how their money was being spent. By 1900 the nation's 46,800 police officers were employed by 243 different forces, but some inspired pruning was already underway.

So the 1960 commission was set up, chaired by Sir Henry Urmston Willink QC, MC, PC, JP, and during the following two years it held ninety-five meetings as well as conducting an overview of the 90,000 police personnel, who cost the exchequer £150 million annually. They noted that of the current 158 forces in Great Britain, 97 had an establishment of fewer than 350.

Eventually, the commission made 111 recommendations, including the Home Office's setting up of a Research and Planning Department (of which Ernie Millen became the unit's detective chief superintendent in January 1960); new authorities were to be established, known as Police Committees, and were to consist of two-thirds elected members and one-third magistrates; whilst the Chief Constable was to submit an annual report to the police authority, who were required to maintain an efficient police force, they had no operational role; the Home Secretary would take on more supervision than previously.

However, the police authorities would be empowered to choose Chief Constables, deputy and assistant Chief Constables – but only from a Home Office shortlist. The Home Office also stipulated that only an officer who had served in another police force would be selected for appointment as a Chief Constable. Police authorities were allowed to require a Chief Constable to retire – but again, only with the Home Secretary's approval.

Amalgamation was the key word; and if the local authorities refused to agree to a voluntary scheme, the Home Secretary would use his authority to enforce a compulsory unification.

Over the next few years, the number of police forces in England and Wales, which had already been chipped away, shrank from 117 to 49. Brighton Borough Police Force was no more. It was subsumed, together with the borough forces of Eastbourne and Hastings and the larger East and West Sussex Constabularies, into what would eventually become, in 1968, Sussex Police, based at Lewes.

CHAPTER 35

Page's Downfall

Bellson, Heath and Hammersley did not fare so well as
Ridge. They had appealed against conviction and sentence,
appeals which were dismissed on 14 May 1958; their
application to the Attorney General to appeal to the House of
Lords was refused on 6 June 1958. Bellson served his sentence
in Pentonville. He had previously been known as 'The Guv'nor
of Brighton', and there was no doubt that he was a powerful and
a rich man; when Albert Dimes was charged with stabbing rival
gang leader Jack Spot, Bellson immediately coughed up £500
for Dimes' defence. He had originally been a supporter of Spot,
but now it was Billy Hill's star which was in the ascendant, and
Hill was backing Albert Dimes. But whilst serving his sentence
Bellson wrote some unwise pieces in one of the Sunday tabloids
and, what's more, he was regarded as a grass because of what he
had said to Vibart and Butler (which had been widely recounted
in the press). He was now *persona non grata* to the criminal
fraternity of Brighton and he returned to London, 'The Guv'nor'
no more. He died on 8 March 2002, aged eighty-six, and was
cremated at Barnet, North London, five days later.

Anthony John Lyons had suffered poor health before, during
and after the trial. He died on 18 October 1961, aged sixty-three,
in the Rayland Nursing Home, 54 Marine Parade, just half a mile
from his flat in Marine Gate. Probate was dealt with by his friend
and surety, Solomon Rubenstein; Lyons' estate amounted to
£730 3s 3d.

As for Hammersley and Heath, following their release
from prison they teamed up once more to become painters
and decorators in the Brighton area; both died a few years ago,
Hammersley in Brighton in 1996 and Heath, ten years after that,
in Teignmouth, Devon.

★ ★ ★

The image of Brighton had taken a mauling, there was no doubt
about that.

The author and historian David Rowland joined Brighton police in June 1958, just a few months after the ending of the trial, but as he told me:

> Even then, I was targeted by the yobs as being one of the bent Brighton coppers. Even at training school, the inspector, the orderly officer, after calling out my name and force made a comment about Brighton having 'bent coppers'. I was furious, but could do little about the comment.

This was inevitable. Some thirty years before, following Wensley's investigation of the Met's major corruption scandal of 1928, tearaways on the streets of Whitechapel, seeing a police officer strolling by would, with great daring, call out 'Goddard!' This happened to Detective Constable Beveridge (later Detective Chief Superintendent Peter Henderson Beveridge MBE), who could be relied upon to memorize the offender's face; and later, when he was alone, he would take the opportunity to quietly 'speak' to the malefactor, usually within the confines of an alleyway. The practice of mocking officers ceased rapidly.

Although Edward Clarke QC had said in mitigation for Heath that he had been convicted of obstructing justice and not of bribery and corruption, there was no doubt in the public's mind as to exactly what had been going on. All the salacious details of the case had not merely been published nationwide, they had gone global, with seedy stories of what had gone on in 'The Bucket of Blood'. Three years later, when Ian Fleming wrote *Thunderball*, his creation James Bond made reference to that establishment; the name was still in the public domain. To a town dependent on its tourist trade it had done immeasurable harm.

Graham Greene's best-selling novel *Brighton Rock* had been published twenty years earlier, but when John Boulting's film was released ten years later, even though Richard Attenborough's portrayal of murderous gang boss 'Pinkie' Brown was as terrifying as Larry Grayson, the violence of the film was still associated with that seaside town. So when the *Daily Herald* published a piece about Brighton on 2 March 1958 which referred to it as 'Little Chicago-on-Sea' that, thought the town council, was the last straw.

Hadn't the witness Betty Lawrence been attacked by gang members and been told that if she gave evidence her tongue would be cut out and she'd 'be chopped into little bits'? She certainly had; commonplace, perhaps, in Chicago, Illinois but not in Brighton, Sussex.

And what about the club that was burnt to the ground? What was the name of the owner? Pagey? 'Bookie' Page? William Page, yes, that was it. And hadn't his club risen phoenix-like from the ashes – and wasn't it illegally flourishing once more? That sort of thing might happen with impunity in East Side, Chicago; it would not be tolerated in Castle Street, Brighton.

Action was needed to redress the balance – to show that law and order was working – and in 'Bookie' Page the council had the perfect target.

★   ★   ★

Two days after the *Daily Herald*'s upsetting headline, a police raid at Page's Castle Club, using a warrant under the Betting Act, discovered a television screen plus a 'blower' connected to the racecourses and a blackboard with runners chalked up on it; in a back room, 246 cash betting slips were found. Appearing at Brighton Magistrates' Court charged with using the premises for illegal betting on 6 March, Henry Warner pleaded guilty, telling the Magistrates, 'After Mr Page gave evidence at the police trial he decided to give it up. I took it over, but he stipulated that I ran it legally. I have attempted to do so.'

Warner, who had been fined on three occasions since 1956 for assisting Page, was fined £75. Stanley Allan Hawkins was fined £25 for assisting Warner, and eleven other men and two women were bound over for frequenting the premises.

Page pleaded not guilty, but the police decided he was not going to slip through the net; on 27 March he was fined £25. Just to give the impression that Page was not being personally victimized, an illegal betting shop in Russell Square, Brighton was also raided – on 21 March the two organizers were fined and twenty-eight frequenters of the premises were bound over.

But it was Page – who of course had not given up the betting game at all – whom the police had in their sights.

On 28 May, his premises were raided again, and the following day, he made this astonishing announcement to the Bench at Brighton Magistrates' Court:

> I need not be here today. Half an hour before the police came to my office at Brighton, a man ran in and said, 'You're going to be raided.' I could have closed up then but I made up my mind to see this through. Everybody is in favour of legalised betting but the police have to enforce this ridiculous law. It's only natural for Englishmen to have a gamble. It is their right.

This self-important rant was par for Page's course, but he had not quite finished. Paying his £100 fine by cheque, he indignantly informed the bemused Bench, 'This is £1,200 you've had from me.'

Walter Henry Lock was fined £5 for being Page's look-out – with the anonymous helper warning Page of the police's intentions, Lock was probably made redundant thereafter – and thirty people in the premises were bound over.

Page was now fifty-four years of age, and one might have thought that he had come to the conclusion that it could be beneficial to keep his big trap shut; but he hadn't.

On 30 July, he was one of twenty-three people who were nabbed at his Castle Road office; the 'blower' system was operating, and a blackboard gave details of the Goodwood runners. Eighty-eight betting slips for the next race were found, together with eighty-seven for the previous races; £58 was found in the office till.

The following day, if the Bench at Brighton Magistrates' Court were expecting another egotistical Page-style speech, they were not disappointed:

> These betting laws are ridiculous. You've heard all about the blackboards and the blower system. There are at least seventeen other bookmakers in Brighton with the same service. I cannot ask, but you gentlemen can – why is it that it is always me who is raided and not the others?

And that, the Bench decided, was quite enough from Bookie Page; he was sentenced to three months' imprisonment.

Page immediately appealed and was released on bail; he went straight to his club and handed it over to another man, saying, 'Any fucker can have this place. It's nothing to do with me anymore; I've finished with it.'

The 'fucker' in question was Herbert Beresford, and on 1 August, the day following Page's generous offer, the club was raided just as bets were being placed on the second race at Goodwood. The following day at court, Beresford was fined £20 and the twenty-one punters who accompanied him were bound over. That raid occurred on the morning of 1 August; in the afternoon, the Bristol Road premises of Nathan Mercado – 'Sid Ki-Ki' to his admirers – was also raided. He was found to be in possession of 262 betting slips from 1,255 bets, and he and twenty-eight others wended their way to the Magistrates' Court.

It looked like the police's no-nonsense policy was paying off. A reporter for the *Daily Herald* reported that 'Brash, brassy, breezy

Brighton, rogue town of Britain . . . has gone respectable', under the banner headline, 'It's "Hove Sweet Hove" for the Bookies'.

Chief Constable Rowsell told the reporter, 'When I came here, the task was a very interesting one. Illegal bookmaking? I'm merely carrying out the law.'

Brighton's betting offices were shutting up – and staying shut. The illegal operations were indeed being shifted sideways to the town of Hove, and county councillors and the chairman of the Hove Watch Committee were shocked and furious. In late August, some thirty people had appeared in the local court, and the solicitor appearing for some of the defendants was caustic in his remarks, referring to Brighton's 'sink of iniquity', claiming that Hove police appeared to be instigating a witch hunt and blaming not only the *Daily Herald* but also Sammy Bellson's inflammatory tabloid articles, penned from his Pentonville cell.

And what of Page? He appeared before the Appeals Committee of the Brighton Quarter Sessions on 24 September 1958, when his three-month sentence was varied to one month's imprisonment, he was fined £50 with 25 guineas costs and was bound over to be of good behaviour for a period of two years in his own recognizance of £25. He was also ordered to provide two sureties of £25 each; in default of finding those sureties, he would serve a further two months' imprisonment.

'If he comes here again for this type of offence', said the Recorder, Mr Charles Doughty QC, MP (who had been informed that Page had been convicted of gambling offences on six occasions since 1955), 'the sentence shall be a heavy one.'

And uncharacteristically Pagey, for once, had nothing to say.

★ ★ ★

It would be easy to suggest that, given the disgraceful practices that had gone unchecked for years at Brighton, the whole of the CID office was bent; but it would not be true. There were honest, hard-working officers in that office who diligently pursued investigations which they presented to their senior officers – but often they would hear no more about them. If they did enquire about progress in these cases they were simply told that the details were being collated; they were part of a much bigger job, and when it came to fruition, a huge gang would be rounded up and they, the officers who had first acquired that information, would be part of the arresting team and would receive full credit for their endeavours. Remember, that was precisely the sort of excuse that Hammersley had tried to fob off Moody with: 'Forget about the cigarettes worth £15,000; a bigger consignment will be coming soon and we can nick everyone involved.'

It may seem illogical to the reader that this could go on; but it was true, and to understand why, it is necessary to appreciate the parochial mentality that pervaded provincial police forces at that time. A detective sergeant was the captain of a detective constable's fate – what he said went; and a detective superintendent was so high up the promotional ladder that few of the lowly ranks dared look at, let alone speak to him. Recall Detective Constable Hovey's words at the trial as to why he had not reported Heath's attempts at extortion: 'I didn't, sir, because I thought to do so might have had unpleasant effects on my career . . . I knew that Mr Ridge held Sergeant Heath in very high esteem as a CID officer.'

The position can best be summed up in the words of the late Frank Wensley, an easy-going East End Metropolitan detective sergeant, who in the early 1970s visited a provincial police force to make enquiries and was introduced to a Detective Constable Jones with whom he was going to liaise:

> I shook hands with him and said, 'Hello, mate – call me Frank.' At that moment, a door at the end of the office opened, a bloke came out and shouted, 'Jones! My office! N-O-O-O-W!' and Jones flew off down the corridor. A bit later, he came back all pale and trembling. I said, 'Fuck me, who was that – the Chief Constable?' 'No, said Jones. 'That was my sergeant!'

★ ★ ★

Early in 1959, Mr W.T. Cavey relinquished the post of detective superintendent; he later succeeded Rowsell as Chief Constable and went on to become Chief Constable Cavey OBE, QPM of Cumbria Police.

For the first time the vacancy for a replacement detective superintendent was nationally advertised and it went to Barnsley-based 43-year-old Detective Inspector John James Marshall. Like his predecessor he jumped two ranks, and during the next seventeen years he was promoted to Detective Chief Superintendent, was appointed MBE and was awarded the Queen's Police Medal.

There was little doubt that the morale of Brighton Police improved during Marshall and Rowsell's tenure, the latter increasing the force's personnel from 286 to 328.

The honest cops who gave evidence at the trial, Police Constables Tullett and Knight, were commended by the Watch Committee, the latter being promoted to sergeant and spending his service in and out of the CID. Detective Constable Ray Hovey (similarly commended) was promoted to detective sergeant and spent his whole career in the CID.

It is perhaps surprising that none of those three officers were ever vilified by their contemporaries for sticking their heads above the parapet and having the courage to speak out against the crooked cops, because this is what happened in so many cases in other forces. In the City of London during the 1970s and 80s, when – to my mind – far more serious offences of corrupt practice occurred, including permitting bail to a gang who had carried out a series of armed robberies totalling £597,000 and had murdered a security guard, and culminating in offering no evidence against them at court. Police officers who spoke out against the seriously crooked cops concerned were – in the most benign cases – sent to Coventry. But others were hounded mercilessly, with threats (both written and vocal) against them and their families; some were transferred elsewhere, and one committed suicide. And when – in the middle of these investigations – another half-dozen police officers were caught and sent to prison for ransacking a burgled shop, the wave of sympathy for them from their colleagues was overwhelming. Some were regarded as being 'in the wrong place at the wrong time', others were hailed as heroes and, their prison sentences over, many were welcomed back into the embracing fold of freemasonry.

But no such disgraceful behaviour was ever shown to Hovey, Knight or Tullett. Although Tullett was regarded as being 'a bit on the serious side', not so Hovey or Knight, who were said to be 'the life and soul of the party'. 'I worked with Frankie Knight', David Rowland told me. 'A lovely guy, he was my sergeant in the communications room. There were never any bad feelings aimed at Hovey or Knight. They were two of the most popular coppers in the job.'

Perhaps Brighton Borough Police, one-third the size of their 830 City of London counterparts, were relieved to be rid of their rotten apples and not afraid to say so.

Following retirement, Hovey was employed as head of security at Brighton's Co-operative Store, and later, Rowland worked with him.

The year after the trial, Superintendent Edwin Moody retired from his post at Liverpool Street Station after thirty-seven years of varied and distinguished service; sadly, his retirement lasted a bare fifteen months, and he died at home in Perth.

And the Scotland Yard officers returned to London, where
with the exception of the higher ranks, Hatherill, Forbes-Leith,
Millen and Radford, the rest were further commended by the
commissioner and the Director of Public Prosecutions for 'valuable
assistance in a complicated and difficult case of conspiracy to
pervert the course of justice' – but although we can leave the
Brighton Borough police in safer hands than before, this was not
the end of the story for several of the Yard officers . . .

CHAPTER 36

Some Went on to Greater Heights ...

Let's begin with Ernie Bond, who accompanied Millen on the Rose enquiry. Just prior to the Chief Constable's trial, Bond was posted to the Flying Squad; it was the first of two such postings which would last for four years. He rose steadily through the ranks until, twenty-five years after the Rose enquiry, he was appointed Deputy Assistant Commissioner, 'C' Department (Operations), awarded the Queen's Police Medal and appointed OBE. He was hugely admired by the rank and file. His incorruptibility was never in question; when Wally Virgo, the venal Commander of C1 Department, first came under suspicion, the correspondence from C1's Serious Crime Squad was leapfrogged over Virgo, to land smartly on Ernie Bond's desk, its secrets intact. His retirement ('after thirty years, to the day!' as he told me) left an enormous gap, filled by one of Robert Mark's myrmidons.

William Brereton returned to the Flying Squad and was later promoted to detective superintendent, before enjoying a long retirement. Bill Baldock similarly returned to the Squad, where he served for five years, displaying great expertise in dog-doping cases. He was promoted and returned to the Squad in 1962 as a detective chief inspector for a brief fifteen months; promotion claimed him again, to detective superintendent, and when he retired after thirty years' service he took with him nineteen commissioner's commendations. They had been earned at the sharp end of policing: the arrests of criminals described as 'violent' and 'dangerous' and of those who conspired or participated in armed robbery.

Next, the Terrible Twins; Vibart first.

Within a few months from the conclusion of the Brighton trial, he completed his ten-year tenure with the Flying Squad when he was promoted to detective inspector and posted to 'W' Division, but not before being commended in a case of office-breaking and then being highly commended by the commissioner for outstanding courage in tackling a gunman. That was the repellent Ronald Easterbrook, who had shot a police officer in the face whilst fleeing the scene of a burglary. When Vibart burst into his hotel room, Easterbrook had unwisely tried to reach for a firearm;

Vibart broke his jaw so badly that Easterbrook's enunciation suffered considerably during his denials at the Old Bailey, but he was convicted and Vibart was awarded £15 from the Bow Street Reward Fund and the Queen's Commendation for Brave Conduct.

Butler had also been promoted to detective chief inspector, and he left the Squad a month earlier than his twin to go to 'F' Division, but not for long – within a few months, both were sent to the British Police Unit, Cyprus to advise the authorities on their fight against the EOKA terrorists. Before they even arrived on the island, the terrorists' spokesperson claimed, 'We will kill them as soon as they land' – but the duo managed to fulfil their obligations unscathed before returning to their natural habitat, and the following year, Vibart was highly commended once more for the arrest of a man wanted for the fatal shooting of a police officer.

In March 1960, Vibart assisted in forming what would become C11 (Criminal Intelligence Department) and was promoted to detective chief inspector, while Tommy Butler, promoted to detective superintendent, was back on the Flying Squad.

One month after the Great Train Robbery, Butler was promoted to detective chief superintendent and took charge of the investigation; he also pulled his old chum Vibart from the wilds of 'V' Division to assist him.

The success of the train robbery investigation brought Butler worldwide fame; everybody knew who he was. He was appointed MBE and retired in 1970. Vibart had been promoted to detective superintendent and awarded the Queen's Police Medal for distinguished conduct; he retired one year before his twin.

Neither officer escaped criticism from their contemporaries. Butler was said to be excessively (if not obsessively) secretive, playing his cards very close to his chest. Vibart could be irascible and was said to be a glory-hunter who was all too fond of dishing out physical punishment. One former officer described him to me as being 'an over-promoted, ignorant bully'. There may have been valid criticisms of both men, but the fact remained that while 'The Twins' served on the Flying Squad they were unstoppable, and the scum of the underworld were understandably terrified of them.

* * *

Millen had spent little time as a chief inspector with the Flying Squad; at the end of 1958, he was promoted detective superintendent and as a member of the Murder Squad he investigated one murder after another. Within three years he was promoted to detective chief superintendent to become head of the Flying Squad, and during his two-year stay the Squad's personnel increased by 25 per cent, as did the arrest rate and the recovery of stolen property.

Millen and Hatherill clashed with Tommy Butler when they publicized photographs of the men wanted for the Great Train Robbery, with Butler saying (quite rightly) that this would drive the wanted men underground; he believed (almost certainly correctly) that he would have arrested them sooner through using his informants. However, Butler took over the running of the Squad when Millen was promoted to Deputy Commander, and when Millen retired in 1969 with the rank of Deputy Assistant Commissioner he had served for just short of thirty-five years and had been awarded the CBE.

Perhaps surprisingly, Hatherill never advanced beyond the rank of commander; it was a position he held for ten years, and he retired after an astonishing forty-four years' service, his OBE having been advanced to a CBE. Perhaps even more surprisingly, his retirement lasted twenty-two years.

... and Others Didn't

Next we come to Dick Radford, and what follows also involves George Hatherill once more, as well as, oddly, the Assistant Commissioner Richard Jackson.

It all began some eighteen months after the conclusion of the Brighton conspiracy case. Three youths – Patrick Albert Tisdall, Thomas Alfred Kingston and Sidney Hill-Burton – were stopped at 11.00pm on 5 August 1959 at Finsbury Park, North London by three aids to CID, Police Constables Tonge, Walden and Taylor. At Hornsey police station the youths were charged with possession of offensive weapons – two open razors and a cosh – a charge which all three vehemently denied, alleging the items had been planted on them; Kingston and Tisdall further complained that they had been struck by the officers, and Hill-Burton stated that he had been threatened.

They sought the advice of the solicitor David Napley, who conducted a spirited defence for them at Tottenham Magistrates' Court on 10 August; nevertheless, they were all convicted and fined £10 each.

Napley would later say:

> If they were guilty they should have had a far more severe penalty for possessing such dangerous and unpleasant weapons in a public place for an unlawful purpose. If the magistrates had doubts, but did not want to express them against the police and imposed a light penalty accordingly, it was indefensible.[1]

Despite legal advice not to do so, the three youths appealed to the Appeals Committee at the Middlesex Quarter Sessions, and on 4 November 1959 the matter was heard before the Chairman,

---

1 This, not to put too fine a point on those comments, is bollocks. The author once arrested a youth brandishing a leather belt studded with metal that weighed more than a pound, which he tried to smash into the arresting officer's face. He pleaded guilty and was fined £5. The weakness of sentencing has everything to do with the woolly-minded lay magistrates who deal with the case and nothing to do with the severity of the crime.

Mr Ewen Montagu QC. The prosecution additionally called other officers present at the time in the police station: Inspector Ward, Sergeant Cottam, Detective Sergeant Bolongaro and Detective Constables Rust and Anderson. The Chairman not only dismissed the appeals but varied the youths' sentences to 28 days' imprisonment each.

Napley was convinced of his clients' innocence and on 25 November he wrote to the Home Secretary asking for a public enquiry; by now, his clients had completed their sentences. Ten days later, the Home Secretary forwarded Napley's letter to the Commissioner requesting an enquiry; in turn, the file was forwarded to No. 2 Area Headquarters, where a uniformed officer, Chief Superintendent Fieldsend, appointed Dick Radford (by now a detective superintendent) to investigate the matter.

Radford was an officer whom Napley had known for some time, particularly when he was a detective sergeant at King's Cross, and he gave this patronizing opinion of him: 'I had never had a quarrel with him and regarded him as a congenial if not over-intelligent policeman.'

No transcript of the appeal proceedings was obtained, and Radford did not read the record of the young men given to the magistrates. He did not examine any of the records held at the station, nor did he interview the three accused. He limited himself to answering each allegation made by Napley in his letter of complaint.

It was a sloppy investigation, and Fieldsend was dissatisfied with Radford's report, saying that it gave the impression he had not approached the matter with an open mind and that it contained irrelevant matters; he therefore ordered him to carry out further enquiries.

But while this was going on, Fieldsend examined the contemporary records at Hornsey police station. When the young men were arrested they had been conveyed to the police station in two cars. In one of them was a man whom PC Walden had referred to as 'a prisoner' at the Magistrates' Court. This man was Robert Sidney Watts and he was being conveyed to the station in respect of ownership of some watches to be interviewed by DS Bolongaro – but no record of Watts' detention could be found. In fact, Bolongaro would later say that Watts had been interviewed as an informant – hence the lack of any record of him being at the station.

Fieldsend immediately came to the conclusion that something was being suppressed by the officers, and on 15 January 1960 he took possession not only of all the contemporary documents, but of the enquiry as well.

Radford was furious, resenting the uniform branch's incursion into the CID's field of activity, and was convinced that Fieldsend 'was out to make trouble for the CID, from the start'.

Rust and Bolongaro gave contradictory accounts regarding Watts, and Radford wanted to interview Watts without delay, but Fieldsend forbade him from doing so, saying that an officer independent of 'Y' Division should conduct the enquiry. This caused Radford's resentment to boil over.

AC(C) Jackson became involved and concluded that Fieldsend was 'a man with a grudge who was strongly prejudiced against the CID . . . he is "riding" Detective Superintendent Radford, and I can see nothing in the papers of the investigation to justify the suggestion that he should not interview Mr Watts.'

Radford did interview Watts on 10 February 1960, and although his statement was vague it did suggest that Bolongaro and Rust might well have been in the Manor House public house with the three aids.

But there was no suggestion in Radford's final report to the Home Office that Bolongaro and Rust had suppressed the matter of Watts in their statements; and after the matter was considered by Commander Townsend of 'C' Department, the Home Office officials came to the conclusion that no new evidence had been produced and that no action would be taken on Napley's complaint.

Seeing the report, Fieldsend was furious; he believed he had uncovered a number of disciplinary offences and prepared a memorandum to Commander Pennington of No. 2 Area saying, 'In the whole of my service, I have never known so many irregularities being committed by so few officers in so short a time.' He recommended that the three aids should be returned to uniform duty and that DC Rust should be transferred; he was content to wait for Bolongaro's imminent promotion, in order that he could be transferred from the Division. But none of his recommendations were accepted, and there, for the time being, the matter rested.

In 1964, the case was raised in Parliament. This was after Eric Fletcher MP had received an anonymous letter from 'an unnamed senior police officer' referring to the case at Hornsey and saying:

> In the ensuing enquiry it was revealed that a detective sergeant had committed no less than nine offences against discipline and a detective constable, twelve offences.

The Home Secretary, Henry Brooke, ordered an enquiry, which was headed by William Lloyd Mars-Jones MBE (Mil.), QC. It lasted for forty-six days, and at its conclusion Fieldsend was lauded for 'doing the only real detective work carried out by anyone in the course of investigating this complaint', whilst AC(C) Jackson and Commander Hatherill were criticized 'for acting hastily and not giving the matter the consideration it deserved'.

On 3 December 1964, the new Home Secretary, Sir Frank Soskice PC, QC, was asked in parliament to make a statement regarding the case and he did so:

> In the case of Tisdall, Kingston and Hill-Burton which occurred in 1959, the allegation was that the facts disclosed by an investigation made in 1960 were deliberately covered up in order to avoid embarrassment to the police.
>
> Mr Mars-Jones finds that no one connected with the investigation acted dishonestly; that there was no attempt to conceal from the Home Secretary information relevant to the guilt or innocence to the men and that there was no breach of duty by any official in the Home Office. He does find, however, that five police officers of subordinate rank – three of whom have since resigned – lied about the time and place of their first encounter with the three accused men; that if the evidence disclosed in the course of his enquiry had been available at the trial or appeal the three men would not have been likely to be convicted; and that the investigation of the complaint was neither thorough nor impartial.
>
> Mr Mars-Jones criticises three senior police officers – who have since retired; he attributes some part of the failure of the investigation to friction between a senior officer of the uniformed branch and the CID in the district concerned and at Scotland Yard and he also criticises certain aspects of the arrangements for handling complaints against members of the Metropolitan Police.
>
> In the light of the report, I am recommending the grant of free pardons to the three men concerned. I have referred the report to the Director of Public Prosecutions but he informs me that he would not feel justified in instituting proceedings against the five officers (or former officers), who were found by Mr Mars-Jones to have given false evidence.
>
> In view of an undertaking given by the Commissioner of Police – which was communicated to the House by my predecessor when he announced the setting up of the enquiry – that disciplinary action would not be taken against any serving officer who gave evidence before the enquiry, the Commissioner is not free to take disciplinary action.

The Commissioner assures me that there is now a high standard of co-operation and good will between the CID and the uniformed branches of the force; the situation described in the Report developed for personal and local factors which no longer remain. The procedure for dealing with complaints has been altered in a number of respects since 1960. In particular, under the Police Act, 1964, the report of the investigation of a complaint by a member of the public must be sent to the Director of Public Prosecutions unless the chief officer is satisfied that no criminal offence has been committed.

It has become increasingly the practice to put the investigation of serious complaints against Metropolitan Police officers in the hands of senior officers from other divisions or sub-divisions and in the light of Mr Mars-Jones' Report, the Commissioner has issued explicit instructions that the investigation of complaints of serious crime should be carried out by officers who are not in the direct chain of command over the officer against whom the complaint is made.

The more detailed findings in the Report are being carefully examined in consultation with the Commissioner.

After he agreed to 'give the most careful consideration' to any request being made for an *ex gratia* payment to the three men, the sums awarded in March 1965 were, in Napley's view, 'far from generous'.

So that meant the Home Office mandarins were absolved from any blame, and that, of course, was the main thing.

The same failed to apply to Sir Frank Soskice regarding the discharge of his duties as Home Secretary, at least as far as Prime Minister Harold Wilson was concerned. Soskice was relieved of the office and appointed Lord Privy Seal, a position in which expressing congratulations of the collective feelings of the House was probably less onerous than his duties at the Home Office. He was later elevated to a life peerage as Baron Stow Hill.

William Mars-Jones was appointed as a High Court Judge in 1969 and knighted.

David Napley was also knighted in 1977, as AC(C) Richard Jackson had been in 1963 when he retired from the police.

No such elevations to high office for Dick Radford; he resigned on an ill-health pension on 18 July 1962.

Which leaves Chief Superintendent Fieldsend. Is it possible that he was the 'unnamed senior police officer' who sent details of the disciplinary offences allegedly committed by Bolongaro and Rust to the Member of Parliament? If so, I hope he rebuked himself; for a police officer – senior or not – to send anonymous information to anybody is itself a serious disciplinary offence.

CHAPTER 38

A Fall from Grace

Ian Forbes-Leith's reputation, meanwhile was on the crest of a wave; in fact, it had been even before the Brighton case.

In 1954, as a detective superintendent (Grade II) at C1 Department, New Scotland Yard, he investigated the case of Dr William Spencer Lewis, who had invested money in building societies for his four daughters and had died intestate; his widow, 51-year-old Dorothy Spencer Lewis, and 61-year-old Napoleon Ryder forged a will transferring all the money in her late husband's accounts into her own, and when this was contested by one of the daughters, a further will was forged. Forbes-Leith arrested the charmless pair and had them both remanded in custody at Bow Street Magistrates' Court, after telling the court that a witness had been threatened. At the Old Bailey on 1 July 1954, both were convicted, with Ryder being sentenced to seven years' imprisonment and Spencer to five. Lord Goddard, the Lord Chief Justice, was unstinting in his praise for Forbes-Leith, saying:

> The country is indebted to you for your work on one of the most complicated and difficult cases I have come across since I have been a Judge.

The following year, he was transferred to 'G' Division after being promoted to Detective Superintendent (Grade I), and there he dealt with a burglary on 26 August 1956, when the manse of Wesley's Chapel, City Road, Finsbury was broken into. The perpetrator was 29-year-old Bernard Patrick Gerald Smeeth, who had three findings of guilt as a juvenile (his youth had been spent in Approved Schools since the age of seven, being beyond parental control) and seven previous convictions and had, in fact, been released from prison that January.

Smeeth had tied up and assaulted the sleeping Mrs Esther Broughton Spivey, the wife of the administrator, before stealing her purse and jewellery and then venturing into the room of Mr Spivey's elderly mother.

Sentencing Smeeth to a total of five years' imprisonment, Mr Justice Ashworth told him:

The only redeeming feature I can see in this ghastly case is that
you controlled yourself in regard to the old lady; otherwise,
your conduct was quite unspeakable.

Once more, Forbes-Leith attracted considerable (and
well-deserved) publicity for his work in this case.

Following the enormous success of the Brighton enquiry,
his star was well and truly in the ascendant; he had married at
the age of thirty-six, and following his attendance at the senior
course at the Police College, Ryton-on-Dunsmore in 1952, four
years later, he attended Course 'C' at the Police College. He had
by now collected his Long Service and Good Conduct Medal to
add to his war medals and his Mention in Dispatches, and the
late John Rigby recalled to me how Forbes-Leith enthralled the
students at the Detective Training School with an account of
the Brighton investigation.

At the early age of forty-two – by which time he had been a
detective superintendent for six years – he looked tipped to
go straight to the very top of the promotional ladder; indeed,
there was no reason why he should not.

This was at the time of 'The Big Five', the five detective
chief superintendents, one each in charge of the Metropolitan
Police's four districts and the fifth in charge of C1 Department
at the Yard.

Jack Capstick, in charge of No. 4 District, had already retired
in January 1958 and he was a hard act to follow, having spent
over thirty-two years in police service, much of that time with
the Flying Squad, as the leader of the secretive post-war Ghost
Squad and as a brilliant murder investigator. Known to the
underworld as 'Charlie Artful', as a young constable, just one
inch over the minimum height requirement, Capstick had let
his truncheon do the talking for him when he encountered
the ne'er-do-wells who frequented the shadowy alleyways of
Seven Dials.

Bert Hannam was just about to retire as head of 3 Area, and
within a couple of months Ted Greeno, clutching his MBE and
eighty-six commissioner's commendations, would be vacating
No. 1 District after spending over thirty-eight years of his life
with the Metropolitan Police. Greeno had served as one of 'The
Big Five' for fourteen years and was a legendary fighting man,
Flying Squad officer and murder investigator.

Forbes-Leith's boss at No. 2 District was Detective Chief
Superintendent Steve Glander, a very tough character known
on the Flying Squad as 'The Ambush King', due to the diverse

operations he set up to catch criminals in the act. His ambushing activities extended to describing, to his face, a detective superintendent as being 'a complete and utter cunt', in front of a roomful of astonished detectives. Glander would not be retiring for another two years after almost thirty-six years' service, but there were several vacancies to suit Forbes-Leith.

All of the incumbents had known the toughest aspects of police life; all had been career CID officers, starting on the beat, then becoming aids to CID, before ascending the promotion pole, gaining enormous experience en route.

Forbes-Leith was different from his contemporaries in having been introduced into the police as a 'Jessie', but to be fair, he had clearly made good. He may not have acquired the toughness of the old-time Guv'nors, or developed their armies of informants, but he was a shrewd investigator, he was good in the witness box and there was no reason why he should not progress to the topmost heights.

This was not a view shared by Jack Capstick as head of No. 4 District, which was where Forbes-Leith was posted on 6 May 1957. Some four months after Forbes-Leith's arrival, when 4-year-old Edwina Marguerita Taylor was reported missing then found brutally murdered, it was not he who accompanied Capstick on the hunt for the killer. It was Detective Inspector George Hayler and then uniformed Superintendent Stevenson. And when Capstick needed to snatch a few hours sleep, it was not Forbes-Leith who took over the reins – it was Divisional Detective Superintendent Harold Marshall. Capstick conferred with Deputy Commander Bill Rawlings OBE, MC and with Commander George Hatherill about the case – but not with Forbes-Leith. And when Derrick Edwardson was arrested (and later pleaded guilty) to Edwina's murder, it was Capstick's last case. On the same day that he left 4 District headquarters for the final time, so did Forbes-Leith – on his way to the Yard.

Capstick did not mention his subordinate by name, but there was no doubt about whom he was referring to when, lamenting that the police were dragging their heels in catching criminals, he later wrote:

> For my own part, I am convinced that one of the major reasons is that most of our present chiefs of police received their initial training at Hendon Police College, sponsored by Lord Trenchard in 1934. There they learned a great deal about the laws of the country and acquired a smattering of criminal law,

but about ninety per cent of their studies related to the duties
of the uniformed branch. I have never known one officer who
had received the two years' training at Hendon who later
became adept at thief-catching. Nobody ever learned the art
of catching thieves by attending lectures.

A pretty pointed point of view, if you like. But the fact remained,
those old-time rough and tough CID Guv'nors were slowly
dying out and a new breed was coming in – and Forbes-Leith
was one of them. Because, putting Capstick's grievances to
one side – pertinent though they might have been – if, in time,
Forbes-Leith were to be appointed as Assistant Commissioner
(Crime), think what expertise as a working CID officer he
could have brought to that role. He would be aware from his
own experience of the problems facing junior CID officers,
and he would be a fine administrator. Look at his predecessors.

Sir Norman Kendal CBE had served in the Metropolitan
Police from 1918, as Chief Constable, Deputy Assistant
Commissioner and then Assistant Commissioner; prior to that, he
had been a barrister. He was described as being 'schoolmasterish,
fussy and sometimes, obstructive'.

Sir Ronald Howe CVO, MC served in the same ranks as
Kendal from 1932 onwards; he was an innovative administrator
but had previously worked in the Director of Public Prosecutions'
office. Percy Worth MBE, the Chief Constable (CID) – with his
long experience as an active CID officer – urgently suggested to
Howe the implementation of what became known as the Ghost
Squad, to deal with the sudden upsurge of post-war crime. Pre-
war, 96,914 indictable offences had been recorded annually; now,
following the end of the Second World War, the number had shot
up to 128,954. Howe, with his lawyer's reticence about making
quick decisions, waited over seven months before agreeing to the
formation of the unit.[1]

In fact, since the beginning of the CID in 1878, not only had
there never been an Assistant Commissioner (Crime) who had
been a CID officer, there hadn't been one who had been a police
officer at all.

But had one of the old-time Guv'nors been in the AC(C)'s
chair when the report of the CID's Chief Constable suggesting
the formation of the Ghost Squad arrived, there is no doubt
that any of them – Glander, Greeno, any of them – would have

---

1 For further details, see *Scotland Yard's Ghost Squad: The Secret Weapon
Against Post-War Crime*, Pen & Sword Books, 2011

snatched that report, even before the ink of the Chief Constable's signature was dry, and gone roaring down the corridors of the Yard demanding that the suggestions contained in the report be rubber-stamped by the commissioner, *immediately*!

Forbes-Leith would not become an assistant commissioner or be inserted into the chairs left by any of 'The Big Five'. He – who should have been going somewhere – was going nowhere. His career came to a standstill after 16 May 1959, when a young black man named Kelso Cochrane was stabbed to death in Notting Hill.

★   ★   ★

Having just completed sixteen months' tenure at Scotland Yard's C1 Department, Forbes-Leith was posted to West London's 'X' Division on 4 May 1959 and inherited a serious problem. For the previous two years there had been considerable public disorder in the form of clashes between members of the newly-arrived black community from the West Indies and gangs of white youths. What became known as the Notting Hill race riots had seen petrol bombs being thrown and a variety of murderous weapons being utilized in running street battles. Nine youths were jailed for a salutary four years each for going on what they described as 'a nigger-hunting' expedition, but that did little to stop the violence; in fact, the flames of unrest were well and truly fanned by an ultra far-right party known as the Union Movement, under the direction of its fascist leader, Sir Oswald Mosley.

Now, two weeks after his arrival, Forbes-Leith was woken from his slumbers at 1.15am on Sunday, 17 May to be informed of the brief details of Kelso Cochrane's murder: that he had been attacked and stabbed by youths in Golborne Road. Taken by police car to Harrow Road police station, Forbes-Leith set up an incident room, and more detectives were summoned.

One of them was Detective Sergeant John Merry. He was attached to C3 Photographic Branch and he would be required to photograph the scene and the body. As he left the Yard at 4.45am, having picked up his equipment, he was accosted by a man who handed him a copy of that day's *Sunday Express* newspaper, requesting him to hand it personally to Forbes-Leith and telling Merry his name; he asked him not to forget the name and to pass it on to Forbes-Leith.

But having other things on his mind, by the time Merry handed the newspaper to Forbes-Leith he had forgotten it.

In fact, the man's name was John Ponder and he was a
reporter for the *Sunday Express*. The item which Ponder wanted
Forbes-Leith to see had been printed at 4.00am that morning
and under the headline 'Murder in Notting Hill' it read:

> A coloured man was stabbed to death in a street brawl in
> Notting Hill early today. Three youths were believed to be
> involved in the fight. Detective Superintendent Ian Forbes-
> Leith, ex-Scotland Yard murder squad detective, who took over
> the Division CID only a few weeks ago, was called from his
> bed to take charge of the investigation. He arrived in Golborne
> Road, Notting Hill within an hour of the murder.

It certainly appeared to be quick work on behalf of the newspaper,
and despite the sparse details it demonstrated, if nothing else,
to the public that the police had started working on the case
immediately. The investigation got underway, and two of the
witnesses recounted Cochrane's dying words: 'They asked me
for money but I told them I didn't have any.' It transpired that
the dead man was penniless, but the investigators were quick to
suggest that robbery had been the reason and that a racist motive
did not come into it.

Of course, with considerable justification, nobody believed
this, even though Sir Oswald Mosley denied that inflammatory
language attributed to him was in any way responsible and even
sought to pour oil on to these troubled waters by proposing that
the immigrants should be returned to Jamaica, where they would
be able to 'restore the prosperity of their sugar industry'. It was
the sort of suggestion which the black inhabitants of Notting
Hill did not find particularly helpful and which the members of
the Union Movement undoubtedly did.

House-to-house enquiries were carried out, witnesses were
interviewed, suspects were pulled in and later released without
charge, and the search for the murder weapon continued.

And then, four days after the murder, a letter addressed to
a John Wilson arrived at Harrow Road police station. Since a
constable named Colin Wilson was the only person at the station
with that surname, he opened the envelope and saw that the
letter was from the *Sunday Express* thanking 'Mr Wilson' for his
information regarding the murder. PC Wilson thought it was
a joke and burned the letter. But on 23 May, another similarly
addressed letter arrived, and this one contained a cheque
for £10 and an invoice stating: 'Description of contribution:
Harrow Road murder tip, exc. £10.'

Now in 1959 £10 was serious money – pretty well the equivalent of a week's wages for a newly-arrived police constable – and PC Wilson lost no time in informing Forbes-Leith of the matter. The implications were that whoever 'John Wilson' was, he was accepting payment for supplying the press with information; the Yard was duly informed, and investigating officers were appointed to delve into the matter.

The internal investigation commenced with almost as much urgency as the murder enquiry. All of the police officers involved in any way whatsoever, whether uniform or CID, were interviewed, including Forbes-Leith, and all of them denied being responsible for the leak. The two reporters in question – Ponder and Frank Draper – were interviewed and both gave one fatuous answer after another, completely contradicting themselves and each other. But of one thing Ponder was sure: Forbes-Leith, whom he had known since the Brighton case, was *definitely* not the person who had contacted the *Sunday Express*.

Eventually, it appeared that there were three persons, all of them CID, who at that early stage had been aware of the facts of the case as recounted in the newspaper. One was Detective Sergeant Sidney Cyril Coomber, who as a detective constable in 1941 was one of three men awarded the George Medal for effecting a particularly hazardous rescue in a bombed house by tunnelling under the wreckage, made doubly perilous by a Luftwaffe air raid in progress at the time.

The next was Detective Inspector Ferguson Walker, a tough, hard-working, hard-drinking Scot; and the third was Forbes-Leith.

The three men were seen by the recently appointed commissioner, Sir Joseph Simpson KBE, the first commissioner ever to have walked a beat as a police constable. Like Forbes-Leith, he was a product of the 1930s Police College, but if Forbes-Leith thought that meant he would receive preferential treatment, he was wrong. For a year prior to his appointment Sir Joseph had been deputy commissioner, dealing with all matters of discipline, and he told the three men in no uncertain terms that unless he discovered the guilty party, their careers would go no further.

Six months after the commencement of the investigation, the officers came to the conclusion that Coomber and Walker were guiltless; however, the case of Forbes-Leith, despite his denials, was quite another matter, and a large question mark hung over his head.

★　★　★

The Cochrane murder enquiry was wound down; nobody has ever been charged with the crime.

Meanwhile, Forbes-Leith carried on; when Jean Johnson was found stabbed to death in a basement flat in Marylands Road, Paddington on 6 November 1959, the whereabouts of her husband Clifford were sought, in the hope that he might assist in the investigation.

A fight broke out outside the North Kensington Community Centre on 9 April 1960, and 17-year-old Michael Berry was punched and died as a result. Two days later, Forbes-Leith interviewed Roy Joseph Nardoni, who told him, 'I don't want my mates to get into trouble for this. I did it – let me make a statement.' At the Old Bailey on 25 May Nardoni pleaded guilty to manslaughter and was placed on probation for three years.

On Christmas Day, 78-year-old bakery worker 'Old Fred' Skinner was found dead in a garden in Stracey Road, Harlesden, battered about the head and strangled with his own tie; his wages of a few pounds, including his £2 Christmas bonus, were missing. House-to-house enquiries paid off; the perpetrator, 16-year-old Christopher Duffy, lived in the adjoining thoroughfare, Winchelsea Road, and he had been unwisely allowed home over Christmas from Approved School. Forbes-Leith caught up with him three weeks later at Eye police station, Suffolk, where he had been detained; found guilty of capital murder at the Old Bailey on 20 March 1961, Duffy was ordered by Mr Justice Hilbery to be detained during Her Majesty's pleasure. Young Mr Duffy could count himself fortunate; had he been two years older, since the murder had been perpetrated in pursuance of theft, he would have been hanged.

It was a good case to be Forbes-Leith's swansong; having come to the irrevocable conclusion that after almost eight years in the rank of superintendent his career really would not advance any further, four days after the court case, he resigned.

He had served twenty-five years, twenty-three days and took his pension (much reduced from what it would have been, had he served his full thirty years) of £1,478 4s 2d per annum and obtained employment in the commercial sector.

Denied further promotion or inclusion in the Honours List, Forbes-Leith did win an award befitting the immaculate 'Guv'nor with the Bowler'. In July 1961 he was paraded at the Savoy Hotel after the Clothing Manufacturers' Federation named him as one of Britain's ten best-dressed men. 'I buy only one suit a year', he told the reporter from the Daily Herald, 'but I have fifteen, all as good as new. I never wear the same suit two days running.'

The smartly attired actors Douglas Fairbanks Jr and Nigel Patrick were duly impressed.

Following his retirement, he moved from his home near Regents Park in Devonshire Close, W1, and settled at The Old Cottage, Upper Bourne End, Buckinghamshire. Seven years later, Sir Ronald Howe, who had resigned as deputy commissioner in 1957, expressed his views in print as to the desirability of establishing a national police force, an opinion he had held since the 1930s.

Forbes-Leith agreed with him and in a letter to *The Times* also took the opportunity to say:

> Detectives have a dangerous job, mentally as well as physically. They work with the knowledge that at any time they can be double-crossed by an unscrupulous individual, not necessarily a criminal in the accepted sense. The morale of many a good detective is low because of the lack of confidence of being supported when things appear to go wrong. Strength at the top is vital.

'Double-crossed'? 'Unscrupulous individual'? 'Lack of confidence'? Well, well. It did appear the Forbes-Leith thought he had been let down; and perhaps he had. So who was it that leaked that snippet of information regarding Cochrane's murder to the press?

In my opinion, it was Forbes-Leith himself, but not for any pecuniary motive. He enjoyed a very good press, and when Sid Coomber telephoned him in the early hours to inform him of the murder, I have no doubt that he got straight on the phone to Ponder to let him know what was happening and to ensure that it would be his name that hit the readers of the *Sunday Express* – a bit of self-aggrandisement, nothing more.

And nothing more would have come of it had it not been for the ridiculous matter of the cheque sent to Harrow Road police station and made payable to someone who didn't exist; something that, when he was made aware of it, Forbes-Leith immediately (and properly) reported.

It appeared that a gratuity – certainly not a bribe – had been offered, but if it could be proved that the payment was in respect of a matter – leaking information to the press – that was, in itself, a disciplinary offence.

Knowing what I do of Forbes-Leith's character, I do not believe for one moment that he had any thought of reimbursement for that snippet of information; but if he had admitted the truth of the matter, not only would his career not have advanced, there was also the strong possibility of demotion following a disciplinary board.

So he admitted nothing – and in so doing he provoked the disapprobation of his senior officers.

Sid Coomber's career did not advance either, but only because he failed (or didn't want) to pass the necessary examination. He was a much admired officer at Harlesden police station and a mentor to a young detective constable who with good advice was propelled in the right direction. His name was Leonard Read, and as Detective Superintendent 'Nipper' Read he later went on the smash the Kray empire.

After Coomber's death in 2005, his George Medal, Defence Medal and Police Long Service and Good Conduct Medal were sold at Bonham's on 5 July 2005 for £3,290.

Detective Inspector Ferguson Walker's career did flourish; he retired as Commander of No. 2 District.

And Forbes-Leith, who could have gone so far had it not been for his desire for a bit of self-promotion (plus profound stupidity on behalf of the *Sunday Express*), died on 6 December 1992, aged seventy-six; he had been largely forgotten.

CHAPTER 39

Conclusions and Suppositions

So was it worth bringing the Brighton case at all, a trial that cost £50,000 and resulted in three men out of five being convicted, an investigation which meant that people like Ernie Waite, a persistent receiver of stolen goods on an industrial scale, walked away scot-free? That someone like Alan Bennett who – quite apart from his other peccadilloes – could boast of the bribes he had paid to venal police officers and ostentatiously flaunt £500 in a bundle of notes before a jury? Was it worth all that?

For what it's worth, I believe the answer is 'yes', absolutely no doubt about it. When stepping out to snare crooked police officers, a disgrace not only to themselves but also to their fellow members of the force in which they serve, stern measures must be taken. If that means dealing with some people who might be regarded as being slightly disreputable at one end of the criminal scale, and the scum of society at the other, then the nettle has to be grasped.

When 'Nipper' Read sought to bring down the Kray brothers he knew precisely what he was going up against, because just a few years before, he had arrested Reg and Ron Kray for blackmail and, despite the most compelling evidence, they had walked out of court free men. Now, in 1967, instructed to bring down their criminal empire by the Assistant Commissioner (Crime), Read told the lawyers in the DPP's department that if he could assemble a lorry-load of archbishops to provide evidence to bring down the brothers, he would willingly do so. Since venerable gentleman of that persuasion did not figure in the Krays' immediate social circle, he would have to 'go down into the sewers' to find those who did; but, added Read, if the lawyers thought that prospect too distasteful, they should say so immediately and he would save himself an exasperating job; the Krays would then go free. Grudgingly – and fortunately – the lawyers agreed.

Many people – including some police officers – considered the concept of using supergrasses distasteful. Having arrested some of the most violent criminals for some of the most despicable robberies, where the most gratuitous violence has been used against men and women and defenceless children and elderly people, then permitting these criminals to give evidence against their contemporaries, after they had admitted all the crimes they had committed, in exchange for reduced sentences, could understandably be felt to be abhorrent.

Understandable – but in my view necessary. I was part of the supergrass system and I witnessed at first hand the successes that could be gleaned from that unpalatable work. Many supergrasses implicated dozens of fellow armed robbers, and one in particular named 277 of them, 159 of whom were charged with serious offences – the reduced number being because, given the strict rules of evidence, corroboration was required to bring charges.[1]

But it was not just a matter of arresting armed robbers (many of whom became supergrasses themselves) on the strength of a supergrass, and recovering firearms and stolen property; it was much more than that. Because many of those grassed up had been best friends of the supergrass, and others their relations or best men at their weddings – one I arrested, having previously grassed up his father and brother, now grassed up his mother as well – it sowed the seeds of mistrust and meant that nobody in the gangs of armed robbers could feel safe any longer.

And the proof of the pudding is displayed in the far smaller numbers of armed robberies nowadays.

Does the end justify the means? Not necessarily always; but in the Brighton case, I have no doubt that it did.

*   *   *

And that brings us full circle back to Alan Roy Bennett, the man who kicked it all off because he was sick and tired of paying bribes to the police, especially in order to exculpate him from crimes he had never even committed – or had he?

The £1,000 missing from Alan Walker's bedroom at the Astor Hotel? What nonsense, said Bennett – he had been at Ascot all day. In fact, Walker had given him £150 to put bets on for him, and so he had – and had lost £120 of it and returned the remaining £30 to Walker. This doesn't ring true to me, and despite having a former detective's nasty, suspicious mind, which isn't sufficient to obtain a conviction, I have no doubt that Bennett swiped the remaining £850 as well.

---

1 For further details of supergrasses, see *Scotland Yard's Flying Squad: 100 Years of Crime Fighting*, Pen & Sword Books, 2019

As for the dishonoured cheque in Leeds, it was, I believe, a racing certainty that Bennett had presented that cheque and that this could have been proved to conviction.

Regarding the attempted breaking at Folkestone for which Bennett was arrested and charged, although the matter was discharged at the Magistrates' Court, this was not because witnesses were produced to say he was there; it was because Bennett produced witnesses to say he wasn't.

This brings us to the £8,000 burglary at Bournemouth. Bennett had the ideal alibi; it could not have been him, he said, because on the day prior to the burglary he had gone to Belgium – and there was his passport to prove it. Or did it? Bennett could have gone to Belgium on the previous day, got his passport stamped, then returned the same day and carried out the burglary the following day. Bournemouth airport was nearby for a swift exodus; it was then known as Hurn Airport, and although many of the international flights had transferred in 1949 to the newly-opened Heathrow, some services still operated out of Hurn. Using a false passport and carrying a bag full of swag would demand iron nerves; but Bennett possessed nerve, charm and arrogance in abundance. After selling the jewels on the continent (thereby providing the finance for his Rolls-Royce) Bennett could then have disposed of (or secreted) the false passport and returned to the UK using his genuine one.

Is that too pat? Altogether too fanciful?

Well, no, it isn't.

*   *   *

Bennett appeared at Bow Street Magistrates' Court on 29 January 1959 charged with obtaining a false passport in the name of Graham John Sleeman. Also in the dock were two other men, Stanley Crowther, a barrister charged with making untrue statements to obtain false passports for Bennett and another man named Percy Frederick Lennon (currently serving a two-year sentence in France), and Ernest Kendall, charged with aiding and abetting Crowther.

In his statement to police, Bennett said:

> I obtained a passport as a result of meeting somebody in the Strand in about May 1957. I had been acquainted with this particular person and knew he had no money. He asked me to loan him £50. He was desperately in need and asked if he could do a service. He said he could get me a passport in

another name. I was experiencing considerable difficulty with certain members of Brighton police force who I thought were hounding me unreasonably in order to get money from me. I thought it might be better for me to leave the country, rather than face further blackmail or a prison sentence for something I had not done. I gave this man £25 and later another £50. Shortly after this meeting, I went to Scotland Yard. I did use the passport to leave the country to go to Spain in order to escape the glare of publicity. It was destroyed abroad.

This statement was full of holes. First, it was a year previously that Bennett had gone to Scotland Yard; by 1957 he was out of the loop so far as the bent cops at Brighton were concerned. Secondly, why destroy the passport? How was he going to return to England without one? And if it really was necessary for him to 'escape the glare of publicity', why not use his own passport?

Next, Bennett refused to name the impecunious character he had met in the Strand; but his co-defendant, Ernest Kendall, did. The man's name was Jasper Addis – the same man whom Bennett named in court as being the person who advised him to go to Scotland Yard in 1956.

*   *   *

Jasper Jocelyn John Addis was born in 1904, educated at public school, had been articled as a solicitor with Addis & Edwards, 10 St James' Place, SW1 and had apparently served as an acting staff captain during the Second World War. He was certainly wearing the uniform of a Second Lieutenant when he appeared in court in 1940 alleging that he had been duped into claiming money for payment in respect of non-existent trade directories; the sum involved was £5,674.

By 1943 he must have resigned his commission, because he successfully appealed at the London Sessions against conviction for neglecting his duties as a fire-watcher, for which he had been fined £15 with 15 guineas costs.

Three summonses brought by the Board of Trade alleging failure to submit returns from 1943 to 1945 in respect of The London Finance and Guarantee Salvage Corporation Ltd were dismissed at Bow Street in 1946, when Victor Durand (that very dodgy brief who would go on to defend Sammy Bellson in the Brighton case) managed to convince the Magistrate that his client was not the Jasper J.J. Addis named in the files. However, since Addis had now been struck off from acting as a solicitor, three more summonses were brought by the Law Society alleging that he had defended people on criminal charges when not qualified to do so. This matter was adjourned after Addis claimed he had had a nervous breakdown.

Addis – keeping up the pretence that he was still a solicitor – was then employed by financier George Dawson and helped himself to large amounts of his employer's money. Arrested, he took out a summons against Dawson alleging that his employer had threatened to murder him. Once more Victor Durand appeared for him, but Addis insisted on cross-examining the prosecutor from the witness box at Marlborough Street Court, to such an extent that the infuriated Magistrate, Mr Rowland Thomas, bellowed, 'Get out of the box and try to behave like a gentleman!'

Addis was bound over in the sum of £10 to keep the peace for a year, but there were more pressing matters awaiting him at the Old Bailey on charges of false pretences and fraudulent conversion. Lord Goddard, the Lord Chief Justice, would stand none of his nonsense, and in the middle of the trial, on 21 June 1954, Addis jumped bail. He was not caught until a month later, and on 6 October, in front of the Recorder of London, Sir Gerald Dodson, he was found guilty of four cases of fraudulent conversation. He was sentenced to two years' imprisonment, after the Judge had been told in mitigation that Addis had given the government information regarding Dr Arthur Albert Tester, the Irish chief of the Romanian Gestapo; he had, apparently, been Addis' client. He had certainly lived at Addis' address at 10 St James' Place.

But what was not revealed in court was that Addis was the subject of an MI5 file; in it, amongst his other peccadilloes, was the information that he had been (and still was) a supplier of false passports.

* * *

That being the case, did Addis supply Bennett with a false passport in connection with the Bournemouth burglary?

It's all supposition, of course; I'm probably doing Messrs Bennett and Addis a grave injustice.

Meanwhile, the court case closed with Bennett – at that time living at Queen's Gate Terrace, South Kensington – and his two co-defendants being sentenced to three months' imprisonment each.

Epilogue

Nannestad is a municipality in Akershus in the county of Viken in Norway. The name Nannestad comes from the contraction of two words in old Norse, 'Nanni' (a male name) and 'staðir' (meaning homestead or farm), and the place boasts a twelfth century church.

It was there that Wenche Bennett died, on 30 March 2012; she was eighty-seven years of age and she was laid to rest in the churchyard, having lived a not uneventful life.

But what of her flamboyant husband, the multi-named Alan Roy Bennett?

He mysteriously went right off the radar, perhaps clutching a handful of passports all in different names and maybe destined to commit undetected crimes worldwide.

Is that a possibility?

Who knows?

Bibliography

Capstick, John	*Given in Evidence*	John Long, 1960
Cox, Barry, Shirley, John & Short, Martin	*The Fall of Scotland Yard*	Penguin, 1977
d'Enno, Douglas	*Brighton Crime & Vice 1800–2000*	Wharncliffe Books, 2007
Fido, Martin and Skinner, Keith	*The Official Encyclopedia of Scotland Yard*	Virgin Books, 1999
Fraser, Frankie, as told to Morton, James	*Mad Frank: Memoirs of a Life of Crime*	Warner, 1994
Jackson, Richard	*Occupied with Crime*	Harrap, 1967
Kelland, Gilbert	*Crime in London*	Harper Collins, 1993
Kirby, Dick	*The Guv'nors*	Pen & Sword, 2010
Kirby, Dick	*The Sweeney: The First Sixty Years of Scotland Yard's Crimebusting Flying Squad 1919–1978*	Pen & Sword, 2011
Kirby, Dick	*London's Gangs at War*	Pen & Sword, 2017
Kirby, Dick	*Operation Countryman: The Flawed Enquiry into London Police Corruption*	Pen & Sword, 2018
Kirby, Dick	*Scotland Yard's Flying Squad: 100 Years of Crime Fighting*	Pen & Sword, 2019

Kirby, Dick	*The Racetrack Gangs: Four Decades of Doping, Intimidation & Violent Crime*	Pen & Sword, 2020
Kray, Reg	*Villains we have Known*	Arrow Books, 1996
Millen, Ernest	*Specialist in Crime*	George G. Harrap, 1972
Morton, James	*Bent Coppers*	Little, Brown, 1993
Napley, Sir David	*Not Without Prejudice*	Harrap, 1982
Olden, Mark	*Murder in Notting Hill*	Zero Books, 2011
Pearson, John	*The Profession of Violence*	Panther Books, 1973
Read, Leonard with Morton, James	*Nipper*	Macdonald, 1991
Rowland, David	*Bent Cops: The Brighton Police Conspiracy Trial*	Finsbury Publishing, 2007
Swain, John	*Being Informed*	Janus Publishing Co. 1995
Thomas, Donald	*Villains' Paradise*	John Murray, 2005
Thorp, Arthur	*Calling Scotland Yard*	Allan Wingate, 1954
Wilson, Pamela Sydney	*Home was a Grand Hotel: Tales of a Brighton Belle*	Book Guild Publishing 2008

Index

Ackerman, Mr 34, 37–43,
    127, 129
Adams, Dr John Bodkin 112
Addis, Jasper Jocelyn John
    17–18, 207–8
Anderson, DC 190–3
Ashworth, Mr Justice 195–6
Astbury, Mrs Elsie 72

Baldock, D/Supt William,
    BEM 52, 185
Baldwin, Councillor George
    Bernard 59–60, 171
Barnard, Harold Frederick
    Charles 21, 165
Bellson, Samuel Pisoner
    'Sammy' 19–23, 55–6, 72–3,
    76–168, 174
Bennett, Alan Roy 9–18, 47,
    53, 56–60, 61–92, 93–168,
    205–11
Bennett, Wenche 'Winkie'
    9–18, 85–7, 121–2, 146,
    152, 157, 162, 211
Beresford, Herbert 180
Berry, Michael 202
Betts, Reginald 26–7, 91, 154
Beveridge, DCS Peter
    Henderson, MBE 178
'Big May' 92
Blythe, William Patrick
    'Billy-Boy' 55
Bodger, PC Charles Ronald 16
Bolongaro, DS 190–3
Bond, DAC Ernest Radcliffe,
    OBE, QPM 5–8, 185

'Bookie Page' – see Page, W.A.
Bosley, Solicitor, John 62–3,
    71–110, 172
Boyd, Clerk of the Court
    Leslie 165
Brabiner, Mrs Alice Florence
    25–30, 55, 65, 77, 90–2,
    125–6, 139, 153, 154
Breffit, CC Reginald,
    OBE, MA 53
Brereton, D/Supt William
    52, 185
Broadbent-Speight,
    DS Arthur 14, 89
Brooke, Home Secretary
    Henry 192
Brown, Alan – see Bennett, A.R.
Brown, Allen Roy –
    see Bennett, A.R.
Burt, Commander Leonard
    James, CVO, CBE 50–1
Butler, Home Secretary
    Richard Austin, KG, CH,
    PC, DL 174
Butler, DCS Thomas Marius
    Joseph, MBE 39, 53,
    55–6, 65–6, 72, 105,
    134–5, 144, 150–1, 158,
    185–7

Capstick, DCS John Richard
    'Charley Artful' 196–8
Cavey, CC William, OBE,
    QPM 109, 182
Chapman (Lawyer),
    Mr C. 108

Cherryman, Mrs Blanche
    Josephine 14–15, 86,
    122, 140, 146, 149–50,
    153, 162
Christie, John Reginald
    Halliday 75
Clapham, Revd Harry 5
Clarke, Edward, QC
    112–68, 178
Cochrane, Kelso 199–204
Cook, DC 45, 47, 103
Coomber, DS Sidney Cyril,
    GM 201–4
Cooper, D/Supt Charles xvi
Cottam, PS 190–3
Crane, DC Richard George 18,
    90, 105–6
Crippen, Dr Hawley
    Harvey 111
Crowther, Barrister Stanley
    207–8
Cullen, Desmond P. 148–9
Cullen, Alderman, Thomas
    148–9
Cushman (Solicitor),
    Mr Stanley 57–8, 68
Cushnie, (Magistrate),
    Mr H., MBE 72

Dacre, (Magistrate),
    Mrs Elizabeth 68
Davies, CC Glyn 172
Davies, Lord Justice 171
Dawson, George 209
Day, Jill 21, 133
Dennis, William Edward
    'Ginger' 55
Devlin, Mr Justice 108
Dimes, Albert 174
Diplock, Mr Justice 71–2
Dodd, Town Clerk, Mr W.O.
    58–60, 68, 109, 171
Dodson, Recorder of
    London Sir Gerald, KC 209

Donovan, Mr Justice
    111–68, 173
Doughty, Recorder Sir Charles,
    QC, MP 20, 181
Draper, Frank 201–4
Duffy, Christopher 202
Dunstan, DS George Richard
    89, 123
Durand, Victor, QC 112–68,
    208–9

Easterbrook, Ronald Leonard
    185–6
Edwardson, Derrick 197
'Embezzling Vicar' –
    see Clapham, H.

Ferguson, Alan Roy –
    see Bennett, A.R.
Ferguson, Austin Roy –
    see Bennett, A.R.
Ferguson, CC Major Sir
    John, CBE, QPM,
    CStJ, DL 49
Ferguson, Mrs 12
Fieldsend, Ch. Supt 190–3
Fletcher, MP, Eric 191–3
Forbes-Leith, D/Supt Ian
    James 50–2, 55–60,
    61–92, 106–8, 153, 166–7,
    195–204
Fraser, Francis Davidson
    'Mad Frankie' 55

Glander, DCS Stephen Arthur
    'The Ambush King' 196–7,
    198
Goddard, SPS George
    xv–xvi, 178
Goddard, LCJ Lord Rayner
    108, 195, 209
Goldie, Recorder Mr Noel B.,
    KC, MP 12
Grant, DS 33

Greeno, DCS Edward,
MBE 196, 198

Haigh, John George 75
Halland, DAC Lieutenant
Colonel G.H.R., CIE,
OBE 50
Hammersley, DI John Richard
6–8, 16–18, 21, 22, 33–6,
37–48, 68, 75–168, 177, 182
Hammersley, Mrs Vera 166
Hancock, Mrs Rose 134
Hannam, DCS Herbert
Wheeler Walker 196
Harkess, Mr J.W. 112–68
Harman, Lord Justice 171
Harmsworth, Anthony,
QC 8, 109
Harris, (Solicitor), Mr A.P. 68
Hatherill, Commander George
Horace, CBE 49–52, 58,
62, 63, 65, 67–8, 187,
192, 197
Hawkins, Stanley Allan 179
Hayler, DI George 197
Heath, Mrs Gina 166
Heath, DS Trevor Ernest 6–8,
11–18, 22–3, 25–30, 33–6,
37–48, 60–92, 93–168,
177, 182
Hemming, (Solicitor),
Mr G.V. 68
Hendy, DI Roland 38–40,
47, 103
Hilbery, Mr Justice 202
Hill, Billy 72, 78, 174
Hill, Supt Thomas xxi, 21,
68, 105
Hill-Burton, Sidney 189–93
Holt, Alan Roy –
see Bennett, A.R.
Holroyd-Pearce, Lord
Justice 171
Hopper, PC 19

Hovey, DS Raymond 28–30,
103–5, 134, 139, 155, 162,
168, 182, 183
Howard, Billy 77–9
Howard, Gerald, QC 75–168
Howe, AC(C) Sir Ronald,
CVO, MC 198, 203
Humphreys, James William
'Jimmy' xvi
Hylton-Foster, Solicitor
General Sir Harry Braustyn
Hylton, QC 75–168

Jackson, AC(C) Sir Richard
Leofric, CBE 49, 53,
63, 189–93
Johnson, Clifford 202
Johnson, (Solicitor) Howard 5
Johnson, Jean 202
Johnson, DCI Robert 98–9,
132–3
Johnson, HMI Sir William,
CMG, CBE, QPM 67–8

Kalber, PC John 51–2
Karrouze, Mrs Iris 25–30, 91,
125–6
Kelland, AC(C) Gilbert,
CBE, QPM xvi
Kendal, AC(C) Sir Norman,
CBE 198
Kendall, Ernest 207–8
Kennard, Arthur William 48,
109–10
Kensett, Norman 33
Kerry, PC Norman 35, 99
Ketley, Frederick 35–6, 98
Ki-Ki – see Mercado, N.
Kingston, Thomas Alfred
189–93
Knight, PS Frank 22–3, 105,
134, 139, 155, 163, 165,
168, 183
Kray bros. 78, 205

Kray, Reg 78
Kye-Kye, Sid – *see* Mercado, N.

Laskey, Miss Betty 53
Lawrence, Geoffrey, QC
    112–68
Lawrence, Mrs Gwladys Mabel
    Elizabeth 'Betty' 25–30,
    55, 77–9, 91–2, 126, 139,
    154, 168, 178
Leach, Harry 19–21, 55–6,
    113–14, 137, 144, 145,
    147–8, 152
Leach, John 19–21, 22, 55–6,
    114, 141, 145, 152
Lennon, Percy Frederick
    207–8
Lessells, Tony 10
Lewis, Dorothy Spencer 195
Lewis, Dr William Spencer 195
Lock, Walter Henry 180
Lynn, (Magistrate), Colonel
    S. 68
Lyons, Anthony John 9–18,
    25–30, 55–60, 62, 68,
    75–168, 174

MacDougall, DCS Colin 4
MacManus, Mr J. 112–68
Maher, Frank 42
Manningham-Buller, Attorney
    General Sir Reginald 63
Mark, Commissioner,
    Sir Robert, GBE xvi, 185
Marrinan, (Barrister), Patrick
    Aloysius 55, 112
Mars-Jones, William Lloyd,
    MBE (Mil.), QC 192–3
Marshall, D/Supt Harold 197
Marshall, DCS John James,
    MBE, QPM 182
Martin, Mr O. 112–68
Mason, Mrs Mary 15, 77, 89,
    122–3, 143

Matheson, Mr 32, 128
Mathew, DPP Sir Theobald,
    KBE, MC 165
McConnach, CC William,
    MBE 172
McIntyre, Donald QC 112–68
Mercado, Nathan 146–7, 180
Merry, DS John 199
Millen, DAC Ernest George
    William 'Hooter', CBE 4–8,
    52, 68, 72, 174, 186–7
Mitchell, Roy John 19, 34,
    131–2, 154
Mocatta, Mr Justice 172
Moffatt, Mr H.W. 72
Montagu, Chairman Ewen,
    QC 190
Montgomery – *see*
    Bennett, A.R.
Moody, Supt Edwin 37–47,
    101–3, 132, 167, 182, 183
Moody, DCS William
    'Wicked Bill' xv, xvi
Morgan, WPC 19
Mosley, Sir Oswald Ernald,
    6th Baronet 199–200

Napley, Sir David 189–93
Nardoni, Roy Joseph 202
Newman, Mrs Margaret
    Elizabeth 89
Nott-Bower, Commissioner,
    Sir John KCVO, KPM 53

Owens, 'Sister Connie' 5

Page, William Albert
    'Pagey' 21–2, 98,
    110, 133, 146–7, 148, 179–81
Paling, (Lawyer), Mr G.R. 60
Paolella, Francisco 48, 109–10
Parr, CC Stanley, CBE,
    QPM 173
Parsons, Mrs M. 134

Pearson, Mr Justice 108
Peck (Lawyer), David 82–168
Pennington, Commander 191
Pilley, Michael 78
Podola, Günter Fritz 75
Poiner – *see* Bennett, A.R.
Ponder, John 200–4
Popkess, CC Captain Athelstan
    Horn, CBE 173–4
Powell, DS Frederick 18, 90
Purchas (Lawyer), Mr F.B.
    91–168

Radford, D/Supt Richard
    Alfred Jennings 53, 55–60,
    61–3, 68, 106, 189–93
Ransom, Florence Iris
    Ouida 111
Rawlings, D/Commander
    William, OBE, MC 197
Ray, Max 'Maxey' –
    see Betts, R.
Read, ACC Leonard, 'Nipper',
    QPM 204, 205
Rees, Stanley, QC 75–168
Richardson, Frederick George
    'Hicksy' 42–5, 127, 142, 149
Ridge, CC Charles Feild
    Williams xx–xxi, 5–6,
    10–11, 20–2, 30, 32, 46–7,
    56–60, 61–92, 93–168,
    171–6, 182
Rigby, DS John 196
Roberts, Michael 19–20
Rose, Frank 3–8, 47, 52, 53
Rose, Richard Isaac –
    see Rose, F.
Rosenbaum, Isaac – *see* Rose F.
Rossi, Robert 'Battles' 55
Rowland, PC David 178, 183
Rowsell, CC Albert Edward,
    OBE, KPFSM 71, 171,
    181, 182
Rubenstein, Solomon 72, 174

Rust, DC 190–3
Ryder, Napoleon 195

Sabini, 'Darby' xx
Sargeant, Tim 59
Scott, PC Peter 51
Senior, Supt A.F. 50
Simpson, Commissioner
    Sir Joseph, KBE 201
Skelbeck, Miss Hilda
    Mary 110
Skinner, Frederick 'Old Fred'
    202
Sleeman, Graham John –
    see Bennett, A.R.
Smeeth, Bernard Patrick
    Gerald 195–6
Soskice, Home Secretary
    Sir Frank, PC, QC 192–3
Spiers, DS George 38, 102
Spivey, Mrs Esther
    Broughton 195–6
Spot, Jack 55, 174
Stevenson, Supt 197
Stratton Bros 111
Streatfeild, Mr Justice 171
Stroud (Solicitor), Mr L.J. 8
Swaby, James Thomas 28–30,
    77, 103–6, 133, 139,
    154, 162
Swaby, Sheila 28–30, 77,
    103–6, 134, 139, 154
Swain, DCS John, QPM 50

Tarff, Mrs Olive 35, 98
Taylor, PC 189–93
Taylor, Edwina Marguerita
    197
Tester, Dr Arthur Albert 209
Thomas, (Lawyer), Mr R.L.D.
    68, 72, 75–168
Thomas, (Magistrate),
    Mr Rowland 209
Thorn, Arthur 26–8, 92

Tilling, DI Frederick John 17, 89, 123
Tisdall, Patrick Albert 189–93
Trenchard, Commissioner The Lord, GCB, OM, GCVO, DSO 50, 197
Tullett, PC Vernon 22–3, 105, 168, 183
Tonge, PC 189–93
Townsend, Commander 191–3
Turner, Maxwell, QC 75–168
Tyson, Alderman, Charles 71, 73

Vibart, D/Supt Jasper Peter, QPM 39, 46, 53, 55–6, 72, 105, 134–5, 144, 150–1, 158, 185–6
Virgo, Commander Wallace 185
Vokins, (Magistrate), Mr Harold 66, 68, 76–110

Waite, Ernest Edward 31–47, 66, 77, 93–103, 126–68
Walden, PC 189–3
Walker, Alan 13–14, 82–3, 86, 115, 138, 140, 152, 157, 206
Walker, Commander Ferguson 201–4
Ward, DC Dennis Andrew 45, 103

Ward, Insp. 191–3
Warner, Henry, 179
Waterhouse, Keith 9
Waterman, Harry 11, 89
Watson, Mrs Joan 32–47, 66–7, 97–103, 128–68
Watson, William 35–6, 98–9
Watts, Robert Sidney 190–3
Webb, Harold Roy 'Rubber Bones' 52
Wensley, DS Frank 182
Wensley, CC (CID) Frederick Porter, OBE, KPM xvi, 178
Wheeler, Solicitor, Cyril 65–66
Whiffin, Mrs Elizabeth 72
Williams, D/Supt., Gwyn 37–8, 46, 65–6, 101, 108–9, 123, 142
Willink, Sir Henry Urmston, QC, MC, PC, JP 174
Wilson, PC Colin 200–4
Wilson, Prime Minister Sir Harold, KG, OBE, PC, FRS, FSS 193
Wood – see Bennett, A.R.
Woodman, CC Philip John 172
Worth, CC (CID) Percy, MBE 198
Wright, DI Leonard 38–9, 47–8, 102
Wyatt, Edward George 37–8, 101